"EDINBURGH 1910"

*A Publication Without Parallel
in the Literature of Missions*

The Reports of the Commission
OF THE
World Missionary Conference

This is far more than a report of the re-remarkable Conference held in Edinburgh.

Eight most important commissions were appointed two years before the convention date. Each commission presented its report in written form, giving the results of its world wide correspondence and study as related to its special subject.

Each separate volume excepting the ninth forms the report of a commission as finally revised after the fullest discussion and criticism in convention.

The ninth volume contains a summary, addresses, and index of the whole.

The set presents a library on missions far more important and comprehensive than anything ever attempted before.

*Nine Volumes, Each 75 cents net; postage, 9 cents.
Complete Set, $5.00 net; postage, 70 cents.*

ECHOES FROM
EDINBURGH, 1910

AN ACCOUNT AND INTERPRETATION
OF THE WORLD MISSIONARY
CONFERENCE

BY

W. H. T. GAIRDNER

AUTHOR OF

"D. M. THORNTON ; A STUDY IN MISSIONARY IDEALS AND METHODS"
AND "THE REPROACH OF ISLAM"

WITH AN INTRODUCTION
BY
JOHN R. MOTT, LL.D.

NEW YORK   CHICAGO   TORONTO

Fleming H. Revell Company

LONDON   AND   EDINBURGH

New York: 158 Fifth Avenue
Chicago: 80 Wabash Avenue
Toronto: 25 Richmond St., W.
London: 21 Paternoster Square
Edinburgh: 100 Princes Street

PREFATORY NOTE
ON BEHALF OF THE COMMITTEE

THE Conference at Edinburgh was, as is well known, mainly a consultative gathering. Its primary purpose was the study of the great missionary problems of the present day by leaders in the missionary enterprise at home and abroad, in order that they might see more clearly what was immediately required for the fulfilling of the charge to "disciple all nations." But as the plans for the Conference matured, it became evident that indirectly another great end would be served by it. The dignity, immensity, and importance of the missionary enterprise appeared in fresh and impressive aspects. Facts rose into prominence which were seen to be of vital importance for the whole Church of Christ. The very holding of the Conference was seen to have a significance which, if it could only be brought home to the imagination of the Church, might give it a new and thrilling vision of the work before it.

Hence the resolution was taken to issue a volume written for the people of the Church, a volume which might present the gist of the Conference in such fashion as to make vivid to those who were not present at it what the Conference really was and did and saw and reached after and believed and hoped—a volume which should be at once a narrative, an interpretation, and a summons. What was desired was that the Church should see the Conference in its relation to the present position and advance of the Kingdom of Christ in the world, so as to see at the same time its own urgent and imperative duty.

After full consideration, the Committee invited the Rev. W. H. T. Gairdner, B.A., of Cairo, to undertake the task of writing this book, and they were greatly encouraged by his acceptance of it. They have to acknowledge the kindness of the Committee of the Church Missionary Society in releasing him from other work and allowing him to prolong his visit to Scotland that he might accomplish this service. It was thought best that Mr Gairdner should be perfectly free to present the message of the Conference in the way that seemed to him most true and impressive. The Committee accordingly have no responsibility for the views expressed in the book. At the same time the Committee desire to record their grateful appreciation of the sympathy shown by Mr Gairdner with the object they had in view, and of the enthusiasm and industry with which he devoted himself, both during the Conference and in the subsequent weeks, to the service so generously undertaken by him, and now in this volume so admirably fulfilled. It is theirs to send the volume forth ; and they do so with the earnest prayer that, by the blessing of God, it may give to many thousands of readers a new vision of the central place of Christian missions in the current history of the world, and of what God would have them now to do for the coming of the Kingdom of Christ.

INTRODUCTION TO AMERICAN EDITION

THE World Missionary Conference, held at Edinburgh in June, has been characterized by discriminating Christian leaders as the most notable gathering in the interest of the world-wide expansion of Christianity ever held, not only in missionary annals, but in all Christian annals. Judged by the impression which it has made upon those who came within range of its direct influence, this is doubtless an unexaggerated estimate. The messages, the work, and the meaning of such a Conference must therefore be a matter of universal interest and concern. Many will wish to obtain and study with thoroughness the nine volumes which contain the reports of the Commissions of the Conference, together with the abstracts of the debates upon these reports. A far larger number of Christians, including all who desire to keep abreast of the most vital developments in the progress of the Christian religion, will be eager to read some adequate interpretation of this truly notable event.

Those who are responsible for the Edinburgh Conference have been most happy and fortunate in securing as its special interpreter Mr. W. H. T. Gairdner, of Cairo. His intimate relation to the Student Christian Movement of Great Britain and Ireland and to the World's Student Christian Federation before he went

INTRODUCTION

to the mission field prepared him in an unusual degree
to understand and to appreciate the various Christian
communions, and likewise the place of the different
nationalities and races in the complex enterprise of
Christian Missions. His subsequent career as a missionary in the Levant, at a station which, in a unique
sense, is on the highway of missionary activities and
missionary travel, has brought him into contact with
the missionary problems of the two great non-Christian continents, Africa and Asia. His brilliant and inspiring book, "The Reproach of Islam," is well known.
By his catholic spirit, by his sympathy with the whole
range of the varied missionary life of the Christian
Church, by his power of vision and by his marked
ability to express in an effective and entertaining manner what he sees and feels, he has been enabled to give
us a discerning and fascinating portrayal of the life,
work, and significance of the Conference, and, what is
much more important, to cause us to catch its spirit
and to receive, in a measure, some of the wonderful
impulses which so profoundly stirred all who had the
privilege of being present during the memorable days
in Edinburgh.

JOHN R. MOTT.

CONTENTS

EDINBURGH 1910

CHAPTER VIII

CHAPTER IX

CHAPTER X

CHAPTER XI

CHAPTER XII

CHAPTER XIII

CHAPTER XIV

CHAPTER XIV. CONCLUDED

LIST OF ILLUSTRATIONS

Ad Maiorem Dei Gloriam

THE words on the opposite page represent all that the writer feels, and desires more deeply to feel, with regard to this book.

To have had the writing of it seems to him to be the greatest privilege he has ever had, or perhaps will ever have.

But there is one thing that remains to be said. The name of J. H. OLDHAM—which recalls a friendship extending from earliest Oxford days at Trinity down to "Edinburgh 1910"—should, the writer thinks, have stood on the front page, as joint-author of a work of which he has assuredly been the "onlie begetter." But since this is not to be, let his name stand alone on this page. From him came initial inspiration; formative sugges-tion; and indispensable criticism. *Quid plura?*

W. H. T. G.

6 WELLINGTON SQUARE,
   AYR, *August* 1910.

INTROIT

In the depths of endless space there burns a star, one among the unnumbered myriads of the host of heaven ; a solitary star, without the dazzling company of either consort, or cluster, or constellation. Most glorious is this star ; yet its glory might scarcely so much as be noted by a traveller through the void, by reason of the far more excellent glory of vast numbers of its starry peers. It is, indeed, but a solitary star of the tenth degree, or less by far ; for one star differeth from another in glory.

Round this unconsidered member of heaven's host is whirling a family of yet far lesser spheres, dark save for such portion of the central radiance as falls on each. Were our traveller through space able so to adjust his perception, as even to notice things so infinitesimal in the relative scale of being, he would at most take note of some three or four of these parasites on the central glow. On these three or four his casual gaze might for a moment fall :—it could hardly but miss four others, far more diminutive still, spinning in the innermost orbits round their lord, merest specks in space, motes in the sunbeams, grains of the star-dust that floats for ever in the void.

And yet to the Third of these Minor Four is clinging a multitude of beings endued with life and self-motion— some of them also with thought and memory and reason ; in virtue of which, certain of these last are saying that their race is akin to the Creator of all the stars and all the constellations and the space in which these burn

—because (they affirm) it has been created after His likeness and in His image !   Nevertheless, the children of that
race are for the most part at enmity with each other, and
are injuring themselves and one another in many grievous
and shameful ways.   And, therefore, some of them are
further affirming that their race has sinned against its
Creator and Father, and is by this a fallen race.   But
stranger still (they say), the Eternal Word, through
Whom were all things made, for their sakes once struck
His being into bounds, and became one flesh with their
kind ; and after walking with wondrous grace and holiness
for a while in a certain corner of their tiny sphere, shed
at last His blood and gave His life for that whole world,
that it might be redeemed back to the image of Him who
created it;   and finally reassumed the ineffable life which
He had from all eternity : having first commanded those
who from Him had caught new life to spread the news of
the heavenly deed from that corner to every other corner
of their world, until the whole of it should be full of the
glory of God as the waters cover its sea. . . .

And what was there that should draw the Eternal Word
out of His eternity to tabernacle on Number Three of the
Lesser Satellites of Helios, that unconsidered star ?

The same question might be with as much justice
urged were that satellite not the David, but the Eliab or
the Abinadab of the planetary family ; and were the star
which gives it light and heat not the Helios, but the
Sirius (or whichever were the absolute cynosure) of all
the heavenly host.   For the unique marvel were still the
existence of spiritual beings, personal as God, incarnate
in flesh, capable of knowing themselves, their world,
and their Maker ; who are in His likeness, being par-
takers of the divine Reason.   Size in this regard were

of no account ; for Spirit is not to be sized. The
nonspatial is not to be reckoned in terms of space.
And, therefore, whether the tiny sphere, that spins
and whirls there before the gaze of the celestial
traveller of our fancy, be the One and only one he has
met or will ever meet on whose stage the drama of conscious being is being played ; or whether it be but one of
Ninety-and-Nine other worlds that need no repentance :—
though it were enormous as Arcturus,or minute as a marble
peopled by conscious atoms :—still would these spirit-
consciousnesses be nearest of all to One who is Spirit ;
still would the agony of their spiritual conflict, the
trembling balance of their spiritual destiny, bring down
to their aid the strong Son of God, from Whom came
all things, and to Whom, as to its goal, the whole
creation moves.

It is not, in truth, unfitting that an account of a great
Missionary Conference which took place in the year
of grace 1910 should begin with an exordium such as
this. For the scientific enquiry (so characteristic of
the age), the slow synthesis of which has enabled us to
take a right view of our planet in space, is just that which
enables us to view it and realise it in itself. If we now
can see it as one unit among others, it is this that enables
us to see it also as a unit in itself, a single whole. And it is
because the world has at last come to be realised as a
single whole that the enterprise of carrying the Gospel
to all the world is gradually being invested with a new
realisableness in the minds of men. And it is because
that enterprise is being thus invested with a new realisableness that a World Missionary Conference met in
Edinburgh in the year 1910 with a new sense of its own
world character, a new vision of the goal, and a new

desire to be born again into a knowledge of God commensurate with the superhuman task.

In order to see our world as a unit, in fact, which it is imperative to do, we must not stand mentally in Britain or America or wherever we happen to be, and view it thence, with the result that nearer things inevitably bulk more largely than the remote, and that thus the unity of the whole is disturbed. But we must place ourselves by the side of that celestial traveller we have fancied . . . and behold ! how there swims into our ken a gloriously yet mildly radiant sphere ! . . . Through its translucent envelope of atmosphere its seas stand out dark and clear, its ocean-circled continents luminous and white. One after another the familiar shapes emerge into view, slipping out of night's dark shadow into the light of the sunward side, white as a lily, and as fair, against the dead black of space. *There* is the world once visited by the Son of God ! There is the world which as one world is known to-day and must to-day be won for its Maker and its Redeemer.

A vision of Earth ! Known as a unit in this our day ; every day more and more closely and organically knit by the nerves of electric cable and telegraph wire ; more richly fed by the arteries and veins of railway-line and steamship ocean-way : one nation in extremest Orient thrilling at the words of some orator at furthest sun-setting, almost as they drop from his lips ; so that its inhabitants, for all the differences of tribe and race, become daily more convinced of the unity of their humanity :—one world, waiting, surely, for who shall carry to it and place in its empty hands one Faith —the only thing that can ever truly and fundamentally unite it or deeply and truly satisfy it, bringing its one human race into one Catholic Church, through the message of the

"One Body and One Spirit,
One Lord, one Faith, one Baptism,
One God and Father of all, who is over all, and through all, and in all."

Such was the vision which called together the World Missionary Conference of 1910 ; such was the vision splendid which was seen with ever more luminous distinctness as the Conference proceeded ; and such is the vision which any narrative or account of the Conference must seek to convey to the whole Church of Jesus Christ, since on the whole Church's welcome and obedience to the heavenly vision depends its realisation. Thus, only thus, may be fulfilled that prayer of all the ages

AS IN HEAVEN, SO ON EARTH,
THY KINGDOM COME.

IONA,
July 1910.

EDINBURGH

Showing the

CHAPTER I

WORLD HISTORY AND THE WORLD MISSION

THE part that the world-wide enterprise of Christian missions is playing in moulding the history of the world is already a large one, and is destined to increase more and more.

This interlacing of world-history and the world-mission is a phenomenon which, as was lately well said by one in highest position, will increasingly compel the study of the statesman and all who keep watch on the course of the world. But it has also another aspect. If missions help to make history, world-history also reacts on the world-mission, deflecting the currents of its effort, giving definiteness to its ideals, causing modifications in its methods. Just because it is a mission that seeks to save the world, it is necessarily sensitive to the occurrences of the world. And when there occurs one of those rare events which, like an earthquake-shock, affects every political seismograph all over the earth, it follows, with equal inevitableness, that the whole enterprise of the world-mission feels the thrill, and recognises the call to meet a new emergency and a changed situation.

Such an event is that which has lately taken place in the Far East, the event, which, it might almost be said, ushered in the twentieth century Up to that time, from the earliest days of European commerce with the Orient, nay, except for the parenthesis of the Saracen

9

and the Turk, from the days of Alexander the Great himself, the tides of empire and domination, of political and commercial supremacy, had rolled from West to East. India was under a western flag : China, with one-fourth of the human race, was (it seemed) on the verge of dissolution, and the only question seemed to be whether she was to become a far-eastern Turkey, the Sick Man of Asia, or was to be partitioned among the Powers of the West. The Pacific was no less a western ocean than the Atlantic. With America dominating its eastern sea-board, and Russia and the other Powers its western, the circuit of world-influence seemed to be complete, and western Power appeared to dominate and monopoli the entire globe.

And then, Port Arthur fell, the Battle of Moukden s fought, the Trafalgar of the Korean Straits was deci ; and the entire aspect of things was changed.

The little Island Kingdom, which alone had ver seemed quite to fit into the former world-s eme ; which, in the war with China in 1894 and the lief of the Legations in 1900, had made Europe feel t there was one element in far-eastern politics that as proof against absorption ; that little Island Kingd emerged victorious from a decisive struggle with a we ern Power, and in so doing upset settled views based the records of tens of centuries.

The tide of western advance and domination, which had seemed more like an unchangeable phenomenon of nature than a resultant of human actions and states, was checked, rolled suddenly back. To the Oriental it even seemed as if the tide metaphor might be given its logical extension :—as the turn of the ebb is only the signal for the long irresistible flow of the returning flood, was not that decisive event, in like manner, the sign that the tides of influence, of trade - supremacy, of political ascendency might henceforth be reversed and flow, as before Marathon they had flowed, from East to West! Back from the East westwards ran the electric thrill of some such thoughts as these, creating national longings and aspirations where formerly there were none, and multiplying the intensity of those that had already existed. All talk about the partition of China ceased with astounding abruptness,—the world looked awestruck on, as the sleeping Colossus roused itself, woke, and stood upon its feet! . . . Korea, Manchuria, Malaysia, Ceylon, each in its own way, felt the thrill. A new thought, a fresh aspiration seemed to give a sense of unity even to racially and religiously-divided India. Vague and ignorant might be the talk that went the round in the bazaars of the cities and even in the villages of India, but it was not the less significant. The same talk might have been heard in Cabul and Teheran, and in the cafés of Constantinople and Cairo, and God only knows how much further west and south. It was more than a mere coincidence that the quinquennium that followed the event saw the rapid development of nationalism in Egypt, and coups d'état in Persia and in Turkey. In Europe, Russia herself, the blind instrument of this whole revolution, reacted to its impact. And the Ethiopianism of Africa, whether Southern and Christian, or Northern and Mohammedan, in all probability felt its influence too. . . . It was evident that the East had awaked, and this because it was not the fussy thunder of Western legions that for the hundredth time was annoying her slumber, but because she was for the first time responding to an awakening call of Nature from within! The swirl of the world-tide, which for five centuries had been creeping up to the Orient and encompassing it round, had now in fact swept it for good and all into the current of the unified life of all mankind.

2.

The last great, united Missionary Conference had
met in 1900, the year when the regiments of " the
Powers " *and Japan* were advancing to the relief of the
Legations in Pekin.   Was it not palpable to those who
sat down to plan the Edinburgh World Missionary
Conference of 1910, that the Church of Christ was face
to face with a new emergency and a changed situation ?
Humanity was awaking to self-consciousness : it became
tenfold more urgent to say to humanity *Ecce Homo* !
The world was realising that it was a unity :—was that
unity to be or not to be in One Lord and one Faith ?
Were the gigantic forces, so contrary and so violent, now
liberated end loosened all over the world, merely to be
left to fight and clash their terrible way to future settle-
ment ? or was the inconceivable acridity of such a conflict to be modified and mitigated and humanised by
Orient joining Occident in the faith of Christ ?   In that
case it might be, aye, *might* it not well be !, that Japan
with her traditional non-aggressiveness, China with her
Confucian contempt for war, and India with her tradition
of potent passivity, might when christianised teach the
West the supreme Christian lesson it has never been able
to learn, in taking their mighty stand upon the principle
that henceforth world-evolution should proceed *humanly*,
and competition itself, freed from its nature-tradition
of cruelty, become just one aspect of human co-operation !   The Yellow Peril of Eastern power might thus
free the Yellow Peril of Western gold from its mysterious
curse, and be to the world the source no longer of peril
but of peace !

3.

Now it was open to those who promoted the World
Missionary Conference that met at Edinburgh in 1910

to take one of two courses, and to give to the Conference one of two general aims. Similar general conferences, held previously in 1854, under the leadership of the great missionary statesman Duff, in 1860, 1878, 1888 and 1900, gave precedents for following either of these two lines— either that it should be deliberative and consultative, or that it should be mainly designed to bring the subject of missions in a striking way before the public—which in this case meant little more than the public in the part of the world in which the Conference should be held. In the first case it would have the character of a deliberation, in the second a demonstration.

The considerations that have been explained in the preceding paragraphs make it clear why those men felt that they had no option but to plan a Conference of the former type, and it is remarkable that precisely the same conviction had simultaneously forced itself on the minds of the leaders on both sides of the Atlantic. The crisis of the enterprise, caused by such a radical change in the situation that faced the Church all over the world, demanded most of all, and first of all, that the Church should " do some fundamental thinking." Thought, lavishly and immediately given ; enquiry and study on an unprecedented scale ; information contributed from every quarter, thrown into the common stock, carefully digested, co-ordinated and presented, and then debated by picked representatives of all missionary forces at home and abroad ; conclusions patiently and deliberately formed as a result of these proceedings ; and finally (it was hoped), common action taken in accordance with those conclusions,—all this is what appeared to the leaders to be necessitated by the unprecedented situation. . . As one of the ablest of their thinkers put it, writing while the preparations for a Conference on the lines indicated were in full swing :

" The very character of the World Missionary Conference is determined by these [world-] changes. It is felt everywhere, by all the Missionary Boards, by the missionaries themselves, and in a vague way by private members of all denominations. It was impossible to arrange for another Conference of the old type, at which an elaborate programme of addresses should be, as it were, performed before admiring crowds. The sense of a difference in the atmosphere was too definite, too widespread, too significant to be ignored. In some way the result of one hundred years of missionary endeavour, and the effect produced by the penetration of Asia and Africa with at least the beginnings of Western civilisation, have brought the Church to a new sense of the vastness and complexity of the work which now lies before it. We have climbed the foothills which hid the supreme ranges from our sight. But now we see them there, and a more or less complete change on our outfit and our methods must be promptly arranged if the real task is to be accomplished."

Was this deliberate choice of a *business* Conference, the consequent drastic limitation of the numbers of the representatives attending it, and the definite foregoing of " performing before admiring crowds," to mean that the crowds were not to be influenced, the attention of the general public not caught, the interest of the Church masses not engaged or deepened ? The Conference has come and gone and already it is evident that these great and important results have by no means been sacrificed by the fidelity to which it limited itself to its single aim. Like Solomon it sought wisdom,— *to know* ; and its sessions had not closed before it was evident that the other things which it had not directly sought had been added unto it.

To know *what* ? The work abroad, of course,

with its thousand facets ; the nature of the supreme crisis that faces the Church ; the Church Catholic itself, to which the whole enterprise has been committed ; and—God.

For those who most deeply had realised the crisis, and the paramount necessity of ascertaining the facts more clearly, preparing more wisely, and working with at once greater lavishness and greater wisdom, realised more and more clearly that the knowledge which needed most of all to be increased was, simply, the *knowledge of God*. For two things came home to them with a force amounting to revelation ; first, that the task revealed by the renewed study of the situation demanded an experience of GOD in CHRIST that the Church does not yet possess : and second, that such a deepened experience is possible, because there are in God, as revealed in Christ, depths and heights that are knowable though still unknown. And it became their inspiring hope that the God who revealed His power once to the first great Conference, which, united in heart and united in place, waited upon Him, would use this one also as His medium for another such revelation to His waiting Church upon earth.

The spirit in which the Conference assembled can best be understood through the following words, addressed by the leaders to the delegates, and others, eight months before it met :—

" In proportion as the Conference represents a sincere and earnest attempt on the part of the Christian Church to understand and perform its duty in the world to-day, in a deep and literal sense its possibilities are as illimitable as God Himself. It is strange how hard we find it to hold to that faith in the goodness of God which is implied in any theistic belief, and which lay at the heart of all that Jesus Christ taught ! We do not in the depths of our souls believe that God's desire for the advancement of the kingdom of truth and righteousness is stronger and deeper than ours. Were we inwardly so persuaded we could not doubt that, if in the face of the present opportunity our hearts fervently desire to witness yet more glorious days than the great past, in which the good news of Christ proved its power to captivate the nations of Europe, something far beyond the present achievement and attainment of the Church is also the will of God. Can anything stand in the way of the accomplishment of that good will but the unbelief of the Church? Is it true that, as Christ taught, God's infinite power is at the command of those who in childlike trust seek to do that will? The issue to which the consideration of the world task of Christianity drives us back is *whether the Church really possesses Christ's thought about God, and, if not, whether it can get it back*. The only limits to the new visions which the approaching Conference may unfold, and the new faith and devotion which it may inspire, are those set by our own unworthy and impoverished conceptions of GOD."

Were these high hopes fulfilled by Edinburgh, 1910?

No Conference of ten days; no gathering of mere representatives of the Church Militant, could do more than claim, when the Conference closed, that their eyes had seen the wonderful *beginning* of their fulfilment. That much they did claim. But it was just in order that that beginning might be continued, and those high hopes might altogether be realised, that the Committee caused this book to be written and sent forth, if so be that the Christian body might thus be brought into touch with what its representatives experienced in Edinburgh, 1910.

CHAPTER II

THE idea of preparing beforehand for a great religious Conference by educating the delegates was not an entirely new one, when the leaders of that of 1910 sat down to think out their plans in the summer of 1908. Recent important Conferences in the Mission Field, such as the Decennial Missionary Conference at Madras in 1902 and the Centenary Missionary Conference at Shanghai in 1907, had appointed special Committees to carry out investigations and prepare for the work of the Conference before it met: and the Committees of the Shanghai Conference had printed and circulated to delegates papers dealing with the subjects which had been entrusted to them. Moreover, only a fortnight before the leaders met at Oxford, had closed the great Pan - Anglican Congress, at which five thousand delegates from every Anglican diocese had met for conference in London: in this case, a remarkable propædeutic had been carried out for the three years that preceded the Conference, in the shape of a series of numerous short papers, written by acknowledged specialists on the many subjects which were to be taken up at the Conference, and sent *seriatim* to all those who desired to prepare their mind for the discussions themselves. But in this case there was no co-ordinating element,—no Committee sat to reduce this mass of information and thought to organic unity : and herein, as will be seen, was the advance made by the

B   17 leaders of Edinburgh, 1910, in the scheme of preparation they now sat down to work out.

The very character of their aim, in truth, made such a scheme inevitable, for it is palpable that if the characteristic of the Conference was to be *study*, and deliberation on the basis of that study, a lengthy and arduous preparation was made thereby inevitable; for no such research could possibly be undertaken by the few individuals who are usually asked to " read papers " on these occasions. And even were that not impossible, it would be impossible for them to pour out, or their auditors to take in, the result of their research, during the limited time which is available at even the lengthiest of conferences.

It is clear, too, that inasmuch as the aim of the Edinburgh Conference was at once more defined and (really for that very reason) more elaborate than that of the Pan-Anglican, the contribution of howsoever valuable a series of papers on each topic, by the most adequate of writers, would not in itself be sufficient. There must also be a co-ordinating element, which should both have the material collected on a clearly and most carefully defined plan, and also co-ordinate it and reduce it to shape when collected; the result to be presented in the most highly organic and intelligible form to each delegate some weeks before the first day of the Conference, and, at the Conference itself, to be laid upon the table and discussed in as much detail as possible.

2.

Such in general were the lines laid down at the International Committee which met at Oxford in the July of 1908. It proved a memorable occasion : five members from the North American Continent, ten from

Great Britain, and three from the Continent of Europe sat for four days, from early morning to late in the evening,—and the discussion of business was not always interrupted during meals. Complete harmony and a sense of the guiding presence of God—which were later so noticeable at Edinburgh—were given as an earnest to that Committee, and enabled it so to work that by the end of those four days, the foundations of the Conference had been well and truly laid.

The Committee wisely decided not to let the great enquiry which it was planning range aimlessly over the whole field, and so miss, perhaps, attaining definite and useful results ; but to select a limited number of subjects of cardinal importance and special immediate urgency, and to direct a searching enquiry towards these alone. The eight subjects which were thus isolated for the purposes of this research were as follows :—

I. Carrying the Gospel to all the non-Christian World.
II. The Church in the Mission-field.
III. Education in relation to the Christianisation of National Life.
IV. The Missionary Message in relation to Non-Christian religions.
V. The Preparation of Missionaries.
VI. The Home Base of Missions.
VII. Relation of Missions to Governments.
VIII. Co-operation and the Promotion of Unity.

Eight " Commissions " were then appointed, each consisting of some twenty members,—a hundred and sixty of the ablest men and women in America, Britain and the Continent. To them was to be entrusted the exceedingly arduous and exacting work of collecting and systematising the information on these eight subjects. Now the men who were to be asked were naturally some of the busiest men in the two continents, and the demand which it was proposed to make of them was almost audacious ; yet nothing in the history of the Conference was more remarkable than the response made to the invitation of the International Committee to join those Commissions, though many members of the Committee hazarded the guess that if fifty per cent. of those who were to be invited should accept, there would be reason for congratulation. Mark now the event. Out of the original list of nearly one hundred and sixty names only eleven declined the invitation, in practically every case for reasons which made acceptance impossible. We may thus gauge the importance of the work which had been offered them, and the possibilities which these persons immediately discerned in the Conference and this preliminary task alike. We shall also see in a moment what their acceptance of this task was to mean for these devoted men and women.

3.

The names of their Chairmen show at a glance the quality of the personnel of these Commissions. For the CARRYING OF THE GOSPEL TO ALL THE NON-CHRISTIAN WORLD the name of John R. Mott at once commends itself as appropriate ; a man who had twice been round the world and had visited all the chief mission-lands ; a man who combined to an extraordinary degree the power of thinking in terms of detail and of thinking in terms of continents ; who believed in the watchword, " The Evangelisation of the World in this Generation " ; for he belonged to that type of which someone speaking of Cromwell (was it not Carlyle ?) said, that it is the most " dangerous " of all, the *practical mystic*. . . . . Over the Commission of THE CHURCH IN THE MISSION-FIELD presided Dr J. C. Gibson, of the Presbyterian Church of England China mission, a man who had been thirty-three years a missionary in contact with the rapidly-growing Church of the most potentially powerful mission-land in the world ; who had further come into contact with men engaged in missionary work in every land, and had already in his writings revealed his high gift as a missionary statesman . . . . Of the Commission on EDUCATION IN RELATION TO THE CHRISTIANISATION OF NATIONAL LIFE, Dr Gore, the first Bishop of Birmingham, was Chairman, a Platonist to the core in intellectual attitude, steeped in that archetype of all educational philosophy, the Republic of Plato, in which the greatest Athenian some four centuries before Christ discussed the very theme that had been propounded for this Commission in the twentieth century after ; how, by means of an education shaped by the heavenly ideal, great leaders of the City of God might be trained and great national and social organisms thus built up informed by the same ideal : a man whose enthusiasm for religious education at home, and (as the Report on his Commission was to show) abroad also, was simply the Christianisation of his Platonism ; and whose passion for the Civitas Dei of Catholicity was owed, perhaps, as much to the *Politeia Platonis* as to the *Epistola S. Pauli Apostoli ad Ephesios* . . . To the chairmanship of the Commission on the THE MISSIONARY MESSAGE was appointed Professor D. S. Cairns, of Aberdeen, a man of the rising school of Christian thinkers, whose writings had proved him to be sensitive to an unusual degree to all currents of modern thought—" every wind of doctrine,"—which, however, do not carry such thinkers about, but rather straighten and accelerate the course of their philosophy towards CHRIST, the Wisdom of God and the Power of God. The fittingness of such a choice

for the Commission is obvious, when we reflect that its main task was to see and to show how the eyes that are keenest to perceive the light that lighteth every man in non-Christian religions, will also know the God-appointed entrance for their penetration by God's Incarnate Word, who is that Light, even Christ. . . . It was also well done to appoint Dr Douglas Mackenzie to the chairmanship of the Commission on the PREPARATION OF MISSIONARIES, a man with a rare mind of equal philosophic breadth and reverential depth : bearing a historic name, son of the great missionary Mackenzie of South Africa, he had grown up not merely in an atmosphere of missions, but in an atmosphere of missionary statesmanship, and in manhood had not disappointed the hopes to which such circumstances gave rise : further, as Principal of the well-known Hartford Theological Seminary, in Connecticut, he had to apply his mind daily to the problem of the training of leaders for " the great employ."
. . . The Commission on HOME BASE OF MISSIONS sat under the presidency of Dr James L. Barton of Boston, a man whose vast experience in all aspects of Mission work, and whose important post on the historic missionboard of which he is Secretary, were in themselves an assurance of absolute competence to undertake this supremely important work. . . . The Lord Balfour of Burleigh was one who had already, like his great ancestor in the days of Old Mortality, had experience of Governments,—with passages, too, that were courageous like that ancestor's, only suitably to these politer days : an ex-Cabinet Minister and great public figure in Church and State alike, who more fitting to occupy the chair of the Commission on MISSIONS AND GOVERNMENTS ? . . . And for the Commission on CO-OPERATION AND THE PROMOTION OF UNITY, the Committee had at hand another notable public servant, who, as Indian civilian, in a posi-

tion second only to that of the Viceroy, had given a lifetime to studying, in the sphere of Indian politics and administration, how to instil and to practice both the principle of co-operation and that of unity ; and who had in his high position followed the example of the greatest Anglo-Indians—an Edwardes and a Lawrence, and many another—in showing himself under every circumstance a Christian first of all. . . .

These names of the Chairmen must be taken as true samples of the personnel of the eight Commissions as a whole. Here we see public men of the highest calibre, politicians and statesmen in the civil, the ecclesiastical, and the missionary spheres, giving not only their names but also (as we shall see) lavishly of their time and effort to the enormous task of these Commissions. It was only purposes of obvious convenience that determined the fact that all these eight belonged to the English-speaking race. But among the Vice-Chairmen or members were men like Professor Warneck of Halle University, Professor Meinhof, Dr Julius Richter, and Herr Ober-verwaltungsgerichtsrath Berner—to name only four. There will be more to say about such great names as these when the personnel of the Conference itself is passed in review.

The list of Commissions might be gone carefully through, and name after name, as outstanding as these mentioned for Christian character, and service, and intellectual ability, might be easily mentioned. But *ex capite Herculem.*

4.

The constitution of these Commissions involved a correspondence with missionary societies on both sides of the Atlantic and of the Channel ; the drawing up of the sets of questions which were to be sent out for answer (an all-important matter, if any good return was to come from the enormous expenditure of these men's time) involved a still more prolonged cross-correspondence back and forth ; the names of the hundreds of correspondents on the mission-field, to whom those questions were to be sent, had to be obtained from Societies in many different countries. The labour was enormous, and there was (we are told) " real danger that the questions would not be issued soon enough to give missionary workers time to reply." It must have been a grim struggle from that July to the new-year ! . . . But the bulk of the question papers were at last ready and sent out by February 1909.

Yet this was only the beginning. There were now exactly sixteen months till the Conference. In that time (1) the question papers had to reach their missionary addressees, many of them in the remotest parts of the world ; (2) an orthodox interval had to be allowed for, during which these papers were permitted peacefully to rest, unattended to, in the missionary's drawer, or reproachfully eyeing him from a pigeon-hole in his desk (*experto crede*) ; (3) in the pressure of the missionaries' life, in sickness sometimes, travel or great heat often, at great sacrifice invariably, these questions were answered in writing,—and the reader may judge what this means in quantity and quality when he learns that some missionaries wrote replies in which they embodied all the experience and philosophy of a life-time's work. In all, upwards of one thousand papers, representing a whole case-full of books in print, were received by the even more unfortunate Chairmen of Commissions ; (4) and then the members of each Commission, who probably did not receive all their material till the late autumn before the Conference, had to peruse the sets of answers, varying from one to five hundred in number. . . . The further process of these Herculean labours must be illustrated by a specimen account (taken from the records of the Commission on Missionary Education) printed in a paper sent to the delegates two months before the Conference :

"The Executive Committee of the Commission met in London for five days last November to consider the preliminary drafts prepared by different members of the Commission on the basis of the large amount of material that had been received from the mission field. Previous to this, the Vice-Chairman of the Commission had come over from America, and held prolonged conference with individual members of the Commission regarding its work. After the meeting in London a fresh revision was made of the first drafts, and these were sent over to the American members of the Commission, and also to a small number of the leading educationalists in the different mission fields. Criticisms and suggestions have been received from the latter, and the American members of the Commission met in New York for four days, sitting for ten hours each day. They arranged that a large amount of additional work should be done on the draft Reports by the American members of the Commission, and also that Professor E. D. Burton of Chicago, who has just returned from a two years' tour round the world for the express purpose of studying educational missionary work, should come over to Great Britain to represent the views of the American members at the meeting of the Commission in London on April 5th and 6th. At this meeting, the Report will be put into final shape for issue to the delegates of the Conference."

The strain must have been, in fact, tremendous. At one time it seemed as if the Reports of the Commissions would not be able to be put into the hands of the delegates before the Conference, but in the end each tryst was kept. And though the members of Commissions (and afterwards the delegates who had to read the Reports) sighed, often and deeply, for even three months more time, still the Reports were sent out some weeks before the opening day on June 14th. And so in railway-train, on P. and O. and Atlantic liner, the spectacle of the long folio printed documents might have been seen, in the hands of a thousand delegates, coming from East, West, North and South, as they tried to accomplish the feat of mastering eight volumes of closest thinking, each averaging from 200 to 300 pages of ordinary print, in a period that amounted to perhaps half a week per volume.

Thus the World Missionary Conference represented *work*, plentiful, hard, and honest, whether on the part of the Conference office-staff (whose enormous labours have not been even touched on above), or the Committee of the Conference, or the eight Chairmen, or the eight Commissions, or the twelve hundred Delegates.

And yet no labour or preparation could possibly have been commensurate with the profound issues which the Reports had unfolded, and which the great Conference now assembled to discuss.

CHAPTER III

At the foot of an old winding street that slopes steeply up to a precipitous acropolis of rock, there stands in one of the cities of the North a little, old, grey mansion, with the pathetic ruin of a little, old, grey chapel by its side. Built on the narrow platform of a little plain, which is inserted, as it were, in among a huddle of grey hills,[1] this mansion is overhung and overshadowed alike by the steep slopes and sheer crags of those hills on the one side, and by a city of abrupt alternate ridges and ravines on the other. Such towering surroundings, were it ten times grander and more spacious than it is, would surely have humbled it. But, indeed, it is in itself neither spacious nor grand :—a traveller who has fared through the Continent and England, and has in mind the regal palaces and no less regal baronial halls that he has passed, might take it, perhaps, for the mansion of some old local barony little known to fame. . . .

Strange little, old, grey Palace of the kings of that grey, small northern land ! In *site*, how fit a symbol for a kingdom that is scarcely more than one narrow midland plain, crouching between two masses of barren mountains and moors : in *aspect*, how fit a symbol for that small, dour people whose entire realm numbered, and still numbers, scarcely more than a single earldom

---

[1] So R. L. S.

or duchy of some of its great neighbours ; which, never-theless, through its sons has made its life felt to the very ends of the earth !

For that little, grey mansion has for centuries seen the courts of Kings and Queens ; it is the Palace of the Kings and Queens of Scotland ; the Palace of their royal capital of EDINBURGH !

Fit symbol, shall we say then, in honourable in-significance and tremendous import, for a Council now assembling in this capital city, on the service of a Monarch whose glory has before now shown its un-concern for all grandeur of exterior, and before now, through the few and the contemned, has wrought among men a world-wide work ! Is there not another small Royal City, with rocky acropolis set among the ravines and grey limestone hills of far Judæa ? There that Monarch had at Salem His tabernacle and His dwelling in Zion. And it was from JERUSALEM that, led by twelve Galileans, this very enterprise started, for the business of which a Council is now mustering in this city of the North.

* * * * * *

The aspect of the city has often recalled to the minds of those that visit it another city, which also was the centre of the national life of a small, free people. As the eye rests on Arthur's Seat the mind may well hark back to where Lycabettus overhangs and overshadows another rocky Acropolis. From the acropolis of the Castle-rock you may descend by the Propylæa of Castle-Hill. The ridge of the Lawnmarket and Canongate shall be your Mars' Hill, and the great civil and ecclesi-astical Council-chambers, which there are wont to sit in judgment, shall together do duty for Areopagus' venerable Court. You descend into a ravine—let it

THE PALACE

be the Agora! Again you ascend the Calton's opposite slope—it is the Pnyx! . . . From her heights ATHENS, too, looked, over her Piræus port, to the deep-violet line of sea that crowned her Attica. That sea, once, to Athens vainly but gloriously dreaming, appeared but a highway on which her triremes might carry her to world-empire and glory beyond all dreams. She knew not that the sway which her city was destined to establish over the world for ever was not to come with observation; for it was not her triremes that were to win it for her, but the power of the spirit of her living thought. . . . The physical parallel between Athens and Edinburgh is, in truth, a guide-book common-place; but it might have suggested to the Delegates now ascending to their Areopagus on the Mound this thought,— the same that was the life-principle of one who "stood in the midst of Mars Hill"; the same for which Athens stands and witnesses; the same which makes little Holyrood a symbol,—that neither by might nor by power, but by Spirit, might EDINBURGH, 1910, play an incalculable part in establishing a yet more spiritual sway than that of Athens among the nations and peoples of the world.

· · · · · ·

As those Delegates ascend the slope of the ridge on which stand, in a group together, a Cathedral and two Church Assembly-Halls, more memories in this city of memories crowd upon the mind. . . . There stands the old Cathedral Church—in the centre of the ridge, midway in that narrow winding street, between the palace at its foot and the fortress at its head. A Cathedral it is, by right of history and of fact; yet many a parish-church in the richer South is the more imposing:— which reveals this Cathedral own-sister to the little

grey Palace beneath, Church and State alike yielding
one identical symbol. . . . Of how many things does
it speak, this little Cathedral, the true Heart of Mid-
lothian, set so firmly in the very heart of the old City !
The Conference, that at the noon of this day came to
worship within its walls, will but endorse, through
its Commissions and its Reports and its Debates, the old
Cathedral's silent testimony that at the heart of all
civic or social or national life, if it is to be great, must
be the Church of God . . .

Yet here rush discords in. For the silent voice of
this Cathedral Church tells further that the Church
of God is to-day a broken unity. Alas ! though the
Conference met to pray there that noon, it was not to
open its proceedings by a solemn and official celebration
of the Communion of the Body and Blood of Christ,
as was the practice of great œcumenical gatherings of an
undivided Church ! Not yet might those old walls see
that sacramental sight :—walls which in the four centuries that have passed have heard the dissonances of
antagonising litanies ; have seen the Missal of one
Church, and the Service-Book of a second, give
way, amid the conflict and violence of consciences
honestly moved, to the form of worship maintained
to-day by a third. A broken unity, a broken unity !,
stands here confessed. . . .

Yet it is something that on this night, a bow-shot
from the old Cathedral, shall meet in Conference twelve
hundred Christians called by many names ; and that
there shall be heard, in an Assembly Hall of that third
communion, the benediction of the Primate of the second ;
and that in the ears of the Conference shall be read,
from the Italian Bishop of the first, a letter likewise
invoking Heaven's benediction on all gathered there, and
on the work they have set their hands to in the name of

the Lord. . . . Peace then ! little Cathedral Church :—
the restoration of that broken unity may not even yet
have come within the range of men's waking vision, but
does it not, to-night, come to them at least as a true
dream ?

.   .   .   .   .   .

Just beyond the Cathedral is a noble Church, with
spire to the towering height of which is added the full
height of that towering ridge.   It is one of the two
Councils or Halls of Assembly which stand together
there.   Assembly Halls may change, but the General
Assembly of the Kirk of Scotland is an entity that
abides : so, as that Kirk's Assembly-Hall to-day, this
Church on the Mound carries the mind back to yet two
more unforgettable scenes upon which this city of
memories has looked. . . .

It is the year 1796, just one century and fourteen
years ago.   A General Assembly of the Kirk of Scotland
is in session, and the unwonted crowding of the building
shows that a subject of supreme moment, and keenly
divisive of opinion, is being debated.   For the General
Assembly has been prayed by the Synod of Moray and
the Synod of Fife, formally to consider a scheme of
Foreign Missions put forward by the first purely missionary society ever formed in Scotland,—founded only
that year in Edinburgh.   Yet from the outset of the
debate it is evident that the overture is to be rejected.
Though ably supported by several speakers, it has
against it the most influential leaders and notables
of that Assembly.   One of them has arisen, and has
delivered a long, most carefully prepared oration, in
which argument is piled on argument to defeat the
motion, because the speaker " cannot otherwise consider
the enthusiasm on this subject than as the effect of
sanguine and illusive views, the more dangerous because

the object is plausible." He ceases speaking and sits
down. And then a venerable figure rises, a man who
on the most ordinary occasion is wont to rivet his
hearers' attention, so deeply from heart and living
conviction comes his rough eloquence :—how much more
to-day, then, when he is fighting a losing battle for
what nevertheless he knows can never be a losing cause !
On that day it is given him to utter five rugged words,
which annihilate the flowing periods of the former
speaker : not one who heard them will ever forget
them ; indeed they will never be forgotten. Pointing
to the great Bible on the table in front of the Moderator
of that Assembly, he simply says,

" *Moderator ! rax me that Bible !* " . . .

The scene vanishes ; and it is again an Assembly Hall
in this old City. The sacred volume still lies in front of
the Moderator's chair. It is still " raxed," to one and
another, who from its pages seek to inspire or exhort
the vast concourse gathered there ;—but for other
purpose than to convince them that God's word gives
them the warrant to carry the Gospel to the ends of the
earth. For it is even from thence that these people have
come ! They have come from thence to declare how to
the ends of the earth has reached the line of that Gospel !
. . . Who are these sitting among them, aye, among the
leaders of them,—Indians and Africans, and Chinese, and
Koreans and Japanese ? These are they who have come
to give one final endorsement to the truth of ERSKINE'S
grand old protest, and to point forward, also,—to what ?

*   *   *   *   *   *

Is this the last of the symbolic memories that come to
this Conference from Edinburgh's past ? There is yet
one more ; and it, too, has to do with these two Halls
of Assembly upon that fateful ridge. . . . Where the

narrow ridge is narrowest, why do these two stand so stiffly, almost back to back? Once more the past calls us, back to the year 1843, midway between that other scene of yesterday, and this of to-day. Again an Assembly Hall is in session, and again it is crowded from the floor to the roof. Once more excitement is strong to its intensest pitch; for another supreme decision is this day to be made. The Moderator rises; with deep earnestness he offers prayer; then he reads from a document which he holds in his hand in a slow, emphatic manner. It is a protest. It reaches its impressive close; he flings it down on to the table before him, and then—solemnly departs. A great company of adherents rise, and leaving the rest sitting there, follow him through the streets of the grey city, three in depth, for a full quarter of a mile. And in a separate place they constitute another Assembly, while the old one sits on as before. And thus it is until this day. . . .

But to-night, in the new Assembly Hall which thus arose after that Disruption, a Missionary Conference, a general assembly indeed !, is to meet ; and, in the Moderator's chair will sit, as President of the Conference, one of the distinguished sons of the very Kirk from whose Assembly that disruption broke forth ! And night after night both Halls are to be thronged by a great company of folk, without distinction as to either nation or communion, for the one purpose of them all now is to carry the Gospel of their Master to the whole world, obedient to His command. . . .

.   .   .   .   .   .

So the Delegates pass up the slope on this evening of the 14th June 1910, towards their council-hall on that historic ridge. There, on its sky-line, dark against the late, mellow radiance of the never-ending northern

c

summer day, are the corona of the old Cathedral, the
spire and twin towers of the two Assembly-Halls. . . .
It may be that they still speak of a broken unity : but
surely, on this perfect evening, with a changed accent !—
Is it to be the work of carrying the One Gospel of the One
Lord to this One Human Race that is to add to these
unities yet one more, the unity of a One Catholic Church ?
So through the aisles of that old Church may one day
roll the harmony which shall ensue when all the discords
that have rushed in shall have been resolved, making
that harmony thereby all the more full and sweet.

.   .   .   .   .   .

EDINBURGH ! city of memories, of symbolic pictures
from the past ! . . . Is " Edinburgh " to be also, one
wonders, a city of hopes, the symbol and indicator of
something that is yet to be ?

NEW COLLEGE

Within which is the United Free Church of Scotland Assembly Hall, the scene of the Conference;
with the spire of the Church of Scotland Assembly Hall behind.

CHAPTER IV

THE Assembly Hall of the United Free Church of Scotland, in which the delegates now took their seats on that midsummer evening, is attached to the buildings of New College, the theological seminary founded by the great Chalmers, for the training of candidates for the Free Church ministry. The whole edifice is built on the steep flank of the ridge that has already been described ; so that the slope (called the Mound), by which the front gate is approached, is really continued within the buildings themselves, the front quadrangle being on a lower level than the whole of the premises fronting it, to which there leads a long steep flight of steps. The buildings that surround the quadrangle are consequently of great height, and darkly overshadow the small sombre court itself. Yet, high as are these overshadowing buildings, even over them appears the tall spire of the Established Kirk Assembly Hall rearing itself into the sky. Built, as we have seen, at the very top of the ridge, it looks down into the well of the quadrangle far beneath from what seems a simply towering height. In that quadrangle stands the silent effigy of John Knox. From the Assembly Halls to St Giles, from St Giles to Holyrood, this name dominates all,—nay, the whole city itself,— as that spire towers over all from the apex of the ridge. And the delegates entering by this deep, stone court, passed daily where that statue stood motionless, with rigid pointing arm and hand.

2.

Ascending now the flight of steps that fronted them, they passed through a vestibule, and then, by a series of corridors running round the Assembly Hall, into that Hall itself.

The council-hall was a striking one,—broad and spacious rather than lofty. The galleries, which ran round all four sides of it, brought the topmost row of their steep banks of benches almost level with the roof, by skylights in which the hall was almost entirely lighted. Thus it was no mere phrase that night to say that the House was crowded " from floor *to ceiling*,"—from the thronged benches of the floor, to the densely occupied galleries with their " overbellying crowds." The seats on the floor of the House were in blocks, oblong not wedge-shaped, slanting inwards towards the long rect-angular space in the centre, which was filled with the cross-benches, a square inclosure, and finally the Pre-sident's chair. The Chair thus faced the entire audience, with other chairs of honour to right and left, on a raised daïs. At a lower level was the square enclosure with a table in the midst, round which sat the Business Com-mittee of the Conference, with the Chairman of the Committee in their midst just below the President, and on his right the General Secretary of the Conference. Behind them were the cros -benches for the reporters. The Continental delegates took their seats in the front benches to right and left of the reporters. The rest of the delegates filled the remaining benches indiscrimin-ately, to the very farthest seats beneath the galleries.

THE QUADRANGLE

3.

When the appointed minute had arrived, the Lord
Balfour of Burleigh, President of the Conference, entered
the hall, accompanied by the speakers of the evening.
The President took his seat in the Moderator's chair,
with the speakers in the seats of honour to right and left.
The moment of inauguration was when the President
called upon the venerable Principal of the New College
to offer prayer to GOD.

In reading the accounts of great Œcumenical Councils
of the past, one is struck by that invariable feature of
their solemn inauguration,—the celebration of the
Eucharistic Feast with which they consecrated their
whole proceedings. In this world-conference meeting
that was not to be. And the fact, borne in on the soul,
wounded and hurt it. (Yet there was hope in the very
pain, for perhaps only such wounds can lead to healing.)
But as far as a human prayer could bring that Conference
into living touch with the sacred past and the Lord, with
the Communion of Saints and their King, so far was the
Conference brought by the prayer at that time offered.
Deeply experienced in solitary prayer ; steeped in the
liturgies, the private devotions, the spiritual language and
literature of Fathers, Doctors, Mystics, and Saints in all
ages, that white-haired Principal's prayer filled the place
with the aroma of the devotion of ages. . . . The Communion of Saints, the spirits of just men made perfect,
the general assembly of the first-born, encompass
the Conference like a cloud of witnesses, as the leader
solemnly commemorates and gives thanks for noble
men from many an age, and many a communion. " He
who holds the Book with the Seven Seals is opening one of
the Seals at this very hour ! ", he cries. And then comes
the thanksgiving for " Origen and Athanasius and the

great Alexandrians that gave us our Creed "; Augustine and à Kempis and Brother Lawrence ; (. . . and there was intercession here for " the Greek and Roman churches that they might have grace, grace of reformation and revival, such as we ourselves need ") ; . . . Bishop Andrewes, " who taught us how to pray," and Jeremy Taylor and William Law ; John Knox and Samuel Rutherford, Bunyan and "Baxter with his 'Saint's Rest'" ; and Spurgeon and Maclaren and M'Cheyne and Chalmers of New Guinea, Duff and David Livingstone. . . . It was a eucharist of thanksgiving, a solemn commemoration, which brought the Conference very near the Head and His universal church ; bringing nearer too, it may surely be, that united Eucharist and Communion which shall one day be.

4.

The Lord Balfour of Burleigh then rose. And just as Dr Whyte's prayer had been a reminder of the first act of the old Councils, so the President's very first sentence recalled another of their historic features. In those old days the solemn opening of a Council by the Emperor and the stately charge that he gave to it were essential and memorable features. And, for all that times are changed beyond all recognition, the Conference now assembled in the royal capital of a Christian king was not to lack a right royal and Christian message. " Gentlemen," said the President, " I am charged with a message from his Majesty the King, which you will doubtless receive with due honour and respect."

The Conference at the word rose and stood.

" *The King commands me to convey to you the expression of his deep interest in the World Missionary Conference to be held in Edinburgh at this time.*

" His Majesty views with gratification the fraternal co-operation of so many Churches and Societies in the United States, on the continent of Europe, and in the British Empire, in the work of disseminating the knowledge and principles of Christianity by Christian methods throughout the world.

" The King appreciates the supreme importance of this work in its bearing upon the cementing of international friendship, the cause of peace, and the well-being of mankind.

" His Majesty welcomes the prospect of this great representative gathering being held in one of the capitals of the United Kingdom, and expresses his earnest hope that the deliberations of the Conference may be guided by divine wisdom, and may be a means of promoting unity among Christians, and of furthering the high and beneficent ends which the Conference has in view."

5.

To the ears of the Conference the message rang with a true personal interest.[1] *" Defensor fidei "* is no doubt a very formal title—necessarily so in these changed times : but the spirit of it surely permeated the stately simplicity of these gracious words.   With a single accord and impulse the whole Conference, monarchists and republicans alike, sang GOD SAVE THE KING.

That message was the climax of the honourable and distinguished greetings given to the Conference :—the Municipality had welcomed it the evening before ; the National Church had opened its Cathedral to it at noon ; the University of Edinburgh had that day

[1] There were three other messages of unusual significance and importance which at different times were read to the Conference.   Two are given in the Appendix to this chapter.   The third will be noticed later on.

for the first time in its history honoured the leaders
of a Missionary Conference with its highest honorary
degrees ; and now the Prince of the Realm in which
it met had greeted it. A Conference so saluted would
have indeed been unworthy had anything but a noble
dignity characterised all its proceedings.

But before the end of that first evening there was
not one that was not deeply conscious that the Conference
had been welcomed at its outset by a Greater and
Mightier, Who is above all and over all.

6.

Three speakers spoke at this opening meeting, the
Lord President ; the Archbishop of Canterbury ; and—
if true oratory means beauty and truth in both thought
and utterance—then a prince of spiritual orators,
Robert Elliot Speer.

The first, we have already seen, is a great public
servant, sometime an honoured Cabinet Minister,
a notable Churchman. In this his first address, as
in his last, the ring of personal conviction and
passionate interest were unmistakable, when he spoke
of what the Conference stood for and what it hoped to
do ; the variety of the problems it had met to sift and
discuss with scientific regard to the facts ; the greatness
of the opportunity in the awakening world of to-day. . .
And time and again he struck the note of unity ; " the
thought not without its grandeur that a unity begun
in the mission field may extend its influence, and react
upon us at home and throughout the old civilisations " ;
the things which make sure common ground, "the
fatherhood of God, the love of the Son, the power of
the Holy Ghost, the purity of the Christian life, the
splendour of the Christian Hope." Such an address

struck a noble note, and those that followed carried
the assemblage yet higher.[1]

7.

No more powerful figure had the American foreign-
mission movement produced than the man who had
been chosen to speak that evening. Tall of stature,
and beautiful of countenance, with a powerful voice,
which for all its rasping resonance was capable of the
tenderest of cadences ; with a facility and golden beauty
of expression that was but the obverse of the great
beauty and spirituality of thought ; Johannine at once
for fire and for tenderness :—no wonder if it had been
claimed for Robert Speer that he was among the foremost of America's orators. The word has been soiled
by ignoble use ; but there has at all times been an
eloquence which, because wholly used for God, simply
seems to be a true spiritual charism. Such was that
of the man who had that night a subject intimately
dear to himself, wholly appropriate to this inauguration,
the Leadership of Christ. He began as always with the
personal note, the cherished reality of CHRIST to the
soul . . . the reality of His personal leadership ;
how simple fidelity to this leads on, invariably and inevitably, to the enterprise of giving Him to all the world.
" No one can follow Him without following Him *to the
uttermost parts of the earth* ! " he cried. And then,—the
Church has only imperfectly realised this leadership,
or it would have counted and found possible the things
that are impossibilities to her to-day ; overcome the
difficulties with regard to which this Conference, at
least, is under no delusions. And then the close led
back to the beloved figure of the CHRIST :—" We know

[1] In the following account the order in which they actually spoke is
reversed.

how great the undertaking is ; but we know also that
centuries ago One sat down before that undertaking
undismayed, though failure in the eyes of the world
was written clear and full across the face of it, and
saw far away through the centuries the result that could
not be for ever stayed : "—let only (pled the eloquent
voice) the barrier of unfaith that keeps us and that
Leader's almightiness apart, be removed, and " that
living faith will make it possible for Him to make use
of us for the immediate conquest of the world."

8.

Lest it should be thought that words like these were
but rhetoric and as rhetoric must be discounted, it is most
important to observe that the same startling proposition,
with which the address of the orator closed, fell also
that evening from the lips of one whom neither friend
nor opponent would credit with rhetoric ; who in fact
was not, first and foremost, an *orator* at all. Statesman,
courtier, churchman,—the Archbishop of Canterbury
had been called, and indeed was supremely, all of these ;
Scottish by birth and temperament, with the shrewd-
ness of the Scot and his practical grasp of affairs ;
Archbishop not only by position, but also one might say
by training ; spiritual guide to kings and queens ; large
of judgment, broad of toleration, and politic—yet no
trimmer—in matters of hottest controversy ; forced
by the very terribleness of his responsibilities to an ever-
deepening spiritual experience ; *such* was the man to
whom it was given that night to speak one sentence
which seemed to be suddenly touched with the prophetic
fire ; a sentence by which what might have seemed the
rhetorical paradox of the last speaker's peroration
was solemnly endorsed !

It must suffice simply to allude to the first part of that address, every word of it striking enough. It was marked by gracious humility and brotherliness unfeigned. It revealed unmistakable and even passionate conviction that evangelisation is the paramount duty of the Church. There were many orators on both sides of the Atlantic who would have impressed no one by calling that Conference one " which if men be weighed rather than counted has, I suppose, no parallel in the history of this or of other lands " : but coming from a Scots statesman-ecclesiastic, with a merited reputation for sobriety of thought and word, it impressed. But it was the closing sentence that gave the unforgettable thrill : he was affirming with tremendous emphasis that " the place of missions in the life of the Church must be the central place, and none other : that is what matters " ; — and thus concluded :—" Secure for that thought its true place, in our plans, our policy, our prayers ; and then—why then, the issue is His, not ours. *But it may well be that, if that come true, there be* SOME STANDING HERE TO-NIGHT WHO SHALL NOT TASTE OF DEATH TILL THEY SEE THE KINGDOM OF GOD COME WITH POWER "— !

It was the sudden appropriation to the *present* of perhaps the most mysterious and the most thrilling of all the sayings of CHRIST, with a boldness that only momentary inspiration, stinging " with the splendour of a sudden thought," seemed sufficient to account for, —this was the thing that thrilled. Archbishop fell away and was forgotten ; for a man, at long last, is a greater thing than an archbishop. But even man appeared also to fall away and be forgotten,—it seemed almost as if the speaker himself stood before his own word as one taken by surprise. For one supreme moment, it seemed, GOD had stood forth nakedly revealed, and had spoken in HIM who first spoke those words and now lives in the Divine glory.

APPENDIX TO CHAPTER IV.

(1)

MESSAGE TO THE EDINBURCH CONFERENCE FROM THE
IMPERIAL GERMAN COLONIAL OFFICE.

" The German Colonial Office is following the proceedings
of this World Mission Conference with lively interest, and
desires that it be crowned with blessing and success.

"The German Colonial Office recognises with satisfaction
and gratitude that the endeavours for the spread of the Gospel
are followed by the blessings of civilisation and culture in all
countries.

' In this sense, too, the good wishes of the Secretary of
State of the German Imperial Colonial Office accompany your
proceedings."

(2)

LETTER TO THE PRESIDENT OF THE EDINBURGH CONFERENCE
FROM THEODORE ROOSEVELT SOMETIME PRESIDENT OF
THE UNITED STATES OF AMERICA.

" MY DEAR SIR—It is a matter of real and profound regret
to me that I am imperatively called back to America, so that I
am unable to be present in person at the World Missionary
Conference. I regret it the more as, if I had been able to be
present, it would have been as a delegate from the Dutch
Reformed Church of America, to which I belong.

"Nothing like your proposed Conference has ever hitherto
taken place. From many nations, and from many churches, your
delegates gather on this great occasion to initiate a movement
which I not only hope but believe will be fraught with far-
reaching good. For the first time in four centuries Christians
of every name come together without renouncing their several
convictions, or sacrificing their several principles, to confer as
to what common action may be taken in order to make their
common Christianity not only known to, but a vital force
among the two-thirds of the human race to whom as yet it is
hardly even a name. Surely every man imbued, as every man

should be, with the ethical teachings of Christianity, must rejoice in such an effort to combine the strength of all the Churches in the endeavour to Christianise humanity, and to Christianise it not merely in name but in very fact.

"Your Conference represents the practical effort to apply the teachings of the Gospel to what the Epistle of Jude calls 'The Common Salvation.' An infinite amount of work remains to be done before we can regard ourselves as being even within measurable distance of the desired goal; an infinite amount at home in the dark places which too often closely surround the brightest centres of life, an infinite amount abroad in those dark places of the earth where blackness is as yet unrelieved by any light.

"When such is the high purpose to which you have dedicated yourselves it is eminently fitting that your invitation should have gone to all Christian Churches in all lands. I am sure that there will be a general and I hope a universal response. In missionary work, above all other kinds of Christian work, it is imperative to remember that a divided Christendom can only imperfectly bear witness to the essential unity of Christianity. I believe that without compromise of belief, without loss of the positive good contained in the recognition of diversities of gifts and differences of the administration, Christian Churches may yet find a way to cordial co-operation and friendship as regards the great underlying essentials upon which as a foundation all Christian Churches are built. This is one of the lessons which has been particularly impressed upon me by what I have seen of Christian work in Africa, both in heathen and Mohammedan lands. I believe that unity in a spirit of Christian brotherhood for such broad Christian work will tend, not to do away with differences of doctrine, but to prevent us from laying too much stress on the differences of doctrine. It is written in the Scriptures that 'He that doeth My will shall know of the doctrine'; but the reverse of this proposition cannot be found in Holy Writ. Emphasis is to be put upon 'doing the will'; if only we can make up our minds to work together with earnest sincerity for the common good we shall find that doctrinal differences in no way interfere with our doing this work.—Wishing you all success, I am, very sincerely yours,—THEODORE ROOSEVELT."

CHAPTER V

THE DELEGATES

THE next morning dawned bright and clear.

While the delegates are making towards their Hall of Council, rejoicing in the delicious Scottish midsummer, it is fitting to ask who they are; what communities they represent, what races, what nationalities; and from what lands they have travelled to this place. If to say something about the eight Chairmen only was as much as the limitation of space permitted, what is to be said about the twelve hundred delegates? Yet an impression of the historic gathering would be utterly incomplete were nothing to be set down.

I.

These men and women have come from literally all over the world. This Conference, though held in Britain, in Scotland, in Edinburgh, was in no sense a British, Scotch, or Edinburgh Conference — it is hardly too much to say that its official composition would have been substantially unchanged had it been held in London, New York, Berlin, or Shanghai; for in each case the principle which determined the choice and appointment of delegates would have been the same, and thus the personnel of the delegations would have been practically the same. That principle was a rigidly strict one:—all Mission Boards and Societies in all countries were empowered to send a number of delegates that was in exact proportion to their income, and the proportion was so calculated as to limit the total delegation to something over one thousand. It is obvious from this that a Society whose offices were in Edinburgh itself had not the smallest advantage over one situated at the very Antipodes. Absolutely no respect of persons was shown by sternly inflexible stewards to those who presented themselves at the iron gate of New College, demanding admittance to the delegates' conference-hall:—Did they carry a delegate's ticket, or did they not? That settled the question.

2.

It followed from this that the Conference was a true World Conference, as far as it went. And it further followed that, though large, it was essentially a business Conference, and that it meant business. Societies and Boards in distant lands do not incur the expense of sending representatives in order to give them a pleasant holiday-trip. Neither do men willingly carry about in their portmanteaux, and (to the extent of their ability) in their brains, eight Reports packed with thought and information, and demanding the closest reading and attention, unless they come to the Conference—the entire business of which was known to be the discussion *of those Reports*—with at least as much seriousness as Members of Parliament attend St Stephen's. The long two-years' preparation, in fact; the issuing of the eight Reports; and the strict system of representation, ensured something of a conciliar character for this Conference. It was indeed like a Council gravely responsible, in respect both of the research it conducted and the debates it held, and, though entirely destitute of executive authority, in respect of its acts, its findings, and its recommendations : for these, going from such a Council, must inevitably possess moral authority of the most important kind. It was no doubt this feeling of individual and collective responsibility to God and man that gave to the sessions their purposefulness, and to the debates their high tone and standard of ability.

3.

Besides, the large majority of those who attended were persons who were engaged in active missionary work abroad, or administrative work at home ; many of them were specialists, some of them the highest authorities, in their several subjects. The leaders in the administrative departments of all the Churches, Societies, or Boards, were there in force, to see how the work of the Home Base might be strengthened, and the Church rallied as one man to her task in all its length and breadth. Similarly, very many leading missionaries were there, able to inform the Conference as to the exact state of national feeling or missionary progress existing at that moment in their fields of work, and keen to pick up the smallest hint given by theological thinker or practical evangelist, if perchance it might be applied with profit to his own work.

4.

Let us now look a little more closely at these delegates who have come from every point of the compass to this ancient city and now are streaming up the Mound to their council-hall upon the ridge. They are to an extraordinary degree interesting, richly representative as they are of so many races, nations, tongues, traditions, ranks, professions ; and with such experience of service

D

in Church and State, and of adventures in their quest
in many a distant land. To begin with, these 1200
delegates are representative of many communions, and of
some 160 Missionary Boards or Societies. This alone
shows the technical representativeness of the Conference,
if one so may say. The communions whose absence at
once strikes the observer are of course the great Greek
and Roman Churches—the former with its notable Japan
mission, the latter (Church of Xavier yesterday and
Lavigerie to-day) with foreign missions all over the
world. But who, on this ridge of memories and of
hopes, can say what the future may bring forth ?

Nothing was more striking than the Continental
representation. The Anglo-Saxon's ignorance of language probably is (to do that much-abused person
justice) the sole cause of his haziness with regard to the
strength and importance of Continental missions. He
is only beginning to be aware that several Continental
missions are absolute models ; that the Continental
literature on the subject is of first-rate importance ; and
that Germany (characteristically) has done incom-
parable work on the science of Missions. The representation of the Continental Societies was unprecedented.
Statistics show that 'beside the delegates from the
Moravian Brethren—of whom some were from the Continent and some from Britain and America,—there were
delegates from many Societies in Germany, Holland,
Denmark, Finland, Norway, Sweden, France, and
Belgium. The official Continental delegation in all con-
sisted of over 170 members, representing forty-one
Societies !

5.

The *doyen* of missionary scientists and statesmen, Dr

Warneck, was prevented by infirmity from being present, but he wrote an important communication which was read aloud at the Conference. He was represented, too, in another way. Licentiat Joh. Warneck was there, learned son of a learned father. Another great German missionary was there, who, like Dr Warneck, had applied to the subject of Missions the scientific thoroughness of their race—Dr Julius Richter, the great missionary historian. Whoever saw his face, broad with humour and good-humour, was not surprised to learn that he was the life of the Business Committee, whose protracted labours before and during the Conference must have made such spirits invaluable. Another well-known man, Dr Mirbt of Marburg, was there, a man of recognised eminence in the German Universities, a proof that the phenomenon of missions is beginning to demand the attention and the serious study of the University world in Germany, as elsewhere. Ecclesiastics from the Continent, too, are there—Moravian bishops from Herrnhut—name how sweetly fragrant of Count Zinzendorf and of the most missionary Church of all history! ;—and from Sweden, Bishop Tottie, admirably picturesque figure, apparelled in what was not unlike court-dress, with gold cross suspended over the breast, just under the snow-white bands which farther west are no longer seen except in Presbyterian pulpits. Yonder venerable figure, as of some aged viking, reminds us that Norway is still producing the old breed that once harried the coast of Lothian. Danes and Norsemen have sailed for that coast to-day on a very different quest. Another Scandinavian delegate, bearer of a great name, is there—Count Moltke, sometime Cabinet Minister in Denmark, now occupying a trusted position in the Court of that Royal House whence comes the Queen-Mother of the British King. He is not the only figure who has had intimate dealings with Continental ministries : Professor Meinhof, a man valued in the Imperial Colonial Office of Germany, is there ; and Oberverwaltungsgerichtsrath Dr Berner, in all missionary matters the private counsellor of the Berlin Foreign Office. And many other valued counsellors had come from Holland, from France, from Switzerland, from Finland, and from Belgium, none more remarkable than that thick-set figure, well-known for his African travels, M. le Capitaine Alfred Bertrand, a man who was converted not only to missions, but, it seems, to God, by what he saw in Barotsi- land, where he met François Coillard, the Frenchman whose name stands among the highest in the history of African missions.

6.

When one contemplated the English-speaking delega- tions, it was realised to what an extraordinary degree they even by themselves represented a world-wide constituency. For here were delegates from the United States of North America, from Great Britain and Ireland, and from " All the Britains " across the sea—Canada, Australia, New Zealand, South Africa. With these latter " home " and " foreign " missions often become literally one and the same, for Canadian Indian, New Guinea savage, Maori, Kafir, lie at their very doors, or in their very midst. There is another thing that was realised too, as the venerable figure of an Australian chief-pastor, Bishop Pain of Gippsland, rose to tell of Anglicans and Presbyterians sitting in Council discussing as a practical and immediate problem the *uniting* of the two great communions ; it was realised that some great central problems may in the providence of God be first solved on the circumference, and that the latest-born Churches may lead the way for the elder ones towards the longed-for unity.

It was impressive, the proof afforded by these English-speaking delegates, no less than by the Continentals, that the missionary cause has engaged the serious attention of men of the very highest position and intellectual capacity on both sides of the Atlantic. In the Conference were statesmen and other notable public men. The name of one President of the United States was among the registered delegates—Theodore Roosevelt; and although he was, to his own deep regret, prevented from coming, he sent a long and valuable letter which was read out at the Conference. Actually present among the delegates representing his own communion, is a man who, to the majority of the delegates, was of virtually Presidential rank—William J. Bryan, a delegate, moreover, who worked and spoke to some purpose at the Conference. There, too, is a man whose name is honoured all over the States as one who has stood and fought for civic and political righteousness—Seth Low. A sometime Cabinet Minister of a recent British ministry is there, the President of the Conference, the Lord Balfour of Burleigh : once and again he made the whole Conference feel by his words how deeply and personally the cause of Christ in the world concerned him. Might it not be said, that the great Marquis of Salisbury was there in the person of his son, Lord William Gascoyne-Cecil ? There were philanthropists present, like Lord Kinnaird, Sir John Kennaway, and Charles Harford; great Indian administrators who stood for English Christianity as well as English statesmanship—Lord Reay, ex-Governor of Bombay ; Sir Andrew H. L. Fraser, ex-Lieut.-Governor of Bengal, Sir Mackworth Young, ex-Lieut.-Governor of the Punjab ; men of the very highest position and authority in educational science—Professor Michael E. Sadler and Dr

Parkin. Then there were men present who were some
of the great Churchmen of the time—from England, both
the Archbishops of the Church, though both of them
Scotsmen to the backbone—Drs. Randall Davidson and
Cosmo Gordon Lang ; Bishops, some of the greatest on
the bench—Salisbury, Southwark, Birmingham, Durham ;
from Scotland, Moderators and sometime-Moderators of
the Kirk in its several branches ; from the non-Episcopal
communions, notables like Sir George Macalpine and
Sir Robert Perks ; men whose work in theology is
universally known, such as Principals Moore of Harvard, Douglas Mackenzie of Hartford, and Alexander
Whyte of the New College ; Drs James Denney, A. R.
MacEwen, W. P. Paterson, D. S. Cairns, J. O. F. Murray,
C. G. Findlay, and R. F. Horton ; well-known heads of
Anglican theological colleges, such as Dr Frere of Mirfield, or Fr. Kelly of Kelham, with jolly face above the
monk's frock and cowl. All these were not only outstanding men on their own special sphere, but they all
gave proof after proof that the cause of worldwide
evangelisation was to them of the very substance of their
religious life and work. This should be said, lest, as we
come to those whose special sphere was missionary work
itself, it should be thought that there was any difference in passionate conviction and practical enthusiasm between these and those. Inspired orators of
missions were there, like Robert Elliot Speer ; men
with mind-calibre of first-rate statesmen, like John R.
Mott ; men whose writings and administrative work
have gained universal recognition and widest reputation, as Bishop Montgomery, Eugene Stock, Wardlaw
Thompson, Harlan Beach, Arthur J. Brown, and
many others ; editors of universally known magazines
or reviews such as *The East and the West*, which, in its
issue of that month, might well claim to have in some

sense forestalled the Edinburgh Conference itself ; and of women who are doing a work as great in quality as these, Mrs Gladden, reputed one of the finest speakers for Missions in the United States ; Miss Small, whose work in the science and art of training of workers is quite outstanding ; Miss Gollock, of the Church Missionary Society ; Mrs Creighton, whose work is valued both for itself, and because in it and her the Church feels that Mandell Creighton is not lost to it. Then there were laymen, especially from America, alert, burning with enthusiasm, speaking absolutely to the point—these are men who are showing what laymen and business men can do for the cause, both in the special work they themselves engage in, and in the marvellous movement they are inspiring among the business-men and other laymen of the Churches :—their presence and speaking is often to refresh and stir the whole Conference.

7.

What a sum-total of varied and thrilling interest was in the experiences, had they all been told, of the men who were there fresh from active service all over the world ! Men bearing historic missionary names, like that of Gulick ; men from the Far East, builders-up of Christian Churches, missionary prophets and seers, evangelists and physicians—from the Philippines, Bishop Brent ; from China, Bishops Roots and Bashford ; President Hawks Pott of Shanghai ; D. E. Hoste, the successor of a great man now gone, J. Hudson Taylor, and one of the famous Cambridge Seven ; Dr A. H. Smith and Dr J. C. Gibson ; from Korea, G. Heber Jones. Every one of these was a leader of the missionary enterprise in the Far East ; while from the Middle East there were leaders in the Indian educational world, well known to Government as well as to the Church, such as Principal Mackichan of Bombay; veterans like Bishop Thoburn, whose name was universally familiar, Bishop Robinson, and Bishop Oldham of Singapore; men who had distinguished themselves in some special department, such as Dr R. A. Hume of Ahmednagar, and C. E. Tyndale-Biscoe, whose bright and original educational work helps to make history on the frontier; while as for Orientalists, there were Dr St Clair Tisdall, whose books were known of all; H. D. Griswold, the Sanskrit scholar, and " Pundit " Johnson, who had so amazed learned Brahman society by preaching to it in pure Sanskrit. . . . Amongst his Indian brethren, Brother Western, of Delhi, in friar's habit with a rope for cincture, face pale and bleached, bare-sandalled feet; one of a band which, with the spirit and method that derive from Assisi, preaches the Gospel of service in the endless plains and villages of Northern India to-day. Chiefest among chiefs, a venerable figure, in whom length of service, golden wisdom of counsel, pre-eminence of reputation, marked him the Nestor of that Council of Leaders, Principal William Miller of Madras; as he was led slowly to the daïs, with tardy steps and darkening vision, not Nestor himself was ever awaited with more respect to give his counsel to the mustered leaders of the Greeks.

8.

But possibly the most interesting, certainly by far the most significant figures of all, were those of the Oriental and African delegates, yellow, brown, or black in race, that were scattered among the delegates in that World Conference. For not only by their presence but by their frequent contributions to the debates, they gave final proof that the Christian religion is now rooted in all those great

THE CONFERENCE IN SESSION

countries of the Orient and the South ; and not only so,
but that it possesses in those countries leaders who, for
intellectual ability and all-round competence, were fully
worthy of standing beside the men who have been
mentioned, even without the traditions of two millenniums of western Christianity at the back of them.
Seated among the members of the Conference Business-
Committee, which sat round the table just under the
President's chair, was Kajinosuke Ibuka, in whose face,
immobile as a Buddha, lurked the suspicion of the
enigmatic twinkle of an Eastern image when some
missionary delegate, in a confidential moment, tells the
Conference what missionaries think about the Japanese,
or what they suppose the Japanese think about them.
This man is one of the foremost Christians of Japan, a
theologian, a college Principal, one of the nine who were
formed into the first Protestant communion in Japan.
Not far off is his friend and equally notable fellow-
Christian, the first Japanese Bishop (Methodist Episcopal)
Yoitsu Honda, and Tasuku Harada, well known in all
Japan as the successor of Neesima, famous founder of the
most famous Christian College in Japan.   Here too are
other eminent Christians of the yellow race : from Korea,
one who is graduate of an American University, and a
former Vice-Minister of Foreign Affairs, the Hon. T. H.
Yun Chi-Ho, who, with a great secular career before him
has preferred to sacrifice it all, and give his life for Christ
and the Church.   Chinese delegates too, mostly in
irreproachable Western dress ; but one of them, a sturdy
nationalist, Tong Tsing-en, who in the debates is to speak
up for the permanent value of the Confucian Classics as a
subject of Christian study, is in full Chinese costume—
skull-cap and pigtail, and stuffed, quilted jacket of richest
peacock-blue silk.   From India come some whose light-
brown colour and clear-cut features proclaim the Aryan,

and some whose Dravidian blood is shown by their darker skin. Belonging to the former is yonder venerable, one might say high-priestly figure, a pure Brahman by descent, with long, silky-white beard, tall, upright figure, aristocratic, gentle features, and mild Indian voice; a Bengali convert of the great Dr Duff, now an honoured minister in the Punjab; chosen to be the Moderator of the first General Assembly of the Presbyterian Church in India, and yesterday, together with his Japanese fellow-Christian Tasuku Harada, made Doctor of Laws by the ancient University of this city of Edinburgh. And finally, men of African race, one, a negro of immense size glorying in his African race, from Liberia, the only independent negro organised state in Africa.

9.

From these, some idea may be formed of the twelve hundred delegates to Edinburgh, 1910, and of the types, races, occupations and spheres of service which they represented.

On this 15th June they pass again into the quadrangle of New College; in the summer morning the sombreness of the deep well of that court merely tones down the glare of the June sun, creating a suffused half-light, in the subdued brilliance of which every feature and all the movement of the scene stand out,—the intent, animated faces of the delegates, the summer dresses of the women. The beauty of the thing is incidental; yet, it is not out of harmony with the work to which the delegates now address themselves in the Council-hall above, where they sit as a Committee of the whole House, to discuss the Report of Commission I., the Carrying of the Gospel to all the non-Christian World.

CHAPTER VI

ASPECTS OF PROCEDURE

THE House when it sat in Committee bore the same aspect as when it sat as a Conference, the only difference being that the chair was taken by the Chairman of Committee, John R. Mott, who had been chosen to preside at the discussions of the Reports of all the eight Commissions. These discussions were to occupy the morning and afternoon sessions of the eight days of conference; the evening sessions being given, not to discussion, but to hearing papers on certain universally important aspects of missions.

There were many points of great interest as well as of considerable picturesqueness about these " Committees of the whole House," and since it is impossible to write or read about the debates profitably without having some idea of their setting in the mind, it will be by no means lost time to attempt now to picture that setting at the outset.

I.

Each day invariably began with a quarter of an hour of divine worship—the singing of a hymn, the hearing of Scripture, and prayer offered by one appointed to this service. Then, after the singing of another ringing hymn, the notices and other "business" were got through.

And here was a notable thing; the whole of that business occupied a matter of a few minutes, five or

less. This wonder was wrought by the publication
of a Daily Paper which was delivered by first post at the
address of every house in Edinburgh where a delegate
was residing—a triumph of organisation indeed. As
the minutes of the proceedings of the previous day, and
the order of the current day, were succinctly stated there,
minutes and notices were "taken as read," and the
Conference passed straight to the order of the day.
So, within a few minutes of the close of the hymn, the
House was plunged into the consideration of one of
the eight Reports.

This great concentration and business-like application
were highly characteristic of a Conference which dispensed
at the opening and the close with all votes of thanks,
compliments, and other forms of mutual admiration.
The King's Business demanded haste—and application.
And this too explains the intent silence in the atmosphere of which the Conference worked. Insulating the
delegates from the outer world were the corridors, with
"SILENCE" at frequent intervals along their walls.
Like the insulating vacuum of a thermos-flask, this
sound-proof lining kept the interior of the Council-hall
independent of its exterior. Windowless and therefore
without distraction to the eye, soundless and so without
distraction to the ear, deskless and thus without distraction for the hand, it left the delegate no option
(even had he had the wish) but to give his whole mind
to the matter on hand. And at the times of prayer,
when the spirit of devotion was well aroused, the silence
of God was heard within the hall.

2.

Leaving then the buzz of the world outside, one
passed straight from the humming city into the

quiet Council-hall, and there would find the Chairman of the Commission whose Report was being that day discussed bringing forward his Report,—a printed copy of which had been for some weeks in the hands of all the delegates,—and making his statement upon the same. The Chairman of each Committee had also the right to close the discussion at the end of the day, and during the day he might call upon one or other member of his Committee to speak. But the total time allowed to him or his Committee was limited by standing order, and the whole of the remaining time was given to members of the Conference, seven minutes only being allowed to each speaker. The total time available for this general debating was a little over three hours and a half, after making all deductions, so that at least thirty seven-minute speeches were heard each day : probably more, for while several righteous persons took less than their right not one was permitted a moment beyond it. At six minutes went a warning bell ; at seven he was rung down, and there was an end of him, be he Bishop, Moderator, or Peer of the Realm. At most he was permitted to finish his sentence (if it was a very short one) ; but often sentences and possibly even some of the longer words of the language were cut clean in half by the sharp stinging sound of the bell. These curtailments had occasionally a comic side. . . . " And now to come to the most important aspect of my subject,"—(*Bell !*) . . . the most important aspect of his subject became identical with zero,—at least it remained the sole property of the speaker.

The seven minutes rule certainly helped to keep speakers rigidly to the point, and contributed to the suppression of the Conference-Bore. Yet, even with this maximum of 420 seconds, many speakers could not resist the common temptation of using some of them

in deploring the fewness of the remainder : the wise
were those who plunged headlong and even breathless
into their subject and kept up full pressure for the whole
of their time. Some showed that it was possible to
make a great speech in seven minutes ; some showed,
equally, that even after seventy-times-seven minutes the
speech would still have been a small one. But it will be
understood that the level of speaking at Edinburgh,
1910, was, as it should have been, high and on some
days very high indeed.

3.

Yet the allowance, small though it was, was utterly
insufficient to enable all, who wished, to speak. Not
once did the much-suffering Chairman find that at the
end of the day he had no application-cards before him :
on most days when the closure came there was still
a small pile on his desk. On the last day there were
close on one *hundred* delegates whose contribution to
that day's debate will be buried with them. Under
these distressing circumstances the Conference Executive
proposed on the second day to reduce the allowance
to five minutes, and though a large number voted for
the reduction, the motion did not command the necessary
two-thirds majority, and was lost. On the last day,
however, the Executive took the law into their own hands
and cut down the allowance to five minutes :—yet that
was the day on which, though nearly fifty spoke, there
remained twice that who had tried, in vain, to catch
the Speaker's eye.

Such circumstances throw a very severe strain upon
a Chairman, for to him in this case was left the sole
responsibility of the selection,—the unenviable responsibility of having to look purely to the interests

of the debate, and of yet ensuring that neither race nor nation nor denomination nor " school of thought " should feel neglected or aggrieved. It is to be imagined that every fair-minded person pronounced that their Chairman had in this case played his difficult part to perfection. Yet he suffered.—" If these delegates " (he said one morning, alluding to the large number necessarily prevented from speaking on the previous day), " if these delegates feel disappointed, what must be the feelings of ' the Chair ' ! " And behind the half-humorous expression there was a note that conveyed that his duties had their painful and even their unpleasant side.

4.

Yet not one man from either hemisphere could have filled that chair as it was filled by John R. Mott. Like every Speaker he never spoke — that is to say, he made no contribution to the debates themselves, except only on the day on which, as Chairman of a Commission, he had to bring forward its Report ; yet his influence and personality was felt throughout the whole Conference. The whole physique of the man suggested strength, with its frame built on large lines, finely-moulded head, and rock-strong face. When a point of unusual interest was being hazarded, forward would come the big head, quick as light ; the strong square jowl would be thrust forward, the broad brow knit and scowl (if the word may be used for a sight wholly gracious), the dark shaggy eyebrows almost meet, while from under their shadow shoots a gleam from suddenly-kindling eyes :— a very lion preparing to spring at an idea. . . . Thus, too, when he himself addresses an assembly, knits and kindles the craggy tender face ; the voice vibrates with fierce emphases and stresses, while gestures of admirable justness accompany each point made. The single words seem literally to fall from his lips (the trite expression is for once justified), finished off with a deliberation that never slurs one final consonant, but on the contrary gives that consonant the duty of driving its word home. And so for the sentences also ;— the conclusion of each, instead of dropping in tone, increases to a sort of defiant *sforzando*, which, when his earnestness is at its height, can be terrific. Every sentence is brought down like a blow ; and, as when the heavy arm of some stone-breaker bangs blow on blow on the heart of a lump of stone, until it fairly smashes into fragments, not otherwise hammer the sentences of John R. Mott, with careful, scientific deliberateness, until, at the end, the audience finds itself, in a word—smashed. . . . And then the tenderness of the man comes out—as he deals with the fragments.

Such consistent power is vested in no man save him in whom it daily accumulates by habitual communion with the one Source. And that, in fact, has been the secret in the case of this man, and the sole explanation of his unique career as a Christian worker among the Colleges and the Churches, culminating in Edinburgh, 1910. . . .

Yet this heavy-weight fighter in the great Campaign had the lightest touch. That leonine gleam could be also a gleam of humour. Time and again, when the Conference was dragging from weariness, or when an awkward situation was developing and the tension was giving some anxiety, the light touch saved the situation ;—one brief remark, dry-spiced with saving humour, would set things going rightly forward again. An audience which was probably radical and democratic in its general attitude, might not have cared to be told to limit, or even stop, its applause.

But what audience can take it amiss when its Chairman requests it to " *applaud concisely* " ? . . . Neither does an assembly, as a general rule, appreciate an intimation that it, like all assemblies, is apt to become long-winded. But it will even cheer that intimation from a Chairman who, when directing speakers "to look straight at the clock," adds that an acoustical peculiarity which makes this desirable " may possibly have other advantages." . . .

5.

Just beneath him at the Committee table, sat the General Secretary of the Conference, J. H. Oldham, a man strangely contrasted with the Chairman. Small of stature, and of unassuming face and mien, he slipped into or out of his place at the table, as one not merely unnoticed but not meriting notice. The Chairman, though he did not intervene in the discussions, at least gave the important closing address, and his voice was frequently and authoritatively heard ; but the Secretary, from beginning to end, never opened his lips, save to give out formal notices. Why then was it that the first time he rose to give out a notice, the whole Conference applauded as though it would never cease ? Some did so, perhaps, because they wanted to show their appreciation of a triumph of organisation. But those that knew were aware that, more than any one other, the spirit that was in this very unobtrusive exterior had been at the back of that great Conference, not merely in respect of its organisation and its methods, but also of its ideals, its aspirations, and its hopes.

6.

There was something typical about this fact—that the few men who most made the Conference what it

E

was spoke least or spoke never. It should prevent the reader of this book from thinking that this Conference was "dominated by So-and-so's personality." Just one of its most remarkable features of all, on the contrary, was that it was *not* dominated by personalities at all. Men of marked personality did indeed speak, and this book, if only in order to give a truthful impression of the Conference, has had and will have to sketch them in as vividly as may be. But in no sense did they make the Conference. For one thing the notables were too many, as the perusal of the last chapter may have suggested, for any one or any few of them to be able to make a dominating impression. Men accustomed to dominate assemblies were half-lost in the crowd. Leaders of the Churches and the Societies might be seen sitting in the ranks, or in the shadow of the galleries, and rarely or never coming forward to speak. In short, the dominating impression was that the Spirit of God, and no man, was the dominating personality in that Assembly.

And perhaps this explained something else. Not every large Christian conference, convention, or assembly breathes a particularly devotional or spiritual atmosphere during its sessions. Broadly speaking, the spirituality of a conference is very often in inverse proportion to its size. There were several features that combined to make the Edinburgh Conference an exception to this generalisation; but most of all, something which was perhaps its most striking feature.—Every day, at the very time of the day when the audience was at its freshest and most vigorous, this great Conference, which was daily finding its available time insufficient, deliberately suspended its discussion; for a full half-hour the voice of debate was hushed, and the Conference, as a Conference, fell to prayer. At first this half-hour was fixed for the last one in the morning session ; but it was found that this meant that a proportion of the audience found it had to go out before the prayer-hour. Then let them miss a fraction of the discussion, not *that*!;—and the Executive deliberately runs the prayer-hour into the heart of the morning session—the very cream of the day. " We now approach our great central act of worship," says the Chairman. . . . Some acknowledged spiritual leader ascends the daïs ; over the hushed Assembly-Hall his sole voice is heard, leading thoughts and minds towards " The Quiet,"—towards GOD. As often as not even the voice of the leader is still, and this strange intercession-meeting prays in a symphony of united silence, in the close Presence of God. . . .

An object-lesson that came as rebuke to many an individual life there, and to many a better-known conference or ecclesiastical assembly. Religious assemblies are often very far from devout, and, like most persons, are in the habit of saying there is not enough time for prayer.—And this busiest of Assemblies gave half an hour of the cream of the day to its God in prayer.

CHAPTER VII

" CARRYING THE GOSPEL TO ALL THE NON-CHRISTIAN WORLD "

" It is a startling and solemnising fact that even as late as the twentieth century the Great Command of Jesus Christ to carry the Gospel to all mankind is still so largely unfulfilled. It is a ground for great hopefulness that, notwithstanding the serious situation occasioned by such neglect, the Church is confronted to-day, as in no preceding generation, with a literally world-wide opportunity to make Christ known. There may have been times when in certain non-Christian lands the missionary forces of Christianity stood face to face with as pressing opportunities as those now presented in the same fields, but never before has there been such a conjunction of crises and of opening of doors in all parts of the world as that which characterises the present decade. It is likewise true that never on the home field have the conditions been more favourable for waging a campaign of evangelisation adequate in scope, in thoroughness, and in power. Therefore, the first duty of a World Missionary Conference meeting at such an auspicious time is to consider the present world situation from the point of view of making the Gospel known to all men, and to determine what should be done to accomplish this Christ-given purpose. . . . It is earnestly hoped that the way may have been pointed [by the labours of this Commission] to a more scientific study of the fields and problems, and, above all, that enough may have been done to impress the Church with the unprecedented urgency of the situation, and to create a sense of deep solicitude as to the grave consequences which must ensue if the present unique world opportunity be not improved."

WITH these words the Report of the Commission on Carrying the Gospel to all the Non-Christian World opens:

and it was that Report which the Conference now met to discuss on this first morning.

First, the Chairman of the Commission, John R. Mott, rose to present the Report (temporarily vacating the Chair for that purpose). As the Report was a printed volume equivalent to over three hundred pages he " assumed it read," and proceeded to make certain general observations upon it by way of summing up.

" The assumption," grimly remarked the speaker, " may be a large one ! "—but beyond doubt the large majority of the delegates had found time to give a first careful reading to a really great production. Considering its length, the multiplicity of the details and figures it deals with, and the fact that it is the essence extracted from five hundred sets of answers received from missionary correspondents, it is a wonderfully readable and lucid document. This readableness was largely due to the co-ordinating genius of the Commission, headed by its Chairman.

In fact, it may confidently be said that if anyone wishes to get in small compass a world-survey of enthralling interest, touching at every point upon tremendous national and international problems, both social and racial, political and religious, let him obtain and read this Report of this Commission. It is a veritable Bluebook of the *Civitas Dei* ! Could any other Empire than that of the Church of Christ have issued a document so world-wide in scope, so human in interest and of such truly great importance ?

In presenting the Report, the Chairman recorded six outstanding convictions and impressions which (said he), " have laid strong hold upon us during the nearly two years in which we have been engaged in the preparation of our Report." We have here, then, a

division of the subject-matter as it appeared finally to the
minds of the men most qualified, by character and circumstance, to speak on this subject.   And in this chapter,
therefore, we cannot do better than to follow that division :
especially as all the most valuable matter of both the
Report itself, the debate on it, and the evening addresses
that are to be grouped with this Commission, can be
ranged under these same six headings.

I.

" The first of these impressions is that of the *vastness of the task*
of evangelising the world. . . ."

And no marvel, when we consider that this Report
makes a definite attempt to consider the problem of
evangelising two-thirds of the human race, composed of
perhaps a billion souls, and representing a veritable tangle
of races, creeds, languages and lands, scattered over Asia,
Africa, the two Americas, and the Islands of the Sea !
A glance at the index shows that the extensive aspect
of the problem has not been shirked.   In Asia not only
are the Levant, India, and the great yellow races of the
Far East (countries in which there is a traditional interest)
treated of in the Report, but less known or cared for
countries receive careful attention, such as Malaysia,
Formosa, Siam, or great tracts like Central Asia, usually
left out of reckoning altogether.   The Report is weak only
on North Central Asia, as one delegate, speaking of
Mongolia, pointed out : and it was gaps of this character
that the Vice-Chairman of the Commission (Dr Richter)
was alluding to when he desiderated the forming of a
Continuation Committee, or International Board, to
complete the world-wide study and survey so greatly
inaugurated by this Report.   Then there is the section

of Africa, an honest attempt to sift and analyse the congerie of different conditions that obtain in that one Continent :—the survey goes methodically round the coast, noting the districts that are well-occupied, half-occupied, or unoccuped in those seven great divisions of the Continent which the détour discovers. The large island of Madagascar is treated as an eighth division. The Americas are treated from the viewpoint, first, of the aboriginal "Indians," and secondly, of the immigrant Orientals, in the following six great sections—South America, the West Indies, Central America, the United States, Canada, and the Arctic regions. Finally, there are sections on the scattered nation of the Jews, Oceania, and the " unoccupied sections of the world."

No wonder, the speaker said, " the process has been one that has simply overwhelmed us with a sense of the vastness, the variety, and the infinite difficulty of carrying the Gospel to literally all the non-Christian world." But in the same breath he told the Conference of the advantage which such an overwhelming experience nevertheless brought with it, " making the stumbling block a stepping-stone " :—in the first place, it was an effectual cure to parochialism, which is clean against the spirit of Christianity ; and secondly, it was only this infinitely difficult task that would drive the Christian Church to close its ranks, and, further, learn to seek and claim the power of her infinite Lord.

In the debate, it is hardly surprising it was not found possible to touch equally on all the aspects of the world-wide labour. Even in the various parts of a universal task and duty there are grades of urgency, and the debate on this first Commission, and those on subsequent days, showed fairly clearly that the storm-centres of interest and urgency and anxiety in the œcumenical crusade to-day might be roughly defined as (1) India, (2) the yellow

Farther East, (3) Islam as a whole, especially where it is advancing.[1]

2.

"Tne second outstanding impression and conviction of the members of the Commission is that the time is really at hand— not coming—when the Christian Church should bestir itself as never before in the *countries of the non-Christian world in which it is already at work*."

It seems, indeed, a clear proof of God's guiding hand, that the countries upon which He has led the Church to concentrate her forces, such as India, the Far East, and certain leading races in Africa, should be exactly the countries which it is now most critically important, for reasons which could not have been wholly foreseen years ago, to win for Christ !

And the debate deepened the impression of the Report. Dr George Robson, of the U.F. Church of Scotland Foreign Mission Board, who had made a lifelong study of Africa, declared after a most careful analysis of the present state of affairs that the

"instant need is the *trebling* of the missionary force, I do not say to occupy the field—very far from that, but to meet those urgent needs of existing missions which are at this moment sorely burdening the hearts of the too few labourers ! "

And his concluding words,

" the very first thing which requires to be done if Africa is to be won for Christ is to throw a strong missionary force right across the centre of Africa to bar the advance of the Moslem and to carry the Gospel northwards into the Sudan,"

were powerfully reinforced and endorsed by Dr Karl Kumm, who rose immediately after. Coming fresh from an adventurous journey right across a belt of Africa never

[1] *E.g.* in all Africa, in Malaysia, in parts of India and the Russias.

previously traversed (that between lat. 10° and 5° N.,
—the " Moslem fringe "), he spoke of what he had seen
in that borderland between Islam and heathendom,—
tribe after tribe of the sturdiest and hardest-fighting
peoples in Africa becoming gradually Islamised from
the North—in the North Cameroon district, along the
Shari River, and all along the watershed between the
Shari, the Congo, and the Nile streams. The natural
barriers of resistance were gradually being neutralised
by the extension of European authority, British, German,
and French, which tended to give Islam absolutely free
play, while invariably cramping all forces that might
neutralise it. His warning that the Central Sudan is in
a state of religious solution, and that, should a fanatical
uprising take place there after the tribes have been won
for the Crescent faith, it might have very serious consequences, received a good comment from a testimony from
Dr Miller of North Nigeria, quoted later on in the debate.
In this he completely endorsed Dr Robson and Dr
Kumm's indictments of government policy in regard to
Islam, and emphasised the paramount importance of
winning the Hausa race for Christ ; and to this end made
a carefully considered appeal for forty workers to
evangelise that race, by educational methods chiefly,
and use it as a missionary force to stem the tide of Islam.
. . . A Swiss delegate, Mons. A. Grandjean, showed
how exactly the same crisis faced the worker as far
south as Portuguese East Africa ! and related how a
distinguished Governor-General of Mozambique had
written to his mission that it was high time for Christians
of all denominations to unite in facing the common
problem of Islam ! And an evening address, subsequently delivered by another speaker, showed how
exactly the same problem faced the Church in British
Central Africa, in British and German East Africa,

and all along the Guinea Coast. The same speaker, quoting a careful Swiss investigator, Würz of Basel, showed further how the *Senussi movement* of the Sahara is the mainspring of almost the whole Islamic movement in the northern half of the continent, and that in this matter the Church was faced with an " impossibility," which only a mountain-moving faith could remove.

There was not time to hear witnesses from the great successful missions to the heathen races of Africa— especially those in Nigeria, Uganda, British Central Africa, and South Africa ; but it was felt (and the Report endorsed the impression) that in their establishment and extension lies the chief hope of winning what Islam has not yet won, and winning back what the supineness of the Church has lost to that great faith, which is at present running a winning race for heathen Africa. Recent words of responsible German and British [1] writers on African affairs have shown that there is another side to the official pro-Islamic attitude so much in evidence all over Africa, and lend point to a sentence in one of the evening addresses that, unless the present drift is reversed, we shall probably before long *see Islam assuming the attitude of the heaven-sent uniter and vindicator of the African race,* reaping most of the harvest sown by the Ethiopianism of to-day.

In passing from Africa to Asia, Islam is found to be the bridge ; and for this and other reasons that religion makes our best transition to the consideration of the Middle and Farther East.

The distinguished Orientalist, Dr St Clair Tisdall, showed the necessity of strengthening work in Egypt, Persia,[2] the Levant, and other great centres, in order to be

[1] Sir H. H. Johnston among the latter.

[2] The opening doors and expanding situation in the Turkish Empire, and especially Syria, were mentioned with great effect.

ready for the opening up of difficult countries like Arabia and Afghanistan. Dr Zwemer of America and Arabia, a man who more than any other had worked, with very remarkable success, to arouse the interest of Christendom in the Mohammedan problem, emphasised the same thing in the first part of a speech which caused the *Scotsman* next day to write that " Dr Zwemer showed us that it was possible to make a great speech in seven minutes." The second and principal half of his speech, however, was an appeal, inspired by faith and courage, *not only* to strengthen existing centres, *but also* to evangelise the unoccupied ones. For example, he was in favour of opening a mission in Jidda, the port of Mecca ! besides other points on the long Arabian coast ; while a Scottish missionary from Arabia was quoted as challenging the Church at least to *try* the effect of a mission to Mecca and Medina !

It has been said above that the interest of the debate and the Report alike centered in the countries where internal movements were most marked and the actual situation was most critical. This fact naturally caused a great focussing of interest on India and the Far East ; but before proceeding to what was said about these countries, it may be well to quote one sentence which related their problems to the problem of Islam which has just been under consideration.

" I would have you recollect " (the speaker said) " that even were our Japanese, our Korean and Manchurian, our Chinese and Indian problems solved, their present crises happily met and sur-mounted, and a Christian Far East added to the Catholic Church, that great, central, unsympathetic, alien, and hostile wedge [Islam] would cut Eastern and Western Christendoms absolutely in half, insulating them from each other, and exhibiting to God and man not merely a seam, but a rent, from top to bottom, in the seamless robe of the great Catholic Church—the Church of a Humanity wholly, but for Islam, won for Christ ! " . . .

Some exceedingly striking things were said about
India. One of the " findings " of the Report was that
the national and spiritual movements in India to-day
present a strong challenge to Christian missions to
enlarge and deepen their work. Such was the sentence
with which the Report summed up its own important
section on India. And the debate underscored it.
For example, Dr Robert Stewart from the Punjab asked,
in a striking speech, How many missionaries are necessary
to evangelise the country in our generation ? " The
answer to this question," he said, has been given by the
Madras Decennial Conference which met in 1902. The
question was considered there *scientifically*. They made
their calculation that one missionary for every 25,000
would be necessary. This calculation was not merely
a mechanical one ; it was done with prayer, earnestly,
and the Conference made an appeal for 9000 workers
in order to secure this ideal. He showed that now,
in 1910, 8000 of these still have not been sent, and earnestly appealed that that ideal, deliberately held up
by a united conference of Continental, American, and
British representatives, should not be quietly put out
of sight. Another delegate, Sherwood Eddy, likewise
emphasised the necessity of sending to India the very
best minds the Church possesses, for the very best are
not too good for that absolutely invaluable material
lying to our hand in the educated youth of India to-day.

" If we " (he said) " could have a few of the right men rightly
placed among those who are the brain of India, they will largely
mould the future of thought. But it is increasingly difficult to
find such men either in Britain or in America."

An appeal for our best,—for the men who now enter
for the Indian Civil Service ! It seemed indeed clear
at the Conference that such men might *well* transfer

their careers to the work of Christ if they really desire
to mould and shape that great ancient land.

Then China. The Report had written some tremendously strong pages on that colossus of the nations, and
the debate left one with the impression that of all other
countries, perhaps, China is to-day the chief storm-
centre of urgent opportunity in the whole world. And
for this reason : *now* is the time of the rising tide, the
flood-tide, in China ; and the watchmen on the outlook-
tower are warning the Church that the hour is nearing
high-tide, the begining of the ebb ! For example, T. Y.
Chang, a Chinese Professor from Peking, made the
following statements, which, even allowing for an element
of exaggeration, are sufficiently startling :—

" The people of China are now giving away the old, but they have
not yet grasped the new. . . . The minds of the Chinese are now
empty, and this is the time for CHRIST to step in. If you wait four
or five years, *or even three* years, you will find such a change in
China that the minds of her people will be blocked. I beseech you
to take immediate steps. In five years it will be too late ! *Do not
wait until it is too late, as was the case with Japan.* Take steps now."

He meant of course that in the case of Japan the
Christian Church had failed to seize the moment when
Japan as a nation was plastic and as a nation might have
been influenced in her length and breadth for Christ,
and that now Japan had to some extent settled down
to look in other directions for her ideals and her guides.
These moments of trembling plasticity in nations are in
their very nature of the case short, transient periods.
The success of many an experiment in chemistry depends
upon seizing the few limited seconds when *all* the conditions are favourable. And this Conference brought out
with terrible clearness that such is the state of things
in China now ! Professor Chang was not the only man
to bring out this supreme consideration. Bishop Bash-

ford, of North China, bore out his Chinese confrère : Christianity (he said in his evening address) will suffer for centuries *through the failure of the Churches at that time to capture for Christ a nation, Japan, then peculiarly open to the Gospel—a nation destined for a time at least to become the leader of the Orient.* We shall see in a moment that this statement did not in the least imply lukewarmness on the part of the Bishop towards Japan as a mission-field, but simply was intended to force the Conference to realise the super-importance of the opportunity in China to-day. And the Bishop may have been right when he said (speaking of the Far East as a whole)—

" Not since the days of the Reformation, not indeed since Pentecost, has so great an opportunity confronted the Christian Church." " The Far East as a whole stands at the parting of the ways "— and added on another occasion—

" No such opportunity is likely to confront the Christian Church again till the Day of Judgment ! "

It may perfectly well be true :—certainly never before has one-quarter of the human race been all of a sudden thrown violently open to external influences of the deepest and most penetrating sort. Such a crisis may well prove incapable of repetition in the future.

The same speaker, one of the highest authorities on his subject, showed too that China will soon be in the throes of that industrial transition, which England and Europe found dangerous enough, from hand labour to machine labour. And this while she is passing through a fundamental political and intellectual revolution also ! The Bishop made the Conference feel through and through that " it will demand every possible effort of Christian statesmanship and leadership to bring the Empire through this revolution."

And there are strong elements of hope. At least two speakers who knew the country expressed their wonder and delight at the event which had happened so recently in Peking, where special religious meetings had been held among the scholars of four colleges and schools, and in these services " *five hundred and one* young people signed their names pledging their allegiance to the evangelisation of China."

The situation was shown, further, to be equally critical, and even more hopeful, in Korea and Manchuria. The Hon T. H. Yun, a Korean of highest character and standing, showed that the very rapidity with which Korea was becoming Christianised was likely to constitute a danger. He said, that if they had a sufficient, number of missionaries to take hold of the situation, the rapid increase of the converts would not mean so much danger; but, with so few, either European or Korean, there was a danger that the converts might not be taught as thoroughly as was necessary in order to lay deep and wide the foundation of the Church of the future. And another delegate said roundly that some of the best evangelists in Christendom should be sent to Korea. And with regard to Japan, so far from the failure to take full advantage of the opportunity there in the last century being a reason for discouragement now, one missionary to that land said that Christianity is only just coming into Japan: the foundation is ready laid, and the sympathy of many of the leaders is secured. While the very speaker who had emphasised the previous failure was the one who best of all brought the Conference to see the tremendous greatness of the opportunity that still existed. She had abandoned the individualism which she fancied she had learned from Spencer and " had passed almost *en masse* to the Christian conception of the state ": the question was, would she decide " for

international beneficence against national selfishness ? "
Her difficulties had enormously increased through
her continental victories. And the speaker concluded
with a ringing message. He described how the military
spirit is saying to Japan, " Follow on in the path in which
already you have won such glory : exploit these people
to reimburse your losses. Initiate the federation of
the yellow races. Control, and, if the necessity arises,
supplant the Manchu dynasty ; and, as opportunity
offers, rise to the leadership of the Orient." In all
this the speaker seemed to see Satan taking Japan,
as he took the Master, into a high mountain, and showing
her all the kingdoms of the world, and saying : " All
these things will I give thee, if thou wilt fall down and
worship me." But the Christ-spirit, he cried, suggests
continuance in the path of sacrifice ; such justice and
generosity towards the Koreans as presently will make
them proud of the flag of the Rising Sun, as Australians
are proud of the Union Jack ; such respect for the
territory of China in Manchuria as will assure Japan,
without a war, the moral and intellectual leadership
of the Far East. At this time, when the Japanese
have discarded the Spencerian for the Christian
philosophy of the state, when Christian Japanese are
rising to leadership out of all proportion to their numbers,
but when only one hundred thousand Japanese out of
fifty million are Christians, and forty million practically
unreached, the Christian Church should not dream of
retiring from the Empire. She should, he earnestly urged,
push forward her ablest and most apostolic spirits, and
help to capture for Christ, and " *lead to her own highest
destiny, the present leader of the Orient !* "

The emphatic words of the Chairman under this
aspect may close this section. Surely they will now
command the assent of the reader and carry him with

them :—" We believe that while it is certainly true that there have been times when in certain non-Christian countries the situation confronting the Church was as critical as it is at present, there never has been a time *when in* ALL *the non-Christian countries the conditions confronting Christianity were so favourable for a great and well-considered advance as at the present time.*"

3.

" The third outstanding conviction of the Commission is that the time is also at hand when the Church should enter the so-called *unoccupied fields of the world.*"

What and how many those lands are, the Report shows in a long section which makes melancholy reading. It traces the existence of so much unoccupied territory to " lack of an adequate and comprehensive vision : . . . the thought of carrying the gospel to *all* the world has not widely dominated missionary effort ; " and this because there has never been any agency co-relating the operations of the various Societies. It follows from this (maintains the Report), that not until this co-operation and the machinery for it actually come about, will this reproach of a Church that is now in the twentieth century of her history be removed.

In the discussion a few pathetic samples of neglect were given. An Indian delegate surprised everybody with the apparent paradox that *India* ought to be called the " Neglected Continent " : and he backed his assertion first by asserting that, in proportion to their populations, India was less adequately occupied than Africa or S. America ; and secondly (a less disputable and more suggestive statement), that there were vast regions in N. India with two or three millions of population without a single missionary or Christian worker. The

F

states and districts which were *officially* certified as
unoccupied by any form of missionary effort had a
population of one hundred million souls! On the other
hand, only the Madras district, in his opinion, was
anything like adequately manned. And this though
there were fifty millions of people ready to come en
masse into the Christian Church if the workers were
supplied! This being so, he remarked with an indigna-
tion that evoked a loud expression of assent,

"It seems to me to be *criminal* when there are these vast tracts
of country clamouring for the gospel message, for new Missionary
Societies . . . to be planted right in the centre of districts already
fairly well occupied!"

Some cries of *Shame!* amid the applause showed
that this speaker had hit the mark. He concluded by
telling of the hopeful movement by which five or six
of such unoccupied districts were being taken over
for the evangelisation of the country by Indian
missionaries, supported by Indian money, under Indian
management. . . . But he pled for a large increase
of foreign help. The estimate of the *four-fold* increase
of the missionary force in India has already been alluded
to.

Two dim vast regions of unoccupied Asia were also
spoken of that day. The Rev. G. H. Bondfield of the
British and Foreign Bible Society maintained that
Mongolia, Gilmour's Mongolia, was still an unoccupied
territory. He told how one day he and his party
parted from one of their agents, himself not a Christian,
and stood watching him as he went off westwards into
the desert, amongst the tents, *the only worker* to this
day among that pastoral people of 2,600,000 souls.
What a vivid picture!

"'What, you are stepping Westward!'—'Yea.'
. . . Yet who would stop, or fear to advance.

> Though home and shelter he had none
> With such a sky to lead him on ?
> The dewy ground was dark and cold,
> Behind all gloomy to behold,
> And stepping Westward seemed to be
> A kind of heavenly destiny. . . ."

So might it be!—A Swedish delegate, one of the heroic few who occupy Central Asia for Christ, spoke of an area of 2,700,000 square miles with only three mission-stations ! The great unevangelised territories in Africa have been already partially alluded to, but it would take all too long to complete the list. And so for many tribes in South America. But enough has been said to impress whoever has even a little aspiration and desire, that the bulk of the heavy task still remains to be done.

4.

Very logically then,

" The fourth impression which seizes us with great conviction is that if this world-situation is to be met there must be *united planning and concerted effort.* . . . We fall back frankly in front of this task if it must be faced by a divided Christendom. . . . It is our deep conviction that a well-considered plan of co-operation in the missionary work of the Societies represented in this hall, entered into and carried out with a sense of our oneness in Christ, would be more than equivalent to doubling the present missionary staff."

The loud burst of applause that greeted this remark showed how far it was from being a mere truism. And the applause broke out again when the Chairman expressed the hope that animated his Commission, that one of the permanent results of the Conference would be the foundation of some central board or " simple representative International Committee " (a " Hague Tribunal of missions " one delegate called it), which should give body to the spirit of co-operation that more and more animates Christians to-day. This wish, applauded this very first day of the Conference, and applauded time after time when it was again expressed,[1] was one that lay very close to the heart of this World Missionary Conference. How signally and amid what a scene of emotion a great step was taken towards its fulfilment shall be narrated in its place.

Co-operation in the field was also touched upon by one or two speakers, but the subject was generally left to the discussion on the Report of the Commission on Co-operation and the Promotion of Unity. It was already apparent how all these Commissions were leading up to, or following from, each other. It was not accidental that this first Commission found itself bound by natural ligaments to all the other Commissions ; for the carrying of the Gospel to all the world is the one goal ; and all the other seven Commissions were, as will be seen when we come to each, just so many indispensable means to the reaching of that goal. The work of this first day of the Conference was thus the natural prelude to all the days that followed it.

5.

This fifth impression, then, touched upon a subject treated of by the Commission on the Church in the Mission-field.

" The evangelisation of the world, as we have come to see it increasingly, is not chiefly a European and American enterprise, but an Asiatic or African enterprise. Therefore our hearts have been filled with hopefulness and confidence as we have studied the reports from all over the world showing the growing evangelistic and missionary spirit in the Church in the Mission-field. Whatever can be

---

[1] As for example by the distinguished German missionary historian and statesman, Dr Julius Richter, when as Vice-Chairman of this Commission he summed up the debate.

done should be done which will result in still further developing the power of initiative, of aggressive evangelism, and of self-denying missionary outreach on the part of the Christians of Asia and Africa, and in raising up an army of well-qualified native evangelists and leaders."

The debate and the Report both contained much that was stimulating and valuable under this aspect. The marvellous example of the Koreans—the Moravians of the East—showed *what* may be expected when Eastern Christians give themselves body and soul to God. The Report showed that there are the very greatest differences in the extent to which the native Churches in non-Christian lands are animated by the evangelistic spirit of the gospel. But in the great majority of the reports, it said, the note is one of great hopefulness.

The brilliant example of the Uganda Church (the Korea of Africa) and several other bright African Churches was further recollected. A delegate—the only delegate —from the South Sea Islands made a strong impression when he told of the Islanders seeking to evangelise the non-Christian Orientals, Chinese, Indians, Japanese, who seek those Island shores ; and of others who had crossed vast spaces of the seas, to the evangelisation of New Guinea—as is so movingly narrated in the life of Tamate. A delegate from the United Free Church of Scotland Jewish Mission made the Conference realise how much converted Jews had done and might do for the Kingdom : he mentioned Schereschewszky, whose Chinese version of the Old Testament made straight from the Hebrew is still read through the length and breadth of China. . . . The Church in Manchuria was alluded to by Dr John Ross of Manchuria as one that lived on the principle " freely ye have received, freely give," and averred that of the 40,000 baptized Manchurians not more than 100 had come in through the sole means of the foreign missionary. . . . The growing spirit of independence in the Japanese and Chinese Churches was also (the Conference was told) working out in the direction of self-propagation. The recent volunteering of the 501 young Chinese students for active service has already been alluded to. . . .

This being so, it was not wonderful that the discussions about the raising up and training and support of native evangelists produced some good speeches. In regard to their training, Mr D. E. Hoste, one of the "Cambridge Seven" and now Field-Director of the China Inland Mission—a Mission which has a very good right to speak authoritatively on the subject—deprecated "laying hands" on any man just because "a worker" was needed—rather should a Mission go without, until the man with a call to the work was found. Bishop Roots of Hankow provoked a strong outburst of applause by the following words :

" The bitterest complaint which I ever heard against the missionary cause was that of a young Chinaman, who said, ' The missionaries don't want the Chinese to acquire the ability which would enable them to lead the Chinese Church ! ' Now we know that that charge is not true in our hearts, but,"

said the Bishop, and this was what brought out the applause,

" we need to see to it that it is also not true *in the policy and administration of our mission*,"

a distinction *with* a difference that went home to the men in the Hall who had practical knowledge of mission-work !

And, finally, there was an interesting discussion on the knotty point, " How should such workers be paid ? " And it was highly instructive to see the differences of opinion, and of experience also, which this subject brought out. The deeply respected Korean delegate had already testified to his thankfulness that the missionaries had left the *whole burden* on the native Church. Dr Ross of Manchuria, on the other hand, from next door to Korea so to speak, was so impressed with the need of help from any or every quarter that he hinted he would welcome as much foreign money as he could get ! He said that when once it was given to God money ceased to be native or foreign.

A delegate from South India bluntly endorsed this view on the empirical ground of sheer necessity. Dr Gibson of China also had no scruple of paying native teachers with foreign money, but said that in Fukien the native Church really bore 80 per cent. of local expenses, and that the finding of *men*, not money, constituted beyond all question the real problem of problems. A delegate from Japan said that to stop foreign contributions would injure both the Japanese, by curtailing work in Japan, and the Western Church, by curtailing the blessings that they gained by liberality. And Dr Eugene Stock felt the solution was that all European money should be pooled, as it were, with the local funds and administered by the local Church as one Church-fund. . . . This vital topic was continued on the morrow.

6.

" The last impression we shall mention is . . . the conviction that the most crucial problem in relation to evangelising the world is *the state of the Church in the Christian countries*. We are frank to concede that it is futile to talk about making Christ known to the world in this generation or any generation unless there be a great expansion of vitality in the members of the Churches of Christendom. . . . We look forward, therefore, with great eagerness to the deliberations of this

Conference upon the Report of the Commission on the ' Home Base.' *Our* task is hopeless unless *their task* is well done.

" Nothing less than a Church tremendously in earnest can evangelise the non-Christian world " (Report).

For the most part the discussion under this head was postponed to the debate on the Report of Commission on the Home-Base, which very significantly was put down for the last day of the Conference ; for in the last analysis the success of this enterprise depends on the extent to which the Church of Christ rises to the height of her calling and is inspired with the very spirit of her Divine Lord.

But there are certain words of the Report so weighty, so intense with impassioned energy, that it would be a grievous loss not to set them down here. And the reader who has been impressed by the things brought to his notice in this chapter is besought to resist that inclination of the flesh to omit lengthy quotations, and to read this one with the intensest concentration and care. It will repay him. It will remind him of an aphorism uttered some years ago, " We often say, unless we evangelise the masses, they cannot be saved. We need to learn that unless we evangelise the masses—we cannot be saved ! "

This then is the closing appeal of the Report, which it takes little higher critical acumen to ascribe to the Chairman of the Commission and of the Conference himself :—

" For the Church not to rise to the present situation and meet the present opportunity will result in hardening the minds and hearts of its members and making them unresponsive to God. If the situation now confronting the Church throughout the world does not move to larger consecration and prompt and aggressive effort, it is difficult to imagine what more God could do to move the Church, unless it be to bring upon it some great calamity. . . . It is an inexorable law of Christianity that no Christian can keep spiritual life and blessing to himself, but must communicate to those in need.

" The *apologetic value and influence* of a widespread, thorough, and triumphant propagation of the Gospel should also be emphasised. In Christian lands many have lost faith in Christianity as a power to uplift mankind. . . . The foreign missionary propaganda furnishes from the difficult fields of the non-Christian world evidence showing the ability of the Christian religion to transform men individually, to elevate communities socially, and to win whole nations.

" The only thing which will save the Church *from the imminent perils of growing luxury* and materialism, is the putting forth of all its powers on behalf of the world without Christ. Times of material prosperity have ever been the times of greatest danger to Christianity. The Church needs a supreme world-purpose—a gigantic task, something which will call out all its energies, something too great for man to accomplish, and, therefore, something which will throw the Church back upon God Himself. This desideratum is afforded by the present world-wide missionary opportunity and responsibility. To lay hold in particular of the lives of the strongest young men and young women, the Church must offer them some such masterful mission as this. May it not be that God designs that the baffling problems which confront Christianity in the non-Christian world shall constitute the battleground for disciplining the faith and strengthening the character of His followers? To preserve the pure faith of Christianity, a world-wide plan and conquest are necessary. This lesson is convincingly taught on the pages of Church history. The concern of Christians to-day should not be lest non-Christian peoples refuse to receive Christ, but lest they, in failing to communicate Him, will themselves lose Him !

" A programme literally world-wide in its scope is indispensable *to enrich and complete the Church.* Jesus Christ must have *all* the races and *all* the nations through which to make known fully His excellences and to communicate adequately His power. . . . It will be impossible to plan and wage a world-wide campaign without being enlarged by the very purpose itself. The life of the Church depends upon its being missionary. Revivals of missionary devotion and of spiritual life have ever gone hand in hand. The missionary activities of the Church are the circulation of its blood, which would lose its vital power if it never flowed to the extremities. . . .

" Moreover, to have God manifest mightily His power in the Home Church so that it may be able to grapple successfully with *the problems at its own doors*, it is essential that the Church give itself in a larger way to the carrying out of His missionary purposes. Is it not true that when this main purpose is forgotten or subordinated, a paralysis comes upon the Church, incapacitating it for other efforts ? World-evangelisation is essential to Christian conquest at home. The only faith which will conquer Europe and America is the faith heroic and vigorous enough to subdue the peoples of the non-Christian world !

" Christ emphasised that the mightiest apologetic with which to convince the non-Christian world of His divine character and claims would be the oneness of His disciples. Experience has already shown that by far the most hopeful way of *hastening the realisation of true and triumphant Christian unity* is through the enterprise of carrying the Gospel to the non-Christian world. Who can measure the federative and unifying influence of foreign missions ? No problem less colossal and less bafflingly difficult will so reveal to the Christians of to-day the sinfulness of their divisions, and so convince them of the necessity of concerted effort as actually to draw them together in answer to the intercession of their common and divine Lord."

Finally, having described this tremendous five-fold result that will surely be the reward of faithfulness, the eloquent and pleading appeal thus concludes :—

" The cumulative and crowning consideration calling the Church to undertake promptly and to carry forward earnestly and thoroughly a campaign to take the Gospel to all the non-Christian world is seen in the coincidence of the series of convincing facts and providences which have been summarised in this survey. Never before have such facts and movements synchronised. . . . Surely all these facts and factors, together with the perils and possibilities of the Home Church as determined by its attitude at such a time and in face of such an opportunity, constitute a conjunction brought about by the hand of the Living God, and should be regarded by the Christian Church as an irresistible mandate.

" Well may the leaders and members of the Church reflect on the awful seriousness of the simple fact that opportunities pass. It must use them or lose them. It cannot play with them or procrastinate to debate whether or not to improve them. Doors open and doors shut again. Time presses. ' The living, the living, he shall praise Thee.'   It is the day of God's power.   Shall His people be willing ? "

These are surely great, very great words. Well were it for the Church of God were her members to get these words by heart, or the meaning of them. Surely it would be for her healing ! Surely they are the things that belong to her peace !

.   .   .   .

The Chairman of this Commission closed his recital of their outstanding convictions by a recurrence to that tremendous word that had been uttered by the distinguished speaker of the night before, and had evidently fallen with impressive and solemnising force on his own ears, as it had on the ears of all.   " The power," he cried,

" the power is in this room, under God, to influence the hosts of Christendom to enter into the realisation of the sublime hope expressed by the speaker last evening, that before the eyes of some of us shall close in death, the opportunity at least may be given to all people throughout the non-Christian world to know and to accept, if they will, the living Christ ! "

On this day, the prayer hour, the " solemn central act of the day's proceedings," was passed mostly in perfect silence. Only Silence was eloquent enough in the face of the impressions of that day. Let the conclusion of this chapter, then, following immediately on the above words, stand for this same silence of intercession and of consecration.

CHAPTER VIII

ON the first day the delegates had surveyed the task. They turned from that, on the morning of the second, to the one thing on earth that suggested the hope of its possibility.

The public is not even aware that there is such a thing as " the Church on the Mission Field." The man in the street, sure of everything, is sure there is not. Even the statesman whose business it is to be conversant with foreign affairs, has probably overlooked it.

They are hardly to be blamed. There is another who apparently has had some difficulty in fully realising its existence—the missionary.

With *him* it has been as with one who has striven, long and intensely, after some great object dearly desired, hardly hoped for ; and then, when it comes to him, cannot see that it has come. But such a one, when the realisation of the truth dawns on him, rejoices with great joy. For the missionary, when once he fairly, even if imperfectly, realises that the Church in the mission-field *is*, finds in this the pledge of final victory. So, the Apostle on Patmos, looking on the infant " Church in the Roman Empire," anticipated by two centuries the conviction of Constantine, that before that Church heathenism was doomed. With the faith which, with absolute soberness, treats the future tense as a perfect, he had already exclaimed *Vicisti, Galilæe* before the world was even aware of the new organism that had been born into it.

93

It was not so much prophecy as perfected insight into the significance of present facts.

I.

The preparatory work done in connection with this Commission must have helped many of its two hundred missionary correspondents to realise this fact of the Church on the Mission-Field. There, on the table of the Conference, lay the correspondence ; one volume from Japan, three volumes in yellow from China, three in red from India, one in green from Mohammedan countries, and one from the continent of Africa. " In difficulty and suffering," the Conference was told, " some of that correspondence had been written ; by one man at the death-bed of his wife ; by another on his own,"—to him, perhaps, a Patmos on which he saw into the reality of things. The compilation of the Report had evidently deepened the sense of realisation on the part of the Commission. The reading and discussion of it communicated that sense to the Conference at large. And the Report itself, now published, establishes the fact for all who care to know the truth.

And what is the truth ? It is the existence of the Church on the Mission-Field. This fact, of literally incalculable potentiality is thus expressed by the Commission at the outset of their Report :—

" *The Church on which we report presents itself no longer as an inspiring but distant ideal, nor even as a tender plant or a young child, appealing to our compassion and nurturing care. We see it now an actual Church in being, strongly rooted, and fruitful in many lands. The child has, in many places, reached, and in others is fast reaching maturity, and is now both fitted and willing, perhaps in a few cases too eager, to take upon itself its full burden of responsibility and service.*"

" Even where it is known, its extent and significance," the Report continues, " are very much under-estimated."

And Dr Gibson, the Chairman of the Commission, reminded the Conference, in presenting the Report, that the Christians on the mission field are not separate particles of inorganic matter, as if the results of missions could be estimated by weighing these separate particles against the enormous mass of paganism from which they have been separated. That view he took to be utterly wrong, and declared that at this moment the recognition of how wrong it is is one of the vital issues of mission work. What is meant by the organisation of the Christian Church in the mission field "is the drawing together of life to life in its highest form, spiritual life, life in its highest potency." "We all know" (he said), "how science is beginning to teach us how even very obscure and very minute forms of life are, because of their life, of enormous potency in their aggregate and in their united working ; and so it is that we desire the Conference to recognise the enormous force that exists now established in the very heart of the pagan world, in the young Christian Church which missions have founded, but which is itself now *the* great Mission to the non-Christian world." The words are those of a missionary-statesman of the Church in the Far East, at the end of a century of missionary enterprise. One remembers again with a thrill, "the Church in the Roman Empire," and the present insight of him who " saw " on Patmos, at the end of the first century of our era.

Or again,

" You have now what we begin to call not a little but a great Church in the mission field. The stage is being gradually reached, but we think it ought to be now somewhat suddenly and very definitely, with great thankfulness to God, fully recognised. . . . I venture to say that the situation is not generally understood even by Christian missionaries and still less by those that look on from without."

Such are the words in which a world-fact of the most
solemn import and significance was announced to the
Conference, and thereby to the Church at home, the
fruit of its toil and its sacrifice ; to those that " believe
in foreign missions," and those that do not believe in
foreign missions ; to the statesman ; to the public ;
to the man in the street. For in very truth it concerns each of them ! . . . Was the Conference in error
when to its eyes very gradually dawned the vision of
the stone cut out without hands that became a great
mountain and filled the whole earth ? That vision had
surely the highest authority. Who was it who saw a
picture of the Kingdom of Heaven in one small organism
which became the greatest among herbs, a tree in the
branches of which the birds of the air came and lodged.

The entire Report, in fact, is the proof of the fact now
asserted. And the discussion on the Report merely
underscored the written proof. The debate on this day
reached as high a level as at any time at the Conference,
for the men who were speaking were the very men
who had the firsthand knowledge of the fact. The
Conference heard of a body of 1,925,205 registered
communicants in the mission-lands of Asia, Africa, and
other parts of the world : of Churches in Japan with their
constitutions and charters ; of the self-supporting and
self-propagating churches in Korea and in Manchuria.
It listened to a Chinese delegate, Ch'eng Ching-Yi,
claiming that the time had come when China should
range itself with Japan in this matter ; and it assented
to his words with emphatic applause. It realised that in
negro Africa the same phenomena are being seen—a
Church of Uganda so independent in its working that the
responsible secretary of the society in London could
confess he knew little about the details of its finance ;
Churches in Nigeria, Sierra Leone, Livingstonia, Blantyre,

Madagascar ; and to crown all it heard of a Church in those South Sea Islands, which were nearly the earliest object of the modern missionary quest, and for which the martyr missionaries shed their blood (with a Home Church in the distance, grudging and unconvinced) :— those islands, then cannibal, now Christian, might themselves with perfect justice claim to be a " Home Church," for they have their " home mission " to the Chinese coolies indentured for work in their island plantations, and their " foreign mission " to far-off lands across the southern sea ! From a training-college in Mabia some fifty-four Samoans, Tokelan, and Ellice islanders have gone to New Guinea, that savage isle, successors of those first three who, in 1883, sailed to be the colleagues of Tamate, his fellow-missionaries in the Gospel of Christ. Chalmers the Scotsman is not the only martyr of New Guinea. The Polynesian is there too. In Papua sleep saints from Scotland and from Samoa ; in Papua islanders from Stevenson's Samoa sleep their last sleep with their Tamate, far away from his Scotland and their Samoa across the sea.

Such is the new vital organism with which the world has henceforth to reckon—*the Church on the Mission-Field*. In this chapter it will be attempted merely to illustrate this central fact by touching upon points in the debate, and in the Report that cast the most light upon it.

2.

Building up the Individual Life

" The supreme and ultimate object of edification is the development of character," said Bishop Lambuth, the Vice-Chairman of the Commission, later on in the day ; " and to secure the most effective activity upon

G

the part of the Church in the mission field. . . . But corporate life is made up of individual life, and the former is not stronger than the integrity of the units which make it up." This sturdy individualism, which every high social doctrine must, if it is worth anything, have at its core, had been equally strongly stated by Robert Speer the day before, when he said—

" But how can society be built except by men ? It is as strong as the convictions of individual men are strong. We cannot build a better world than we can make out of the goodness of the men who compose that world, and in the end our efforts to mould society resolve themselves into the effort to mould and fashion the individual men who compose that society. These two things we must combine. . . . In this missionary enterprise as we constitute it we are bound to set in the foreground the primary purpose of making Jesus Christ known to His sheep whom He knows *one by one by name.*"

Much, therefore, of great general interest, as well as of technical importance to workers abroad, is found in the Report, and was said at the discussion upon this primary and fundamental question ; aspects of which are the sifting and the instruction of candidates for baptism, and the watching, helping and teaching of the newly-baptised.

The Korean, Yun Chi-Ho, one look at whom ensured the respect for him which his record deserved, had the day before alluded to the increased responsibility, which the extraordinary Christward movement in his country has cast on the " Church at home." " The rapid increase of converts is a danger." Dr Gibson, evidently struck by the remark, alluded to it on this morning. He showed clearly how this was so : such an increase of converts is undoubtedly a great joy, but it is a joy that brings a great responsibility with it, the responsibility of " feeding My sheep." Therefore, *in the interest of the young*

Church on the mission-field, the Church at home needs to send more missionaries to do this shepherd-work.

That success is attending their efforts at character-building the world over was proved up to the hilt in the Report. The very emphasis placed on the exceptions proves the rule. The very disappointment caused by those exceptions shows what is expected. The Vice-Chairman of the Commission summed up to the Conference the impressions relating to this point, which had been made on the Commission by those nine volumes of correspondence lying there on the Conference table ; and described some of the fruit of the Gospel as manifested by the lives of the converts on the field. First, Fear cast out. Second, Speech made pure. Third, Truthfulness. Fourth, Family Prayer—the sheet-anchor of the Christian home on the mission-field. . . .

(Said a Korean missionary on this point :

" Previous to the Pentecostal descent of the Holy Ghost upon the Church of Korea in 1897, prayer was regarded largely as a precious privilege. . . . The Korean Christian now regards it as a primary method of *work* for our Lord.")

Fifth, Liberality. He told the Conference of Chinese schoolboys denying themselves a Sunday mid-day meal, in order to save a few coppers cash for evangelistic work ; and converts from cannibalism in the New Hebrides giving their crop of arrowroot for the publication of their New Testament. Korean Christians in a single year contributed out of their poverty £25,000 for the further-ance of the Gospel, which, translated into the terms of the *wages* of the West, would equal £175,000 !—Sixth, Fervent evangelism. Seventh, the Martyr Spirit under persecution. . . . He described, among the many, Um-Chang, sixty-seven years old, beset on every side by murderous fellows who sought his life but offered to spare it if he would but deny his Lord. He could not. " And while their dull rusty knives were buried in his quivering flesh the old man on his knees could be heard saying, ' Father, forgive ! for they know not what they do.' "

Was this the same Chang, one wonders, as the one mentioned in the Report, whose nephew years later showed yet another " fruit " of the Church on the mission-field ? For *he himself* had, so to speak, to answer that prayer of his old relative for the forgiveness of those murderers. " At one of the meetings," says the Report,

" this evangelist, in a moment of profound spiritual emotion, declared that he had for the first time come to know the Lord. ' Do you forgive your enemies ? ' he was asked by a Chinese pastor. For a moment this was more than he could promise. A Chinese friend arose and went to his side, saying to him, ' I want to help you ; I will do all I can to help you. Forgive them ! ' Still he could not promise, and many silent prayers were offered for him. At last he said very quietly, ' I forgive them. Pray for these men, all of you, that they may be saved ; and pray for me that I may be given the victory over myself and them. I shall first write and tell them of my forgiveness and hopes, and then at the earliest opportunity visit them, and plead with them to repent and be saved.'

" It may seem little that a Christian man should abandon the thought of taking a bloody revenge ; but he was not only giving up the impulse of present passion, but breaking with the traditions of his race, and the teachings of a lifetime."

Such are some of the results of the edification of the individual life in the Church on the mission field.

3.

The Building up of the Community

There were unfolded before the Conference a number of the varied methods that are being used for the corporate upbuilding of the Christian communities on the mission field. The services and meetings of the full, happy, Christian Sunday (reminding one of Justin Martyr's description of the " Day of the Sun " in the reign of the Emperor Antoninus, and the way it was kept by those second-century Christians), worship without tedium, instruction with the appetite for it; day-schools, boarding-schools and hostels ; family worship and village meetings ; conferences for workers and leaders ; Sunday-schools— India in 1908 had over half-a-million officers, teachers and scholars, with Japan close behind ; young people's societies ; visitation of homes and work for the women of the Church; and the definite training of workers for service and the ordained ministry. . . . An illuminating touch was this one, from China :—

" In view of the difficulty that the Chinese experience in getting quiet for prayer in their own homes, a room has been set apart for prayer in some stations. Those attending do not necessarily pray audibly, nor is there any stated leader, and all are free to come and go as their duties demand. This method has proved a means of real blessing."

There was another side to this, a necessary yet painful side : *discipline*. The spirit in which this is dealt was sufficiently shown by the way the Chairman of the Commission introduced it,—there was tenderness in the rugged face and the harsh, kindly voice as he showed how those Christians stand up without any of the help given by hereditary examples and traditions and a Christian atmosphere : how they stand up (to the eye of flesh) *alone*, to face an un-Christian world. Could we wonder if they stumble and fall ? It should be recognised then that this matter of Church discipline is exercised not as a harsh matter of judicial proceeding, but rather as a tender, watchful, vigilant care. Another very important point was this :—discipline is not to be exercised always

by *the foreign missionary*. There was an illuminating sentence about this in the Report,

" We note evidence to the effect that decisions arrived at in these [indigenous] meetings carry a weight which does not in the same degree attach to the verdict of the missionary-in-charge, or of a council mainly European. In a few cases we notice that it is still the European missionary who is the sole officer of discipline, and perhaps this is inevitable in the earliest days of a mission. Plainly, however, it ought never to be regarded as a permanent feature, or be long acquiesced in. If we, as foreigners, discipline the unruly, we may edify the individual, but we fail to edify the community, for we destroy the sense that it is the duty of the community to guard its own morality."

Immense social difficulties that are still real problems within the Church or the mission-field, such as the matter of ancestor-worship, of caste, of polygamy, had been dealt with very fully in the Report. Curiously enough they hardly came up at all in the discussion. Just twice they came to the surface, and each time the exceptionally moved tone of the speaker's voice indicated the travail in which the Church still is with these painfully difficult questions.[1]

[1] Late in the debate a Japanese delegate rose, Dr T. Harada, the great Neesima's successor as President of the famous Doshisha College, and in an admirable speech delivered in English pled for patience in dealing with caste. The problem would be gradually solved as the Indian Church realised the significance of her own faith. " We want faith in God ! Our system and your system are not necessarily the perfect or final type of Christianity, and therefore in the expressions of faith, in non-Christian lands, we must be patient, we must wait for the time of the real expression of their spiritual experience, and that is important not only for the sake of the Churches in non-Christian lands, but I think it is important for the sake of the mother-Churches, because in those and only those our Lord's full personality will be glorified and revealed in all the world."

Golden words ! It was a comment on the truth of the last sentences, that what elicited this gem was just the statement of a difficulty with which a sister-Church (in India) was wrestling....

If, then, it was the Church in the mission-field that more and more must be tended, fed, administered, disciplined, and moulded by its own leaders, palpably the supreme work of the missionary must be the training of those leaders, those workers and ministers of religion, who are to perform all these functions. On this aspect much had been set forth in this Report, and much was added in the discussion. Many points of great importance were made which it is hardly necessary to mention here : such, for instance, as the necessity of separating between the curricula of simple workers and of those who are to lead the life and thought of the whole community ; the need of familiarising the students with the dominant faiths and philosophies of the land; the need of studying the thought-idiom of the people in the theology that is taught and the text-books that are written. (An American delegate "was surprised and saddened to see how much time was consumed in the training of the men in strictly denominational lines ; " and the teaching of that text-book beloved of Cambridge ["England" !], Paley's "Christian Evidences," seemed to him a thing to be deplored. While the Bishop of Birmingham by voice, face, and gesture tried to make a sympathising audience share the horror with which he discovered that the Thirty-Nine Articles figured on the syllabus of a certain Divinity College for innocent candidates for the Indian ministry.)

All this clearly involved the grand question of Education in the mission field, the very subject which very logically was down for discussion the next day. Speaking last of all that day, Lord William Gascoyne-Cecil, with ceaseless play of white, nervous hands, visionary eyes that contemplated space rather than his audience, and leonine head with its mane of tawny hair and beard recalling the great Marquis, made a short speech which really formed the transition to the subject of the morrow.

"Educate !" he said, "that your converts may deal with all these questions. A Church will always be in slavery to others when it is an ignorant Church. An ignorant man is always slave to some one else. Knowledge is power. It is no good altering your regulations and your rules unless you can take advantage of these alterations. If your workers are capable of governing the Church they will govern the Church. If they are incapable they will not govern it. To make them capable you must educate them—not merely a theological but a wide education. Trust them with the knowledge which has made you powerful, and then you can leave your Church and your work, confident that they will work out their own salvation."

4.

That this counsel had already been in no small measure followed in many parts of Mongolian and Aryan Asia, and Hamitic and Bantu Africa, was apparent from the very fact reported that day, that already Churches exist whose workers had been able to take advantage of the privileges which had made them actually or potentially autonomous ; together with others the earnest pressing of whose claims that day seemed to be justified and applauded by all.

The Conference was informed of the highly interesting technical details of the transition that had already been effected in Japan. But of most general interest, perhaps, was the problem of the Churches still some way off, or just approaching, the transition stage. There are many of the former everywhere on the mission field, but naturally this was not an aspect that lent itself to discussion at this Conference. The Report had a good word on this subject :—

"While [the infant Church] remains in pupilage to the Home Church, the relation between the two is essentially temporary, and the organisation of ' The Church in the Mission-Field ' must be regarded as transitional and not permanent. It follows that, until the stage of adolescence is reached, the forms of organisation should remain as simple as the services required of them will permit, in order to conserve, as far as possible, the spontaneity and self-determination of the nascent spiritual life. If too little control is given, the life may develop in wrong directions ; if too much, it may lose the power of developing at all."

More was said in regard to the Churches just approaching the transition. " Do not *wait* to have the Church in the Mission-field demand a larger share in the administration of its affairs " was a counsel from India which was heartily applauded. A missionary from China made the Conference laugh by pointing out that the only way whereby to show that we believe our own statements was by opening the door *and by getting out of the doorway* ; and that very often the foreigner says, " Come in ! " but stands in the light, bulking so large that there is very little room for the native to come in when he tries to do so. Expressions which betray just the wrong mental attitude were held up for the condemnation of ridicule—" ' Bring some of *your* native Christians ! ' " " ' Native agents and native helpers ! '—Helpers of *whom* ! agents of whom ! ' " ; " ' *Rights* of the Boards and the Societies,'—we have no rights except to serve our brother ! " . . . On the other hand the word " native," though laboriously held up for a like condemnation, was continually slipping out of the mouth of speakers of all nationalities. Almost immediately after the Chairman's elaborate denunciation and abjuration of it, a patriotic Chinese speaker was only advised that he himself had violated the taboo by the laughter that interrupted him at the forbidden word. After that, good resolutions broke down with a rush, and with a sigh of relief the delegates, " foreign " and

" native " alike,[1] fell back on the dubious but useful word: whereby it was to be inferred that it is an indispensable word, difficult to replace; and that its soiling by ignoble use is nothing but a call to the Church to redeem it again, rather than hand it right over to the defilers. Perhaps, though, President Harada, speaking in the English that was foreign to his tongue,[2] gave nevertheless a beautiful hint of an alterative word, when, with wonderful insight into the genius of the English tongue, he spoke of " the Mother Churches." The Mother Churches! Why not then the *Daughter*, instead of the Native, Churches!

On the whole, then, it will be understood that the temper of the Conference was significantly in favour of advance all along the line, in this policy of confidence and commitment to the daughter Churches. It hardly even needed the testimony of the first Japanese bishop (Bishop Honda) as to the tried value of that policy in Japan, or the plea, put forward by Ch'eng Ching Yi with so beautiful a spirit, for a larger measure of trust—

" Will it be too great a burden for the Chinese Christians? Surely not! It is our privilege and joy, not our burden. As a little girl, who was seen carrying a little boy on her back [note the Chinese touch], when one said to her ' I see you have a big burden on your back, have you not? ' said : ' That is not a burden! that is my *brother*! ' "

It hardly needed further the equally beautiful plea made by the Korean, the Hon. Yun Chi-Ho, when he applied the principle of co-operation even to the question of the administration of foreign monies, and with finest insight stated the ideal yet practical grounds on which he based his plea : or the caustic witticism of a well-known missionary leader in India, quoted by an Indian

---

[1] The reader may here puzzle over which was which.
[2] In the speech noticed on p. 94, footnote.

delegate, that in the old days Indian converts had been quite willing to be considered the children of the missionaries to whom they owed their conversion ; but now there was a second generation of Indian Christians which had no idea of being the sons of the younger missionaries, though the younger missionaries still liked to regard themselves as the fathers of the Indian Christians !— It did not need these speeches from these oriental Christians to gain their point,—the very ability of speakers and speeches was in itself the best plea of all ;—for the sense of the meeting was clearly for the motion. The blunt words of an American mission secretary went as far, or rather further, than any plea coming from the daughter Churches :—

" Save in a very few countries, no church-polity is in practice to-day on the foreign field. Too much real power has been exercised by the Boards, Societies, and Missions—altogether too much for the conditions which exist to-day."

He went on to show the hollowness of the objection that the Church on the mission field would exercise its power unwisely, and asked amid cheers if westerners have never exercised *theirs* unwisely ? The more he saw of the Christians in Asia, he declared, the more respect he had for them. They were serving Christ, oftentimes amid loss of business and social ostracism ; yet they stand with splendid vitality. And he concluded, " I trust that this Conference will mark the period of transition by a true recognition of the functions and the rights of the Church of God in the non-Christian lands."

Certainly the Mother Churches that day earned the right to appeal in turn, as did the Chairman of the Commission, in the last words uttered that afternoon, to the representatives of the Daughters in the Conference. Addressing them, he reminded them of the sincere cordiality and sympathy they themselves and their views

had been received at that session, and how more than
willingly the principle had been recognised that the
Oriental Churches, just as much as those in the West, have
essential rights, liberties, responsibilities, the source of
which is Christ alone.   And he concluded by an appeal
that they would interpret to their peoples on their return
to the East what were the sentiments with which the
World Missionary Conference was animated, and how
assured therefore is the future, granted only patience,
love, and faith.

5.

" Native Church " and " Foreign Mission "

With these words this chapter might well close.   But
they did not alter, as they did not overlook, the fact that
nevertheless, in all these fields and all stages of their evolution, foreign Missions and native Churches are found coin-
ciding in the same place.   On what principle are their
mutual relations to be adjusted ?   It was interesting
to see how the oriental delegates were the most emphatic
of all that " the Mission " still had an absolutely indispensable place, even in the most developed field :
the same place, in fact, that it had when it entered that
field, of initiating the advance into the regions beyond,
and assisting in the raising up of leaders.   From this
point of view the independence of the Mission, as was
well shown by an American missionary to China, was
every whit as important as the independence of the
Church, so that each may do its own proper work.
Another delegate from the same country to the same
field showed clearly that the Church can claim no right
to restrict or control the work of the missions in any way.
They are free to work where and how they please ;
but if they choose to work within the Japanese Church,

they should do it only on condition that it should be under that Church's supervision. "A tailor," he wittily remarked, "may sew in any way he chooses, but if he is sewing upon my suit of clothes I have a right to direct how he should sew." It is not necessary to discuss here the various solutions by which the spheres of " Mission " and " Church " are harmonised—solutions varying according to the ethos of the various types of ecclesiastical governments, whether Episcopal, Presbyteral, or Congregational. One was left with the impression that oriental heads were in this matter as level as those placed on occidental shoulders. It was, for example, an Indian, J. R. Chitamber, who advanced three powerful reasons against a proposal which at first sight looked like giving the native-Christian worker *more* honour, the proposal to take specially qualified oriental workers on to the staff of " the Mission."

The strong impression that the day's proceedings left was that both in spirit and in form this problem is in course of being happily solved in the daughter-churches of the East. If the spirit is right the solution must follow. If the personal relation is sound the corporate relationship will easily be adjusted. In this connection one of the least forgettable moments of the Conference was an evening address by the delegate from South India, V. S. Azariah, in which he pled for a deep readjustment of the personal relation that sometimes existed (he alleged) in India ; for a more real co-operation of spirit between Western and Eastern,—in one word, for " *friendship*."

The address commanded, to say the least, a by no means unqualified assent in that great assemblage. Possibly some of the men—Indian missionaries they were—whose dissent, and even more than dissent, boiled every now and then to the surface, did not quite understand what the speaker was intending. Or possibly they were

unnecessarily trying to fit the cap on to heads never
measured for it. But, in any case, the address was a
not forgettable feature of the Conference ; and even if it
were mistaken, the courage it evinced and the delicacy
and humour with which the thing was done, entitle it to
recognition. It did not need the speaker's assurance
that it was an unpleasant task ; an electric silence,
broken now by a sort of subterraneous rumbling of dissent,
or startled by thunderish claps of applause, is the least
comfortable of all atmospheres for an orator to speak in,
and demanded all the evident courage of the man to
speak in it. He had been pressed (he said) against his
will to give that address, and had only yielded on
condition that he might speak his whole mind. He
disarmed a possible or rather a certain, criticism, saying
at the outset that his personal relations with Western
missionaries had invariably been " simply delightful."
And this gave the cue to the appeal which was the whole
gist of the speech—that " *friendship* " and no other
thing should regulate the relations between Eastern
and Western. It did not always in India so regulate
them, he felt ; and he gave instances of what he
meant. It was here that a flash of humour relieved the
tension. He was speaking of a glaring instance of something other than " friendship " regulating the dealing
of missionary with native Christians : " of course " (he
continued) " I do not mean to say that this sort of thing
is typical." (Significant applause from the dissidents.)
. . . The speaker looked up ; and then, with a dry
impromptu—" At the same time it would be a mistake
to think that it was exceptional ! " Somehow the
deft reply to the implication of that applause tickled
the Conference's sense of humour, and a general burst
of applause and laughter cleared the air. Speaking
with the subdued intensity that underlay the whole

speech, he closed thus, the rolled foreign *r*'s making the words " friends," " friendship," vibrate through the hall :—

" This will be possible only from spiritual friendships between the two races. . . . Through all the ages to come the Indian Church will rise up in gratitude to attest the heroism and self-denying labours of the missionary body. You have given your goods to feed the poor. You have given your bodies to be burned. We also ask for love. Give us FRIENDS *! "*

Most people, one fancied, were touched by a sincere speech. It could after all do one no harm to be reminded of the difficult ideal of inter-racial friendship. And as for the criticism, what does it matter even if criticism passed on us is false ? The point is, that in *that* we see the impression we have made on those who pass the criticism ; that thus and not otherwise they feel about us. The old couplet—" Oh wad some fay the giftie gie us to see oursels as ithers see us," loses no particle of its point if the vision of those others is most unaccountably mistaken.

6.

" Church ? " or " Churches ? " in the Mission-Field

One more aspect of the subject remained—the supreme one. Under the fourth aspect the Conference had climbed to the conception of these independent Daughter Churches. What about *"The Church* on the mission-field?"

This was the great subject to which had been given a whole Commission to itself, and was to have a whole day for its discussion. Accordingly little was said about it on this day—but enough not to leave the edifice of the day's debate uncrowned. A Chinese delegate struck a ringing note in a speech the object of which was a plea for " Chinese independence," he quickly qualified the word :—" Really there is no independence of the

Church. *All Churches of Christ are dependent first upon God and then upon each other.*" Another speaker, with the same primary object, was equally swift to state a complementary caution : " There is a danger [in this movement in the Chinese Church] because we do not want to see arising in China, or any far-eastern land, a Far-Eastern Church separated in sympathy and in aim from the *Catholic Church of a Christian World.*" Both speakers were congregationalist in church-polity. And it was characteristic of the spirit that informed this Conference of Edinburgh 1910, that it should have been these who gave expression to the shining ideal of Catholicity, of the one *Civitas Dei,* no less than two Bishops of the Anglican communion. Of these two, the first said that the missionary in China must realise always that he stands at any rate for the present as a mediator with the Church Universal, and foreign workers must never withdraw from China until there are Chinese workers able in their own persons *to maintain touch with the Universal Church.*" (Bishop Roots of Hankow). And the other :—

" If we are to hand over Christianity to the Church of China, and Japan, and India with good courage, then we must have done more than at the present moment we seem, I think, inclined to do— to contribute to a definition of what the Church is, the definition of its essential or real Catholic features. Men are conscious that what they used forcibly to assert was essential to Christianity they are no longer willing to assert. Now it follows from that that they ought to be labouring patiently and diligently to know what they are to substitute for the old assertion. . . . I am very far from meaning that it is our business, as Westerns, to define this for Easterns or for Africans. What I mean is . . ."

The bell stung the intent silence and the Bishop of Birmingham prepared to flee. To this speech alone the clamour of the entire audience compelled the granting of an extension, and Bishop Gore finished his sentence :—

" that we have got to put into all bodies of Christians the consciousness that continuous life depends on continuous principles, and that any period of deep intellectual change involves and necessitates fresh effort to interpret in such intellectual forms as admit of statement, and become a bond of union, what we believe to be the real basis of a Christianity that can be copied."

7.

We may fittingly close this chapter with the eloquent words with which the Report concludes a tour of the imagination, a tour and a survey of the great round world and the little churches on its Mission-Fields. As the mind follows the sunrise that scatters the shadow of the night and ushers in a Lord's Day all over the face of the earth, it beholds how " from the rising of the sun to the going down of it, incense and a pure offering ascends unceasingly to God, land answering to land as each in turn takes up the chorus. So under God's ordinances of day and night it has already come to pass that not for one day only, as we commonly say, but for more than thirty-six hours every week The Holy Church throughout all the world keeps her sacred watch in solemn commemoration of the Resurrection of her Lord. The Commission humbly desires that it could so present a true vision of the great Church in the Mission-Field as to give a new inspiration to Christian thought, so that all should sing with a new and intenser emotion our ancient hymn,

" 'THE HOLY CHURCH THROUGHOUT ALL THE WORLD DOTH ACKNOWLEDGE THEE.' "

H

CHAPTER IX

EDUCATION IN RELATION TO THE CHRISTIANISATION
OF NATIONAL LIFE

In the last chapter, which was a narrative of what took place on the second day of the Conference, the importance of an efficient pastorate to lead "the Church on the Mission-Field" was shown to be cardinal. On this more than any other class devolved the duty of interpreting the Christian faith to their nation and so of rendering it indigenous in every land : so that " the glory and honour of all nations " [1] be brought within the circle of the Kingdom of God. " This work," said the Bishop of Birmingham, " will be the work of the Spirit of God *through teachers belonging to the country.*" It was, therefore, immediately obvious that the question of the efficiency of the pastorate, or the reverse, turned upon its training ; and accordingly an all-important section on the training of the pastorate was included in the Report of the Commission discussed on that day.

But the training of the ministry is only an aspect, though the supreme aspect, of the whole question of *Education.* For apart from the fact that the clergy must be " educated " before they can be "trained " (to use the

---

[1] In Rev. xxi. 3 a certain familiar Old Testament quotation is for the first time significantly varied, the usual singular becoming a plural : " They shall be My *nations* "—in the New Jerusalem into which the fulness of a redeemed earth is brought.

terms in their conventional senses), there is the further fact, to which indeed the Bishop was alluding in the sentence just quoted, that the *schoolmaster* as well as the preacher and pastor has an all-important part to play in the Christianising of national life on the mission-field, the bringing of the glory of the nations into the Church. From the schools—with their range from kindergarten to university—come the leaders of both Church and State in all these mission lands ; the ministers, the teachers, all the laymen who are going to lead. In these schools are educated the rank and file of the Christian communities, no less important than those, as we have seen, in carrying the gospel to their own people. These are the men, then, who will interpret the Christian faith to their fellow-countrymen ; and therefore the whole question of education in the mission field becomes at once one of the most vital importance. This, then, was the question which, by the most natural and proper transition, was now discussed on the third day of the World Missionary Conference.

I.

Missionary education, as we may gather from what has just been said, occupies a place of primary importance in the estimate of those who lead the Christian enterprise in all the world. It always has done so ; though the rationale of its importance was not always fully realised. The great Dr Duff was the man who led the way in expounding the philosophy of Christian education in the mission-field, though the lessons he suggested can hardly yet be said to have been fully learned, even by many of the directors of the enterprise at home. Probably this Edinburgh Conference, and the Report of this third Commission, will mark the final stage of the assimilation of those lessons, and education be recognised and studied, as a method entirely parallel with the evangelistic, medical, and pastoral aspects of missionary work.

But if even the directors of missions have only come gradually to this position, it is probably that others are still almost totally unaware of the real place of education in the missionary enterprise. A vague idea that the mission school is useful as a means of teaching heathens or native Christians to read the Scriptures probably represents the general notion. To such the perusal of the Report of this Commission, or of the debate upon it, will come as a simple revelation. It will give them too, perhaps, a wholly new idea of the dignity, the significance, and the thoroughness of the missionary enterprise. It must be the task of this chapter, at any rate, so to interpret both Report and debate that this —whether for the first time or not—may indeed be the impression that is conveyed to the reader.

2.

The Report, to which the Conference now turned, was indeed a masterly document. On the Commission which drew it up were great names—the Bishop of Birmingham, Professor E. C. Moore of Harvard, Professor M. E. Sadler of Manchester, and Sir Ernest Satow, to name only four. It was not only intrinsically important, as it stood, but it was invested with the additional importance of being a first achievement. The Vice-Chairman of the Commission, Professor E. C. Moore, was weighing his words when he said that that Report, like all the others, marked an epoch in this, " that it is *the beginning of a serious endeavour to arrive by joint consultation at a policy*." If it had the faults, it also had the glory of a first beginning, he added. One may judge of its value, not only by the authoritative rank of the commissioners, but by the number, the representativeness, and the ability of the men and women who supplied the material which the commissioners co-ordinated and presented in an organic whole, and from which they derived their far-reaching inferences and conclusions. Two hundred correspondents—missionaries from India and Ceylon, from Japan, Korea and China, from Malaysia and the Levant, and from all over the continent of Africa— replied to the questions sent out ; and the Report in its introduction acknowledged that " many of these [replies] were of very high value." In five great chapters the five principal divisions of the field are reviewed. Then comes a masterly treatise, both historical and philosophical, on the relation of Christian truth to indigenous thought and feeling, and the bearing of education on that relation. Three further chapters, highly informing and suggestive, on industrial training, literature in the mission field, and the training of teachers, lead on to the conclusion of the Report. In spite of this document being a Report—a very formidable word—it is extremely readable : the very character of its materials, and the unconventional range of its enquiry, ensured that much. The historical chapter alluded to above discusses education in the Roman Empire, the educational ideas and attainments of the early Christians, early educational philosophers like Origen, and many other topics of great general interest, in order to lay, deep and broad, the foundation for a science of Educational Missions to-day. It did not need much higher critical faculty to trace the authorship of this delightful chapter, —and the rest of the Report is equally readable,—or to see in it all the educational ideals and experiences successively gained at Oxford, Westminster, and Birmingham.

The resulting blend of living scholarship and living
experience gives it both its value and its charm.

3.

How mighty a force educational missions have been
—and by no means from the purely missionary view-point
—was well demonstrated in the speech with which the
Chairman of the Commission, Dr Gore, Lord Bishop of
Birmingham, opened the debate. And it should be
remembered that he was the mouthpiece of a Commission
that included a great Eastern diplomatist, and a British
educational authority of highest rank, when he spoke of
the " impression which has been produced upon our
minds as to the real and rich and abundant fruit which
the educational labours of missionaries have borne in
every part of the world " : and further, went on to
enumerate some of those fruits.   He spoke of the
diffusion of Christian ideas and ideals " far beyond the
region of any specific church influence " ; the elevation
of outcasts ; the first introduction of the very idea
and ideal of the education of women ; the sustaining
of the ideal of education as a harmonious training of the
whole man, with definite regard to a goal of social
service ; and finally the creation of a bond—perhaps the
one real bond—of spiritual sympathy between the
European and the peoples of Asia and of Africa—these,
he said, were some of the achievements of education
in the mission fields of the world.

And at the end of the morning session, Professor M. E.
Sadler, probably one of the highest educational authorities
living, bore witness to the real importance of the reflex
light thrown by educational missions on educational
science at home. " The educational science of Europe and
America," he roundly declared, " has paid far too little

heed to the experience of the mission field." He spoke of his own profound sense of the value of missionary educators as shown at once by their contributions to the Report and to the morning's discussion. These contributions he called " first-hand experience of the highest value gathered through long years of devoted effort in every part of the world." And it was highly significant that it was this speaker who should have given expression to the hope that

" this gathering may leave behind it some form of permanent organisation which may continuously gather together missionary experience in education, and present it in such a way that it may fertilise the educational thought of the world more fully than it has done at present."

The specific thing which the speaker valued most highly was, as he went on to say, the contribution that educational missions make to the present problem in the West, where education is becoming more and more organised and dependent on public money,—" how to preserve for it amid all the conflicts of belief the power of a spiritual ideal, without which no education can do that which we here feel to be its prime and its most lasting work." It was, indeed, deeply interesting, in days when some who are reckoned advanced thinkers are ridiculing the schoolmaster for meddling with " moral " and " spiritual " affairs at all, to see a great educationist take up his stand for the knitting together of the intellectual side of education with the emotional and spiritual, and after saying

" The great danger of the highly-organised systems of modern education in Europe is that, being hyper-intellectual, they lead often to moral scepticism,"

to hear him citing the experience of educationalists from

the mission-fields as corrective of some one-sided and unphilosophic theories of modern Europe !

4.

After these general considerations, the reader of this chapter will, it is hoped, feel more than an impersonal interest in hearing of the critical problems that face missionary educators in mission lands in their endeavours to mould and Christianise the national life of the peoples to whom they have gone.

Nowhere has missionary education had a more distinguished history, bright with more illustrious names, than in India. Nowhere has it before it a more open field or a more decisive opportunity. The many-sided national movement in India to-day has neither depleted nor emptied the missionary colleges and schools; on the contrary the Conference had it from speaker after speaker—Principals Mackichan and Haythornthwaite, for example—that their classrooms "had never been so crowded," and so "overflowing with students." Facts like these very greatly emphasise the necessity of Christianising this dawning national life. What basis of unity can be found for this national life ? No basis, argued one well-known man, can be found for it in Hinduism or Islam or Secularism or Rationalism. But it *can* be found in Christianity, the faith with ideals of universality, of brotherhood, and of freedom. The Report, therefore, is full of passages which show how educators are re-thinking out their methods, and revising their curricula, some of which have hitherto been too much directed to the attaining London University degrees, and too little to the production of national leaders. It is being realised more keenly that it must be the missionary college that shall kindle the young Indian's patriotic enthusiasm, by teaching him his own language and the history and literature of his own country, lest that enthusiasm be kindled by alien hands and enlisted for disloyal and anti-Christian causes. And, in particular, it is widely felt that the training of Indian teachers must be revised. *Their* training above all must be nationalised, since it is they who most of all have to mediate Christianity to the Indian mind. Speaker after speaker got up and emphasised this finding of the Report—that the supreme need of the hour is for *leaders* to lead India in this her time of crisis.

And here it was notable that this need for improving educational method, so keenly felt and so continually emphasised, seemed only to heighten and give precision to the old emphasis on the *evangelistic* aspect of missionary education. The Conference heard educational missionary vie with evangelistic in insisting that the ultimate aim of mission schools is to win men for Christ. Men so won are far the best present that mission schools can make to India at the present moment, for they are the men who have the moral backbone and grit of character which India above all things needs in her sons to-day.

In the face of all these facts, — the increased difficulties in which an ever intenser competition is involving missionary education ; the universal under-staffing and under-equipping, and the absolute necessity nevertheless for immediately strengthening the staffs, and improving the quality of educational apparatus and equipment in all our schools ;—two things were made transparently evident to the Conference : first, that there must be immediate reinforcements sent for the staffing of Christian schools and colleges throughout India ; and second, that a co-operation and co-ordination of the most definite kind must be practised on the field

itself, in order that the existing forces may be directed
to the very highest advantage.

There was one other aspect of missionary education
in India that was brought into great prominence in
both Report and debate : an aspect that had a most
important bearing on this matter of the Christianising
of Indian national life,—what may be called the ideal
of " diffused Christian influence." Special prominence
had been given to this ideal by the most distinguished
educationalist in all India, the veteran Dr Miller of
Madras. He had written a very strong letter and
issued it in printed form to all the delegates, in which
he declared his conviction that the Indian Church was
still to all intents and purposes a foreign church, and
that it would remain so as long as Hindus of the higher
castes, who are the real representatives of India, remain
untouched by Christianity. And he insisted that
India could never be won for Christ, if it is the lower
castes or outcastes who are relied upon. The higher
castes must be reached, and the only way of reaching
these classes is by diffusing Christian influence amongst
them by means of educational institutions providing
the very highest education. The letter was strongly,
even provocatively, worded, and many references were
made to it in the discussion. One speaker pointed out
that to talk exclusively of the highest and the lowest
classes was to omit the class that contained 65 per cent.
of the nation—the middle-class. The " sense of the
meeting " seemed to be that while fully conceding the
force of Dr Miller's positive contention, and resolving
firmly not to slacken in the smallest degree our efforts to
leaven the thought of the whole Indian community
through well-equipped schools and colleges, a most
effectual way to the heart of the nation was to be found
in the training of leaders for a truly national church.

5.

The first day of discussion had reminded the Conference of the vast problem of Islam, that great non-Christian system that strides like a Colossus over half of Asia and Africa. This Commission on Education now revealed the extraordinary importance of the work of missionary schools or colleges in Moslem lands. In the Turkish Empire there have been no stronger centres of reform than the great American colleges that are found occupying so many strategic centres in Turkey, Anatolia, Armenia, Syria, from Constantinople to Beyrout; colleges which are, moreover, only the crowning stages of complete systems of education ranging from infant schools to professional colleges. They have confined themselves most loyally to purely educational aims and methods; yet their influence has been such that the recent reform movement in the Ottoman Empire has been attributed to it more than to any one other cause. That there is little exaggeration in this statement may be concluded from the following testimony from an eminent traveller, Sir William Ramsay, who says in his " Impressions of Turkey " :—

" I have come in contact with men educated in Robert College, in widely separate parts of the country, men of diverse races, and different forms of religion—Greek, Armenian, and Protestant—and have everywhere been struck with the marvellous way in which a certain uniform type, direct, simple, honest, and lofty in tone has been impressed upon them ; some had more of it, some less ; but all had it to a certain degree ; and it is diametrically opposite to the type produced by growth under the ordinary conditions of Turkish life."

With the proved influence of these colleges fresh in mind, the Conference heard an appeal from that country where the conditions are in so many respects analogous

to those in Turkey,—the ancient kingdom of Persia.
It was impossible not to be impressed by the speech of a
well-known Orientalist and scholar, Dr St Clair Tisdall,
who urged the starting of a similar college in Persia, to
crown the efficient system of mission schools that already
exist in that land, and also asked for a great strengthening and increasing of the mission schools throughout
the Empire. It is surely entirely to be desired that
this powerful appeal will be taken up. Nor are Turkey
and Persia the only realms in the Mohammedan East in
which Americans are doing this great educational work.
In Egypt, as the venerable Dr Andrew Watson of Cairo
told the Conference, an American mission has 190 schools,
with 17,000 pupils, of whom some 4000 are Mohammedans. The first-rate importance of educational missions
in Moslem Africa was further proved by what was heard
from the East Coast, where Islam is making such rapid
strides southwards. The statement of the Bishop of
Mombasa, in East Equatorial Africa, was quoted (to
mention only one high authority)—that the most direct
way of checking Moslem advance and of influencing Islam
for Christ would be by the establishing of numerous
schools in all Islamised districts. To these schools the sons
of Moslem notables would certainly flock; whereas if we
do not start such schools they will start their own, and
these will be bitterly anti-Christian and will hasten the
already rapid advance of Islam. And from the West
Coast came a similar moving appeal. Absent at his
work among the great and important nation of the
Hausas, Dr Walter Miller was nevertheless heard,
through a friend, declaring that with a fairly considerable
force of educationalists, a work of far-reaching influence
and importance could be done in Northern Nigeria, and
from thence all through the Central Sudan.

A large section of the Report was devoted to educational

missions in heathen Africa also. The great problem here was there stated to be the due adjustment of the literary and the industrial elements in the education provided by the mission schools. The former without the latter tends utterly to spoil the negro, while an industrial without a literary education wholly fails to develop the whole man. Readers of Mr Dudley Kidd's recent books, especially "Kaffir Socialism," will remember how much he emphasises the need for " fundamental thinking " on the subject of negro education, and its bearing on the national life of Africans. For India and the countries of the East are not the only ones that have their national movements to-day. South Africa with its Ethiopianism is experiencing the same movement—one attended with special elements of anxiety and danger, not found in countries where there is a uniformity of race, and where a black and a white people do not co-exist side by side. Diverse as are the conditions in the several regions of negro Africa, the same impression was nevertheless left by reports from Cape Colony, Natal, Transvaal, Basutoland, Lourenço Marquez, Nyasaland, Uganda, Southern Nigeria and Sierra Leone, that the " Christianisation of National Life " is everywhere to be effected by the raising up of qualified African leaders ; and that these can only be raised up by an education as thoroughly planned and as ably carried out in its way as the developed systems that exist in the more advanced countries of the mission field.

6.

The interest, already high in the morning, reached its culmination in the afternoon, when the educational problems now facing the Church in Japan and China were set before the Conference.

From the aspect of missionary education, Japan presented to the Conference a situation of very great difficulty and urgency. How great the influence of Christian education has been in the past, was shown by a striking object-lesson. On the benches of the Conference sat the four Japanese delegates to the Conference ; and Professor E. W. Clement, in giving a short summary of their life histories, was more convincing than the Report itself. Y. Chiba, alumnus of the Missionary College of Aoyama Gakuin, and now President of a theological seminary ; T. Harada, alumnus of the Doshisha, honorary LL.D. of Edinburgh, and now President of his alma mater, the most important Christian college in Japan ; Yoitsu Honda and K. Ibuka, both pupils of Dr S. R. Brown, the pioneer missionary, and both of them subsequently Presidents of important educational institutions. These " illustrate in themselves the relation of Christian education to the development of indigenous Christianity in Japan " :—four scholars of Christian schools ; four Presidents of colleges that are helping to mould the national life of Japan! But the Government of Japan has now its own astonishingly complete educational system, spread like a network all over the country. The Government undertakes the education of every Japanese child from the kindergarten, at the age of three, right up to a University degree, and post graduate work beyond that degree. And the influences found in this system are in many respects very injurious to Christianity, and to that Christian character which is the Church's best contribution to Japanese life.

It is, therefore, easy to see how hard such competition as this has hit Christian education in Japan, and how completely the long start of the latter has been neutralised. Either there must now be strict co-operation, greater definiteness of aim, and improvement of quality everywhere,—or extinction. The Report made clear that the educationalists on the field see their way to meet the situation by greater concentration and a more calculated distribution of their work, provided the Church of Christ rises to its opportunity and sends immediate reinforcements, in order to strengthen the educational work of the Church along the definitely limited lines of which the present situation allows. Dr Ibuka, in a short but powerful speech, voiced and justified this appeal. Fully admitting, as a Japanese, the great results that Christian education has produced, he went on to say that existing schools and colleges do not meet the present demand. " Without a single exception " he said (and it was the President of the second best-known college in Japan, the Meiji Gakuin, that was speaking),

" the existing colleges need to be greatly strengthened, both in their equipment and in their teaching force. . . . But there is a second need, which is equally urgent if not more so. I mean the establishment of a Christian University. . . . Its establishment will mark a new era in the history of the nation, and it may be in the history of all Eastern Asia. . . ."

And he concluded by quoting a resolution, passed by a Conference held in Japan in October 1909 representative of all the Protestant missions and Japanese Churches, recommending unanimously the starting of this University. " I know we are asking much," he said, " but may we not ' expect great things from God ' ? " ' Much ' is a relative term. An American delegate (S. L. Gulick) surely spoke both sensibly and significantly when he said : " A million-dollar institution in Japan for higher education will count ten times as much as a million-dollar institution in America for the uplifting of the world ! "

This chapter has already recorded an appeal for a Christian Higher College for *Persia* : here is a second similar appeal from *Japan* : and we shall hear, finally, of a third from *China*. The three together made a not unreasonable total, considering the importance of the Edinburgh Conference and the literally world-wide range of the countries surveyed by this Commission. A delegate was saying no more than the bare truth when he closed his address with the words, " The day of small things in missionary education has gone."

If any testimony was needed to justify this particular appeal from Japan, or to prove the real relationship between education and the quickening of national life in this mission field, it was surely supplied by S. L. Gulick—the bearer of a great name in the missionary history of Japan. Intervening at the very close of this part of the discussion, he exclaimed he had two points to make in two minutes. One of the two has been quoted above. The second was in the highest degree important. It was contained in a letter which he held in his hand, from Marquis Katsura, the Prime Minister of Japan, and addressed to President Harada, of the Doshisha College, who was then present at that moment in the Conference - hall. It was now read to the delegates :—

" Recognising the great service of Doshisha, through its graduates, in our political, literary, and business, as well as religious circles, I am of opinion that your school has been specially instrumental in emphasizing character and manhood in the young men of Japan. It is my sincere and earnest desire that your historic school may attain an even greater development and serve the country still more efficiently in the years to come. I take this opportunity to express my gratitude toward the late Dr Neesima, and to pray for the prosperity of Doshisha."

When the first statesman in Japan bears his witness to the value of Christian education in relation to Japanese national life, it is fitting, surely, to add no more.

8.

Already in the two previous days the Conference had been brought to feel, with an intensity that was even painful, how great, how utterly unparalleled is the crisis which China presents to the Christian enterprise to-day. And the impression was very greatly deepened on this third day. The very fact that China is traditionally a land of educational system, of an aristocracy of letters, of leaders who are leaders by virtue of their learning, made it certain that nowhere would the relation between education and this Christianising of national life be so vital and so all-important as in China.

" No one," said the Vice-Chairman of the Commission, " can be in China without realising the intensity of the intellectual life of that land, and being at once impressed by the thought that any appeal to the educated classes in that land must be made through education ; and that the Christian Church stands no chance in China, save as it can raise up and educate leaders for it-self." He went on to point out the significance and the danger of China's sudden repudiation of the Confucian political system as impracticable. The danger is, he said, lest the Chinese turn with too all-absorbing an enthusiasm to material things, the pursuit of wealth, the study of the means of its production. Now, it is Western knowledge that has brought about this change of attitude. And the knowledge that China is now seeking after what it so long refused, seeking after " practically everything except that which seems to us to be the secret of the welfare of nations," multiplies the responsibility of the

I

Church in the West to share with China that secret also.

Again and again, so the Report informs us, did the correspondence from China recur to this point. "In a country like China," said one writer bluntly, "a Church of ignorant men cannot hope to have influence." And the following sentence is selected from many by the Report itself to sum up the matter :—

"If Christianity does not speedily develop an educated ministry, it will soon fail to command respect or exert any great influence over the people and their leaders. Everything lies within the grasp of Christianity now, if the best talent of the native Church can be given good Christian educational advantages."

It is a crisis. The Christian Church had a start which is now bound to diminish every day, unless a great new effort is put forth. And for this reason : up to the present time the graduates of the Christian schools and colleges were almost the only men of the new education who were available to meet the needs of the nation. On the previous day the Conference had had the most striking testimony to the estimation in which these men are held and the importance of the careers now open to them [1] on all sides. But now the Government has entered the field ; all over China are springing up thousands of schools and colleges which will tend year by year relatively to depress the prestige of the mission institutions. Moreover, certain political disabilities are

[1] A matter which has its difficult side to the churches also : as Dr Duncan Main, the medical missionary of Hang-chow, said, " The demand from Government is so great that we cannot keep sufficient men to carry on our own work. The Government comes forward and says, 'We will give you £15 and the Missionary Society are only giving you £1'"—then with a burst of humorous despair— "and where is the Christianity to-day in China, or anywhere else, that will stand temptation like that ? "

being attached to graduates of mission schools,[1] though even this most serious obstacle can be surmounted (the Report maintained) if the standard of those institutions can be kept high :—real merit in the graduates will ultimately neutralise all disabilities. Thus the position is surely manifestly clear. Every correspondent to the Commission alluded to it. In a sentence, the position is this :

" To-day the leadership of Christian thought, in the making of the modern China, is a possibility ; but each year makes it less possible, for each year sees the opposing forces increase and the pro-Christian influence, by comparison, grow faint."

The reader will recall the almost sensational speech of the Chinese delegate on the first day. And he will now be able to appreciate why such a speech was justified.

Thus almost everything which was said about the situation in India, and the appeal which that situation creates, might be applied without change, but with an intensified note of urgency, to China. As in India, so in China, we learn that " the demand upon Christian schools has suddenly become more than we can meet. In the attempt to meet that demand, the pressure has become so great, and the schools are so miserably staffed, that we are in danger of losing sight of the real end and of failing to meet that which we see to be the real need of the people in this emergency." As from India, so from China comes the clamant demand for an unprecedented reinforcement at this time, and the acute recognition of the need for co-operation on the field itself. These two words in fact almost sum up the solution of the problem—Reinforce ; Co-operate.

But in India a fully developed system of universities and affiliated colleges already exists. In China there

[1] This assertion, however, was contradicted later on in the Conference by a Chinese delegate.

is no such system, and exactly here lies the supreme
opportunity of Christendom, and the supreme call for
co-operation. If Robert College, Constantinople, and
the Protestant College, Beyrout, have been able to accomplish so much, what fruit might not be expected from
the establishing of similar institutions in every province
in China ? Already the missionary Societies in the
field are drawing together their forces, and by the
federation of existing colleges are bringing into being
universities that will train men up to the B.A. standard.
But in addition to these there is call for at least one
fully-equipped University in the complete sense of the
term. This grand scheme has already gone beyond
mere talk : but it can only be carried through by a great
effort of co-operation—not only co-operation on the
field, but even more *at home*.

It was at this point that William Jennings Bryan
intervened in the debate. A storm of applause greeted
him ; but even notables came under the seven-minutes
rule at Edinburgh, and with the fear of the bell in his
heart the great man waved away the applause :—" I
appreciate your welcome," he said, " but I need the time ! "
The speaker was that very evening to hold an Edinburgh
audience for seventy-five minutes in a reasoned defence
of missions, and a passionate personal testimony for the
Christian enterprise and for Christ. On this afternoon he spoke for Christian education in China :—" No
part of our work in the foreign field," he said, " impressed
me more than the work that these colleges are doing."
The cost of them per head is the merest fraction of the
cost in the West, and yet the influence they must exert
in the present crisis is beyond calculation. And then
the statesman spoke out his mind :—

" These countries that are educating the world are
Christian nations, and by sending out these Christian

educators into all lands these Christian nations demonstrate that they are not afraid to lift other nations out of darkness, and put them on the high road to prosperity. It shows that they are not jealous of these nations in their growing strength. We hear of a yellow peril, and we are asked, if China is awakened and people are educated, what will become of the rest of the world? The Christian people of this world believe *that there is but one yellow peril on this earth, and that is the lust for gold!"*

The words gleamed in the subdued light of the hall— "yellow," "gold,"—like the ominous glint of the Rheingold itself. . . . The Conference remembered the time when at one of America's Gargantuan political conventions an almost unknown man leaped suddenly with a phrase into world-wide fame. In that phrase, too, glinted the yellow of the gold—and then, as now, it was used to symbolise and express the speaker's unconquerable suspicion of the commercial spirit, when that spirit is not governed and controlled by the Christian idea of service.

The *first*, nevertheless, though it gained a nomination lost an election. Perhaps its spirit was sounder than its economics. But perhaps, too, in the long reckoning of time and of eternity, that loss—to person and to party—will go for nothing, and less than nothing, were the *second* to inspire that great Republic of the West, now, to-day, and without delay, to christianise the national life of China by one supreme effort of Christian enterprise.

To christianise the national life of China! Would not that, more than any one other thing, mean the conquest of the world for Christ?

CHAPTER X

"THE MISSIONARY MESSAGE IN RELATION TO THE NON-CHRISTIAN RELIGIONS"

THE eight days, on which the eight Reports were considered at the Conference, were divided by a Sunday into two equal groups of four, the first of which, speaking broadly, dealt with the peoples and religions that form the objective of missionary work; the second with problems that chiefly concern the Societies and Boards that prosecute such work, and so with the problem of the home-base itself.

On the last day of the first group a Report was taken which formed a transition from the one to the other. In discussing the Missionary Message in *relation to non-Christian religions*, the Conference was brought back to the world-survey with which it started, but this time from the standpoint of the spiritual attitude of the races and nations previously surveyed. While the discussion of the *Missionary Message* raised vital issues, which led forward to the consideration of the spiritual attitude of the Christian community at the home-base itself.

I.

By common consent the Report that was now laid on the table of the Conference and presented by the Chairman of the Commission, Professor D. S. Cairns, was one of the most remarkable, perhaps the most remarkable, of a great series. No less than two hundred answers were

sent in from the field in response to the questions sent
out by the Commission, and the Chairman testified that
not a few of those were of a length and an importance that
would have justified their separate publication. The Commission, in fact, had been presented with the results of
years of thought, lavished by the deepest thinkers in the
field upon the work of their lives. Such materials could
not have failed to react powerfully on the Commission
which had the task of studying and co-ordinating them.
This is evident on every page of the Report. Towards
its almost lyrical close we read :—

" We cannot conclude the review of these reports from the field
of action without recording the deep and solemn impression which
they have made upon our mind. The spectacle of the advance
of the Christian Church along many lines of action to the conquest
of the five great religions of the modern world is one of singular
interest and grandeur. *Vexilla Regis prodeunt* ! "

Like all masterpieces, the interest of the Report steadily
increases up to the very last sentence. The most striking
and essential passages of the reports from the field have
been detached from their matrix, collected and welded
together, not however into dry synopses, but into
well articulated wholes.—There are successive chapters,
constructed in this way, on Animism, Chinese Religions,
Japanese Religions, Islamism, and Hinduism, which
form the five-fold division of the entire subject-
matter. Here the interest, great throughout, rises
steadily, reaching the highest point in the last division
on Hinduism. Nevertheless in the next and concluding chapter it takes a yet higher flight : the five-
fold division is gone over once more, but this time
to apply to each of the five certain far-reaching principles which had gradually been distilled from the study
of the whole subject-matter itself. And then, finally,
from the heights thus gained, Christianity itself is passed

in review ; the religion of CHRIST—as it was (and is) in Him ; as it has been actually realised ; *and as it might be*, if the Church responds to the Macedonian call of to-day. The paragraphs succeed each other, ever climbing to height on height, with the sure grip and foot-hold of the Alpinist at the last ascents before the top, and with a similar disciplined acceleration, revealing a similar intensification of passion within : until with a shout, if one so may say, the alpenstock is struck into the snow on the topmost peak—the last sentence is reached ; and in the rhythm and beauty of its two clauses not only the cadence but the absolute climax is attained. That sentence—in which the thing ceases to be a report and becomes literature—is no casual aphorism that achieves a random success. The whole material of the Report is in that sentence, fused by white heat and intensest pressure into a gem.

One would be disposed to hazard a prophecy that the concluding chapter to the Report of this Commission will mark an epoch—in ways which it is the chief object of this chapter to indicate.

2.

It was hardly to be expected that the discussion would reach the level of the report. It has already been said that the debates rose or fell to different levels. On the Church on the Mission-Field, for example, the level was uniformly high. On this day the level was moderate. It would have taken the delegates at least twice the time during which the Report had actually been in their hands, to consider it fully and realise its full importance ; and consequently the discussion did little more than illustrate some of its important details. Probably the only way by which its central message could have been brought out at the discussion itself, would have been to read its concluding chapter aloud at the outset of the day, and to spend the rest of the time in listening to a series of comments by chosen speakers, divided by intervals for silent thought and solemn supplication.

In this chapter it will therefore probably be best to continue our examination of the Report itself, mentioning from time to time passages in the discussion that threw light upon it.

3.

The non-Christian religions have been variously regarded by Christian men. Some have considered them as perfect specimens of absolute error, masterpieces of hell's invention, which Christianity was simply called upon to oppose, uproot and destroy. A closer study of Scripture itself, and also of the history of the earliest missions, has, however, convinced most people that this view is simply the exaggeration of one extreme aspect of a wide question. And while of course theories as to the origin and significance of the non-Christian religions still vary, there is a general consensus that, representing as they do so many attempted solutions of life's problem, they must be approached with very real sympathy and respect ; that they must be *studied*, if only to bring the evangelist into touch with the minds of his hearers. More than that, the conviction has grown that their "confused cloud-world" will be found to be "shot through and through with broken lights of a hidden sun." And, these things being true, another conviction has dawned :— Christianity, the religion of the Light of the World, can ignore no lights however "broken"— it must take them all into account, absorb them all into its central glow.

Nay, since the Church of Christ itself is partially involved in mists of unbelief, failing aspiration, imperfect realisation, this quest of hers among the non-Christian religions, this discovery of their " broken lights " may be to her the discovery of facets of her own truth, forgotten or half-forgotten—perhaps even never perceived at all save by the most prophetic of her sons.   Thus " by going into all the world " Christ's Church may recover all the light that is in Christ, and become, like her Head, as it is His will she should become,—*Lux Mundi*.

Such was the working principle which guided the spiritual enterprise and quest now set forth in the pages of the Report of this Commission.   Both the correspondence received by the Commission from all over the mission-field, and the speeches that were delivered at the discussion, revealed clearly that missionaries everywhere do their work animated by this working principle, however variously it is expressed and applied.   As Robert E. Speer put it, in the address that closed the day's discussion, not only did it seem fairer that the Commission should compare best with best, and not with worst ; but also it is the very strength of the conviction that Christ *is* best, that emboldens Christians to call with such confidence on the non-Christian religions to produce *their* best, and lay it down beside the absolute Best of all. "We hold to the truth of the absoluteness of Christianity," cried the speaker, " but does that truth hold us ? " Moreover, practical wisdom itself dictates this course ; for the question is not how the missionary may convince himself that Christ is best, but how he may convince non-Christians—men out of touch with his whole range of ideal and aspiration and thought.   Clearly, nothing but a very intimate knowledge of their point of view will enable him to present to them his message acceptably or even intelligibly.

4.

To what had the Report called the attention of Conference in respect of the five great religious systems into which its subject-matter was divided ? *Animism* was treated of first. This is the generic name for the religious beliefs of more or less backward or degraded peoples all over the world ; a system the chief feature of which is a belief in the occult power of the souls of individuals, and their capability of continued existence after death ; and in the similar power of other spirits, ranging from the spirits of plants or animals upward to those of powerful deities. Negroes all over the continent of Africa ; " Indians " in the Americas ; Aboriginal tribes in India and other parts of Asia ; and Islanders from all the tropical and southern oceans, hold various forms of animistic beliefs. Indeed the religions of China and Japan are, to some extent, but civilised and moralised forms of animism ; indeed it may even be said that queer vestiges of it are to be found in all the countries of Europe, wherever, in fact, the traditional superstitions of country-folk still linger on.

The Commission had had the advantage of a notable recent addition to the large body of literature that exists on this theme, a work by the younger Warneck, named *The Living Forces of the Gospel*, and, as has already been narrated in due place, the Conference had the advantage of the presence of the author in its midst. His address at the Conference was a valuable commentary on the book itself—a rare compound of the close scientific treatment characteristic of Germany, and the rich pietism, no less truly and invaluably characteristic of that noble race. May that race yet more fully join to its scientific pre-eminence its ancient spiritual insight ! Would it not then truly lead Christendom in the spiritual battle

that impends ?—Herr Warneck's experience had chiefly
been gained among the Battaks, the pagan remnant
of Islamised Sumatra. And a mass of other evidence, sent
from parts of the world as widely separated as possible,
went to show the justice of certain important conclusions
drawn out by the young Licentiat.

The most striking one of these was that the purely
theological parts of Christianity are at once the most
effective, the most easily grasped, and the most quickly
fruitful, among animistic peoples ! The missionary
finds the pagan's mind distracted by the multiplicity
of their demons and contradictory cross-currents of unseen
malignity : . . . and he preaches—*One God* : One
accessible Father-Spirit of unalterable good-will to him !
The doctrine comes as an intellectual as well as a spiritual
rest to him—and with what deep feeling did the scholar-
missionary depict the reality of that rest ! Again, he
finds the whole life of the heathen devoted to a complex
and ineffectual system of securing escape, deliverance,
from a literally clinging cloud of hostile influences : . . .
and he preaches to him—*One Saviour and Deliverer*.
Or, he finds him occupied by the thought of the spirits
of his ancestors and other dead people : and he preaches
to him—*the Resurrection* of the Saviour and of men.
The venerable Norwegian missionary, Dahle, told how
this doctrine of the Resurrection, so invariably preached
by Paul to the pagans and animists of his day, comes
home with like tremendous force to the animists of
to-day.

And now what of the *moral* results ? They appear
in due season after this spiritual and intellectual en-
franchisement ! They must be patiently waited for :
they will surely come, when the theological teaching has
had sufficient time to sink into their minds and hearts.
The true idea, One Living God, awakens and informs the

conscience. This is certainly an exceedingly striking comment on the doctrine of those many who say that backward tribes must be civilised first, and that of all mortal things it is useless bringing them—theology.

And here the last chapter of the Report shows the deep importance of the lesson which the Christian faith itself may learn from even animism, surely the humblest of all possible teachers ! " The whole analysis," it says, " is deeply suggestive for Christian theology. It raises the question whether the Christian Church *in civilised lands* is using sufficiently the elemental truths of Revelation—the unity, the omnipotence, the omnipresence, and the availability of God." The animist sees his environment riddled and shot through and through by spirits :— does the Christian see *his* environment steeped through and through by *Spirit* ? a world controlled throughout by the Spirit of a Personal God, with whom the human spirit should be in completest touch by faith ?

This example of the method of the Report, as it deals with the humblest and least sublime of all the five great creeds which it considers, may very well serve us a pattern of its treatment throughout.

5.

The religious crisis in China to-day may be briefly indicated by the fact that at the bottom of its religion, at the bottom of that great and apparently indissoluble system of Confucian morality, is this very animism, in the form of ancestor-worship. And will modern science with its conception of Nature, asked the Report, spare for long the cosmology which goes with the ancestor-worship, the popular pantheon, the superstitions of animism ? In thousands of schools and colleges all over China to-day a curriculum is gradually being introduced,

which as surely as the night follows the day will substitute for the conception of spirit-forces Physical Force,
and for the energies of dæmons the one impersonal
Energy which the whole system presupposes. " What,
then," cries the Report, " can avert the appalling spiritual
disaster of this great race going over to naturalism ? . . .
Who can measure the tragedy of such a climax ? . . . There
is only one force that can prevent this disaster, and that
is the power of Jesus Christ ! " Already, as the Report
goes on most truly to point out, " the one gleam of
Christian idealism which has come to China from the
West, through all the rapacity and violence of national
policy, has been the missionary enterprise. Here she has
at least seen something of the faith that can remove
mountains, and the love that never faileth. But has
there yet been that demonstration of the supreme might
and reality of the Eternal which can alone break the
slumber of her past ages ? "

The last question is in very truth a home thrust. China
is not the only country which is face to face with a
teaching that regards Nature as a closed-system ; Substance as the one ultimate reality ; and all forces and
energies, even life itself with its supreme manifestations
of consciousness and goodness, as so many functions
of that one originless, endless, inexplicable reality—
SUBSTANCE, the alpha and omega, the lord god
almighty of the naturalistic creed. This is the avowed
theology, if such a word has any meaning in this context,
of thousands throughout Europe, and the implicit
substratum of the thinking of many ten times more.
Philosopher, dramatist, and novelist have, in fact, done,
and are doing, far more than pure scientists in making
these doctrines public property,—more even than the
self-invited interpreters of science, the atheist lecturer,
preacher, or journalist. In translations and sixpenny

editions these doctrines are crossing every sea, are finding their way into the heart of India, China and Japan. Some of their teachers have, it is true, attempted to raise these doctrines to the level of a religion : but the attempt never seems to go far or to be sustained for long. And yet, as the Report says, " all history shows that without religion no civilisation can live."

Here, then, is the supreme crisis, not of China only, but of the Church. If the Church can surmount this wave to which *apparently* the whole aggregate result of modern scientific research is giving volume, mass, and momentum, would it ever thereafter have anything else to fear from without ?

The question is a home one to the Church, as appears from an illuminating sentence in the Report :

" Here is the very core of the problem of the future in China. It has been truly said by a distinguished modern thinker (Eucken) that the real strength of naturalism lies, *not in the argumentative case for it, but in the weakness of the spiritual life in the heart of mankind.* . . . When faith fails, naturalism is the one alternative theory and practice, and when faith triumphs there is no place left for naturalism."

And the Report sums up the position of affairs in these profound words :

" Is it not then the conclusion of the whole matter, that what this great race needs above all else is that elemental faith, which is surer of eternity than of time, and which draws from these exhaustless fountains so great a vitality of love for men, that morality ceases to be law because it is the very breath of life."

We shall see, before the close of this chapter, that there have been times when a community did actually rise to the height of this possibility. If formerly, why not again ?—Is Edinburgh, 1910, to prove the beginning of the answer to this question ?

Several speakers brought out very strikingly how

Christianity with its message can directly meet the manifested cravings of China. For example, Tong Tsing-en, the Chinese professor from North China, standing before the audience in the rich blue silks of his native land, showed clearly how completely the Christian ethic, *if lived*, fulfils and satisfies the Confucians at every point of personal, domestic, or social life : how the study of the Confucian classics should therefore by no means be discontinued—they are a national literature which Christianity need not displace just because it fulfils it. He also showed—and it was a striking confirmation of a result that the Indian section yielded— that Christianity could also fulfil the Buddhist demand for purity, for sacrifice, for separation, by separating from *sin* while avoiding the fatal Buddhistic distrust of life itself. Another speaker, from South China, showed how the reverence of China for *fatherhood* was fulfilled by the doctrine of the Father " from whom every Fatherhood in heaven and earth is named "—fulfilling, indeed, the vague Chinese belief in the " Venerable Heavenly Father," about whom nevertheless Confucius maintained so close a reserve. And a younger man from Western China pointed out the point of contact furnished by the social idea of the Christian brotherhood, with the Chinese sense of the solidarity of the family, the nation, and the community, and with the Chinese conviction that the individual neither lives nor dies " unto himself." . . .

6.

Both what the Report brought out in its chapter on the Japanese religions and what came out in the debate, made it evident that practically the whole of what has been said in the preceding paragraphs applies with equal force to the nation which at present holds the hegemony of the East. It is true that there are elements in the thought-life of Japan that are giving to the old ideas, and for some considerable time may continue to give, a greater permanence than they are likely to have in China ; for instance, the mystical regard of the Japanese for the person of the Emperor, which so closely knits that small compact country together and thus helps to establish its fundamental animism. But from another point of view, Japan has already reached a more advanced stage in naturalism, advanced enough, in fact, to make her have serious doubts as to its ability to save for her her moral and social life. Count Okuma has described the welter in which Japanese thought finds itself, having abandoned so much of the old, without taking to itself anything new with which to fill the gap. Equally, therefore, to Japan, as to her great neighbour, applies the beautiful sad sentence from the Report,

" *Never surely was richer freight derelict on the great waters of time.*"

And it is Christianity and no other to whom is offered the opportunity of a salvage beyond all parallel. Once and again the Japanese nation has half-turned to the one gleam of idealism that had reached her in Christianity alone, from the West, and asked herself whether she might not in following that gleam guide her uncertain steps. And still to-day Christianity, if anything, holds the field. Mohammedanism has not a chance, mercifully for humanity, although in the Near East voices are heard inviting Japan to assume the hegemony of Islam. But " Christian morality," the Bishop of Ossory said, "is enshrining itself in the hearts of the Japanese people ; and we have it on good evidence that there must be at least one million people among the educated classes of Japan who think in terms of Christian morality as regards the conduct of the affairs of daily life."

K

Two things more than anything else, it was pointed out, keep Japan back : first the difficulty the Japanese mind has in placing the Emperor in any category that makes him *second*—even to the King of Kings. This surely is a sentiment that can hardly escape gradual modification. But the second obstacle is indeed serious : as Galen M. Fisher, a well-known and successful worker among young Japanese, phrased it, it is " the unpractical nature of Christian philosophy . . . and *its inability to dominate the life of our western civilisation.*" So here once more the same supreme challenge to the Churchwas heard !, the same challenge under another form. On the very first evening Dr Coffin of New York had most uncompromisingly pointed to the failure of western Christianity to solve her social question, as well as to Christianise the foreign and colonising policies of the western nations. And another speaker told of the evil impression made by our cities on Japanese observers and the impossibility they found, in consequence, of believing that the religion of the West had within it the power to be the social salvation of the East : the only off-set to this humiliation being the acknowledged supremacy of the Christian home. But is not this fatal weakness only an application of the radical weakness that the consideration of the Chinese problem had already brought to view, the failure of modern Christendom to rise to faith in a God who is able to transform the social system also when man's faith liberates His saving energies, to sustain it as surely as the solar system is sustained by His might ? If this be so, we have here only one more instance of the salutary reaction of the missionary enterprise on the life of the Church at home. The missionary enterprise may *compel* the Church to seek and find GOD, and in so doing solve her own social question also. In a word, " World evangelisation is essential to Christian conquest at home.

The only faith which will conquer Europe and America is the faith heroic enough to subdue the peoples of the non-Christian world." " Only a gospel that is laid down upon *all* the life of man will enable it to deal with *any* of the problems of mankind."

7.

This chapter does not aim at more than to interpret to the reader the central thought that inspired the whole of the Report of this Commission, and the debate thereon. It is utterly impossible to be exhaustive. It is as impossible to say even a little on all the five important divisions of the whole subject. The sections on Islam and Hinduism, for example, are of greater intrinsic interest, because of greater intrinsic religious and philosophical importance, than those which have been dwelt upon in this chapter. For Eastern philosophy and religious thought had its home in India. It was *Hinduism* that supplied the Commission with both the greater part, and the most suggestive part, of its material. It was in *Islam* that Eastern theism has shown its mightiest power, and actually within the Christian era erected under the very eyes of an impotent Christendom a new theology and a new social system, denying (though all unwittingly) the deepest Christian verities, and professing blindness to the highest Christian ideals !

It must therefore be enough to point out in this chapter, how the consideration of these two, at opposite poles though they lie to each other, simply brought out more clearly the fundamental truth that the entire enquiry has elicited. In the case of Hinduism, both Report and discussion showed that the same heightened realisation of a Living God who is Spirit, which was seen to be the grand desideratum for the salvation of China (and Europe) from a physical, naturalistic pantheism, is necessary to save India. For the pantheism of Hinduism, though it is the very reverse of naturalistic, is for all its spirituality paralysing to effort and joy, to social beatitude and the spirit of service, and to all, in short, that stands for life. While, on the other hand, the very refusal of India to see in the closed-system of the physical universe anything more than a delusion, constitutes a hint, a challenge, an inspiration to Christian thought,—not indeed to deny reality to that universe, but to assert that it is only real *because* there is One who is Spirit transcending it, containing it and not contained by it. But where is to be found the organ whereby that Spirit becomes articulate on earth ? the voice which shall tell to India that with God's infinite Spirit she may be united, and so be redeemed from sin within and circumstance without—not to a Nirvana which is the negation of life, but to GOD who *is* Life ; the ONE in whom social love and joy are perfected ; and in whom self-surrender becomes the realisation of all selves ? Who but the Church of Christ can voice that message, which her Head once and for all has sounded ? It is His Church who is called to be to the human race both voice and eyesight and hearing. Thus once more we are brought back to the same point. The very failures of these non-Christian religions reveal to the Christian church what she has in Christ, available and at her disposal, but as yet unrealised.

And Islam,—perhaps Edinburgh, 1910, will lead Christianity to apply even to Islam, the great antagonist, this same principle, and to find it pointing her this same way. For it was its living faith in a personal God that created Islam, and alone accounts for its marvellous record through thirteen centuries. And it is this living

faith, intenser, more intimate and more comprehensive
than sight, that the body of Christ has to recover, in
order that her witness may be with demonstration and
" with the Finger of God," whether in the lands of Islam,
or of Vishnu, or of Confucius, or of Buddha, or those
whose dim faiths are linked with no great leader's name.

8.

Such was the general scope of the Commission's review
of the great world-religions, and their interaction with
the Gospel of Christ.   No one on completing it would
withhold his assent, one imagines, to what is urged in the
Report as to the necessity of continuing this co-operative
study and survey.   It is not merely that the present
Report was admittedly incomplete—for example it only
treated Buddhism incidentally, the very religion with
which the West, through Schopenhauer, has of late shown
so strange a sympathy.   But not what it omitted but
what it accomplished is the best argument for a yet
deeper study.   Here is a method of studying comparative
religions—not purely philosophical, still less purely
scientific, but Christian and theological through and
through, yet richly fruitful also in speculation and
scientific result.   Should it not by all means be followed
up, and the science of Comparative Religion, hitherto
almost exclusively an instrument of religious scepticism
or equally sterile religious universalism, be recognised as
a marvellous instrument for the recovery of the full
content of the faith of Christ !   Thus did the events of
this fourth day of the Conference voice from yet another
quarter the need of some permanent organisation which
should carry on the work of Edinburgh, 1910, and through
this method of co-operative and co-ordinated study gather
a yet richer and fuller harvest for the Christian Church.

9.

Another deep impression made by this Commission was the need for a completer and deeper training of missionary candidates. Not in the least because a greater cleverness is now thought necessary than heretofore, or because philosophic ability is now to be considered a *sine quâ non*,—for as our modern Friar, Brother F. J. Western, reminded the Conference, " *the chief documents are human,*" and the way to their study is the old way of friendship unfeigned ;—but just because the most direct way into the human heart of both Animist and Hindu and Moslem will be the study of what he holds most precious. That study, the Report has proved, leads into deeper recesses of the heart of the perfect Man, Christ Jesus, and so, in turn, the serious effort to discover what is *in Him*, will satisfy the needs discovered *in them*. Thus this Commission led directly on to that on the Preparation of Missionaries also. Nay, it became clear that not missionary candidates alone but all candidates for any Christian ministry must profit, if these premises are correct, by a study which perhaps has the very deepest contributions to make to the knowledge of Christ and of the New Testament, and to the Catholicity of the future. For the question of Catholicity was a human question before it became an ecclesiastical one, and the full realisation of the spiritual catholicity of mankind may well turn out to lead to the full realisation of a One Catholic Church.

But if these things are true, it follows, as we have seen before, that neither candidates for service abroad, nor candidates for service at home only, are concerned with this matter, but the whole Church itself ; and thus this Commission led directly on also to that on the Home Base, with which the Conference closed. It is Christendom, not the clergy, that is concerned with recovering the full content of its idea of God. And because the length, breadth, height and depth, we are told, must be learned in company " with all saints," the way to this recovery would seem to be for the whole Church to manifest an intenser concern in the needs of Jew and Greek, Barbarian and Scythian, Bond and Free, that we without them should not be made perfect.

10.

Thus (the Report points out in its concluding pages) under the very pressure of the enormous crisis of to-day, the Church may have it in its power to learn lessons of literally indescribable importance. The days of the crises of humanity are Days of the Son of Man. And clearly to-day is such a day. The Report casts about to find in the annals of the past the records of another such day, and each of the two parallels it discovers shows that the courageous facing of the crisis brought with it to the Church a fresh realisation of God. . . . First, when the World burst on the outlook of Israel, terrible in the brute strength of those eastern Empires that made so true and just their apocalyptic comparison with The Beast ; smashing into Israel's elementary theories, in which was construed her knowledge of man, the world, and God Himself. And psalm and prophecy remain to show us that the issue was just this—Atheism, or, Deeper into God ! And the Books of Hosea and Isaiah and Habakkuk— these and their peers—remain to show us also how the second alternative was taken. . . . Again the cycle comes full-circuit, and again a Church, defenceless as a new-planted slip, is face to face with the World. Again the issue is, Destruction, or, Deeper into God ! But to the Church, whose eyes had seen One come victorious out of the elemental war, the issue did not appear as

an alternative ! Gospel, Epistle, Apocalypse show that
no other thought save the calm conviction of completest
victory ever crossed her mind.[1] They make it clear
that these Christians living in time lived above time—
eternity literally lapped them round, shot them through
and through. Living in nature, naturally, they lived
also above nature, supernaturally : it was no question
of an isolated miracle here or there,—one of the
great British archæological scholars of to-day has declared that wherever the enquirer digs in any part of
the records of that first-century Church he strikes the
supernatural. Living in the world they, in fact, lived
in GOD. . . .

The question then simply is—(and let it be understood
again that this chapter from first to last is simply " an
account and interpretation " of a Report and a discussion)—*Is the Church not faced to-day with the same
crisis ?* Once more has the World, nay, Nature, the
Universe itself, smashed ruthlessly into the conven-
tionalised theology of Christendom : it needs no seer
standing on the sand of the shore of any Patmos to see
The Beast rising from the world-tide and presenting
once more the immemorial alternative, " Naturism, or,
Deeper into God ! " The spectacle of the East, with
half a worldful of men, suddenly drawn into the full
current of world-thought is one scene in the vision of
the modern Apocalypse. The spectacle of the West
rapidly surrendering to a radically atheist philosophy
of Nature is the other.

The path of boldness and obedience is ever the path
of safety. May not obedience to Christ's command to

---

[1] Perhaps the solitary exception to this was that timorous community to whom the Epistle to the Hebrews was written—just the
very community whose hold on Christ, and so on the living God, had
never been complete ! Truly the exception proves the rule.

carry the Gospel to all the world once more spell safety for the Church, and give her victory over both these perils at once ?   May it not, in substituting for her conventional ideas a theology that shall once more pervade all life, bring in the East and bring back the West to the fold of the bosom of GOD ?

Thus these reflections, which have in them so much of agonising anxiety, conclude with the word of Hope.   The beautiful close of the Report, in which its whole material seems to have been compressed till it glows, yields a vision shining with the light of a solemn hope : " *Once again the Church is facing its duty, and therefore once more the ancient guiding fires begin to burn and shine.*"

CHAPTER XI

SUNDAY—" the Lord's Day "—marked fittingly the sublimity of the themes considered by the Conference on the preceding day.

On this day the ordinary sessions of the Conference were suspended ; and the delegates rested the strenuous rest of an Edinburgh Sabbath.

Only towards evening, the eve of the day on which the Report on " Missions and Governments " was to be discussed, there was held a meeting which, whether by chance or design, formed a true prelude for the Monday. What was said at that meeting by the Archbishop of York and the Hon. Seth Low may therefore be woven into the account of Monday's proceedings.

I.

On Monday morning—the day on which man returns to work-a-day subjects—it was very fitting that the one Report which took into its purview a work-a-day aspect of missions should come up for discussion. In all the other Commissions, as one speaker pointed out, the Conference kept, so to speak, within the sphere of the Christian Church ; but in the Report now to be considered it was dealing with an external power, the power of the State all over the world. It was one more of the novel features of this Edinburgh Conference, that this unusual subject had received treatment, and a treatment as full and careful as those reported on by the other Commissions.

The same delegate—a member of the Commission— who pointed out the novelty of the subject also emphasised its peculiar difficulty. There was first the enormous variety and incommensurateness of the governments of this world ; and there was, secondly, the fact that the relation of Church and State is a subject which never has commanded a consensus of thinking men, which does not command it to-day, and which perhaps never will fully command it, until the two become one in the consummated Kingdom of Heaven.

Still, the Commission had a clear and compassable task in collecting and collating the actual facts of the case, and studying all the widely different conditions as they affect the missionary enterprise. It was thus able to produce a report that was valuable if only because it made the facts and the conditions available. But it had gone further than this : it had seen its way to make some careful inductions from these data, and thus had taken the first steps towards formulating principles which, if that beginning is followed up, may one day command the assent of both missions and governments, and serve to guide their actions and interactions in the future.

It has already, surely, become clearer that the Christian missionary enterprise merits, and that it receives, the consideration of the greatest of our public men as one of the most significant facts of the present time. Yet how many men—in The Street or out of it—find it hard to shake themselves free from the nineteenth-century feeling about " Foreign Missions " which, for example, Thackeray's novels so faithfully reflect. But would not Thackeray himself (or who- ever's thoughts he expressed) have felt compelled to reconsider the matter had he merely seen the names of the men who formed this Commission on " Missions and Governments," and considered the sweep and scope of the operations which had justified the forming of such a Commission.   Lord Balfour of Burleigh, Sir Robert Hart, Sir Andrew Wingate, the Hon. Seth Low and Admiral Mahan, the Hon. H. L. Borden, Professor Carl Mirbt and Herr Dr Berner, to mention only eight, were names that speak for themselves.   They represented highest mental attainment and highest public position.   They were the guarantee that the subject for which they consented to give their labours was one of the highest dignity and the gravest importance.

The subjects discussed in the Report were indeed of manifest importance.   Not only did it take into consideration the many State questions which the work of missions brings up, but it did not shrink from touching boldly on the whole subject of the relation of ruling races to the ruled, and the relation of the missionary enterprise to both.

Such were the questions that came up in the debate also, and were discussed with an ability and power not exceeded on any day of the Conference.   The debate in fact gave a true idea and a fairly complete transcript of the whole Report, and was besides a vivid commentary upon it.   And for this reason, and because the Report has summarised rather than quoted the communications of the correspondents all over the world, an account of the *discussion*, simply, will be the best exposition of the subject and the Report itself.

2.

Few have not at some time or other heard someone confessing the time-honoured dogma that missions and their agents are the most troublesome of all the things that daily vex the statesman. . . . It was well, therefore, to hear the Hon. Seth Low express at the outset the conviction of his Commission that " a large amount of mutual helpfulness " existed between many missions and the governments within whose territories they are, and that " as the unselfish aims and beneficent result of missions are being more widely appreciated, the good understanding between missions and governments is increasing." That, he said, was " distinctly the impression that the Commission had gained from the total correspondence that they had had." And he went on to say that friends of missions might conscientiously feel justified in asking Christian governments to use their good offices with those of other nations for the free admission and exercise of missionary endeavour, and this not on the ground of religion, but on account of the now proved beneficence of this work, and the common right of humanity not to be denied its advantages !

And this remarkable verdict was immediately endorsed by an ex-Governor of Bombay—Lord Reay— who showed, out of his own experience, that missions were " auxiliaries " of government, and that the services they rendered to it were " invaluable."

3.

The question of Governments and facilities for Missionary Work showed at once the bewildering variety of considerations with which the Commission had to deal. For here were Christian governments which might be favourable, or not unfavourable, or opposed, to missionary work ; governments non-Christian and tolerant of that work ; governments non-Christian and

not tolerant ;—in all the various degrees and shadings
of these qualifications. Perhaps the most *remarkable*
phenomenon was that presented by the government
of Japan, which yesterday was the most intolerant
Government of all, but to-day perhaps leads the way
in the completeness of the religious toleration and
freedom of conscience which it has established.

One of the very first speeches was a moving one by
a French delegate, which made the hearer wonder
why the French government seems so incapable of
being convinced by such testimonies as that of Lord
Reay's, or impressed by such an attitude as that taken
by Japan. He showed clearly that the policy of the
French government in her colonies, though it works
out in a pro-Roman way, is not pro-Roman as such.
It is part of a still-lingering suspicion that non-Roman
missions will bring in anti-French influence. The
deplorable policy that has been introduced into
Madagascar, and the cruel hardships it has inflicted on
the Christian cause there, are instances in point. But
the Report traced this deplorable attitude to a deeper
source ; the French government itself maintains that
that policy is merely the legitimate application of its
secular policy at home. The result is, as that delegate
showed, that French colonies are among the least
evangelised of all the regions of the earth. Nevertheless
he counselled the missions already in occupation not to
be discouraged, but to stay. " Be kind and gentle
to the French officials ; adapt yourselves to the
necessities and you will outlive all the difficulties."
And, in view of the fewness of the French non-Roman
Christians, he besought this World Conference to take
the great French colonies into its purview, not as
French colonies, but simply as unevangelised lands.

How totally different is the attitude of the German

Colonial Office may be judged from the letter it sent
to the Conference [1]; and reports from the missionaries
in German East Africa, South-West Africa, Congo,
Togoland, etc., showed that words are made good by
real helpfulness in action.   And the same thing appeared
in the reports of the Dutch missionaries who have so
wisely confined their attention to the ample spheres
of their vast East Indian empire.   Nowhere did the
relation between a Mission and a Government seem to
be happier than in the Dutch East Indies.   There, too,
a novel experiment had been tried with striking success—
the creation of a Missionary Consul with his office at
Batavia, an official intermediary (without any authority
save that created by his own usefulness) between the
missions in the field and the government, in all questions
where the two spheres overlap.   There can be little
doubt that this experiment will be widely followed.
The only parallel to it was the similar consulship held
by Herr Dr Berner between German Mission-boards
at home and the government of Germany.

The complexity of the whole question was well shown
by the various attitudes that may be taken up by the
same government in different parts of the world.   In
British India the British government stands on the
same level as the Japanese in point of tolerance.   Nay,
it has even solved, in a manner, the problem how it
may be a Christian government and its acts be considered
as such,[2] and yet remain neutral religiously ;   how it
may be favourable to missions and yet, governmentally,
indifferent.   Yet the Native States, which are within

---

[1] See Appendix to Chapter IV.

[2] It was Lord Curzon, no great friend of the enterprise of evangelisation, who, as Viceroy, said that the government of India is Christian,
and that he wished its acts to be considered the acts of a Christian
government.

the British Empire, present an attitude towards missions that is stiffer than that of the Chinese government itself. Once more, in Mohammedan countries the British government seems to take up an attitude quite different; and sometimes it even appears as if the difference was not merely one of expediency, but of principle. In Egypt, it might be argued, the British government must decline, so to speak, to recognise itself. It " occupies," does not govern, the country. (One delegate showed, nevertheless, that some of the ways in which this position worked out were open to strong criticism.)—At any rate the Sudan is more than a mere occupation! But here, in turn, expediency is strongly urged. Yet what shall be said to the announcement of a missionary from the Sudan, of the turning of Gordon College into a Moslem College pure and simple, with Koran teaching, Friday prayers, and college mosque to match? Or that it should be possible for a high official in the Sudan, to say, recently, according to the same delegate (a missionary in whom the Sudan government itself has perfect confidence), " You might as well give it up because we (' we!') make ten Mohammedans to your one Christian!" [1] These announcements were greeted by the Conference with loud shouts of " Shame!"—But the Sudan is partly Egyptian, and also in other respects a difficult exception? The Conference's attention was therefore directed, and not for the first time, to Northern Nigeria, where a good example was given of how any policy but that which obtains in British India is apt to become *in practice* flatly anti-missionary and pro-Mohammedan.

[1] His precise meaning was not explained to Conference. Presumably he alluded to the *de facto* result of general government policy among the pagan tribes or the influence of the army upon the Sudanese recruits?

The testimony from Northern Nigeria spoke for itself :

" There is a real open partisanship of Islam. Practically no attempt has been made in educational work, and that of missionary societies is looked at coolly or even thwarted. Bolstering up of Moslem duties, reviving of customs which have been allowed to lapse, gradual levelling up of pagan districts, so as to accustom them to Islamic law, all show the trend, and make it obvious to Christian and Pagan that the British Government has no use for either of them, but only for the Moslem."

The Conference was further told that it is a recognised saying among the Pagans and the Christians in that part of Africa that the government is really favouring Mohammedanism, and the best thing to do is to become Moslems, otherwise they will get no road-making and no work. The officials openly went on the assumption that " Islam is the religion for that part of Africa." (Yet on their own confession they " get no trouble except from the Moslems.") The Conference unmistakably felt that fairplay and not private opinions ought to govern official attitude to Christian missions. And again cries of " Shame ! " were heard when another well-known delegate, speaking with a serious sense of responsibility as the Chairman of the largest Missionary Society in the world, showed how intolerably the policy works out by which missionaries are debarred from entering a province until the Moslem Emir had given his consent ! . . . It was evident that here was a situation which revealed the need for a strong international board of missions that should have the task of thoroughly sifting every case, and then of making representations to the government concerned. The sense of this need had been increasingly felt and expressed from the very first day of the Conference.

L

The complexity of the whole subject was further illustrated by another curious comparison :—the British Government is sometimes seen *applying* to another government for facilities on behalf of missions—as in the case of China ; sometimes *being applied to* by its own subjects (and not always with satisfactory results as has been seen) ; and sometimes being applied to by *other* than its own subjects. In this latter relation, the Conference was amused by a speech, full of sterling sense and sly humour, from a Swiss delegate—the subject of a nation " fortunate enough to have no colonies." He showed how the Swiss missions in South Africa get their way with British and Portuguese governments by the simple device of conforming to British and Portuguese regulations on every possible occasion, and addressing officials in the British and Portuguese languages respectively,—which they take the trouble to learn, and to teach to their African schoolmasters ! And he charmed the Conference with a word of warning to his Anglo-Saxon friends . . . nobody else (he said) would give it, " so the little Swiss man must say it. Do not expect everybody to speak your language ! Do not expect every colonial governor to be friendly to you when you address him in English. With us Swiss people you may do it and we shall try to answer in English if we can. But with other nations, especially in the colonies, it will not do ! "

It was very pretty banter : — the " dear and powerful Anglo-Saxon friends " felt the tingle of its mild yet just perceptible sting, and enjoyed the delicate sensation.

4.

There were many valuable things said in regard to missions and non-Christian governments. There are still a few countries where facilities for missionary work are utterly denied, and where it is inadvisable to demand them, such as Nepal, Bhutan, Afghanistan. In China the problem has been practically solved. And there was the protest of one delegate against the assertion of the Report that the attitude of the Chinese Government was one of "hostility to Christianity." He said that he had personal knowledge that the Chinese government is far from hostile to Christianity, and that any instance of opposition should be rather described as "*apparent* hostility." The situation in Turkey revealed more serious features. Here there is nominal religious freedom. But practically the individual is totally and absolutely deprived of freedom in one cardinal matter, the freedom to change his religion. And the missionaries in Arabic-speaking Turkey had sent an important appeal to the Conference, in which they declared that since educational missions had confessedly conferred upon the Ottoman Empire very great benefits, and had helped to make possible the era of freedom, the time had come to urge on the Ottoman government the duty of bringing Turkey into line with the free nations in respect of liberty of conscience ; that, further, a necessary element in such liberty is freedom to every man to profess the religion his conscience approves ; and that it is indispensable, in order that this principle may be actual and effectual, that it be proclaimed throughout the empire. As it had been decided by the Business Committee that no special motions should be submitted to the Conference, there was no opportunity to put the one submitted by the Ottoman missions. . . . The need of a permanent Board for considering and taking action in such matters became more manifest than ever.

The difficulty, nay, the impossibility, of laying down

principles that would apply universally was well shown
by a question that is sometimes one of burning interest
in mission lands : the claiming or accepting of indemnities
for violence and injury. In China, for example, experience has conclusively shown that this compensation
for loss of life should be absolutely tabooed. The
Secretary of the China Inland Mission, that mission
glorious with the crown of many a red martyrdom,
impressively stated, amid the murmured assent of the
Conference, the unalterable principle, *No Compensation
for Martyrs*. In most cases, it seemed, compensation
for even loss of property should be refused. In India,
on the other hand, it is quite possible that the only
way of supporting loyally the responsible government
would be by the acceptance of such indemnities. The
Vice-Chairman of the Commission quoted with approval
from the wisdom of Captain Bunsby ; the bearing
of every general observation emphatically lay, he said,
in its *application*. Similarly, in the matter of appeals to
Consuls in countries where extra-territorial rights are
recognised : in China, he observed, it is nearly always
advisable absolutely to forego that right ; in Turkey it
seems to be considered by the authorities themselves
as due to their dignity that such appeals *should* come
through the Consul !

And here the Conference listened to a wonderfully
illuminating address from the Chinese delegate, Dr
C. T. Wang. Into the seven minutes of his admirably
phrased speech he packed a whole vade-mecum for the
foreigner in China. It was a revelation of the Chinese
point of view. As one who was both a Chinaman and
a Christian he made, with striking effect, a sturdy
declaration like this :—

" Let it be understood from the very first . . . that China has her
religions, and a *Government* to which loyalty, respect, and justice

should be given by all Chinese, Christians or non-Christians, as well as by the European, American and Japanese powers."

(it was the first time one had ever heard this trio of names bracketed together. Significant!). Speaking as a Chinaman, he was impressive in his demonstration of the lamentable blunders which foreign intervention is apt to create—the confusion worse confounded, the hopeless defeat of the very aim itself. He, moreover, corrected in the most business-like style four statements of the Report, relating to alleged discrimination on the part of the Chinese Government against the Christians. In one case he maintained the perfect right of his Government to do as it had done. But it was most of all impressive to hear him, speaking as a *Christian*, warn missionaries never, " even in the most extreme cases," to " extend their protection to the Chinese Christians," and to make this principle clearly known " to the would-be converts from the very beginning before they are received into the Church." A loyal subject, he considered, is one who, "independent of the help of a particular religion, abides within the laws of his or her country." There spoke the first-century Christian ! In this sturdy nationalist and good Christian, with the crisp, terse speech and quite frank non-respect of persons, one saw the Church which is to be a *Chinese* Church, and which in being so is to win its country for Christ.

5.

If a Chinaman gave the Conference a vade-mecum on the general question of etiquette for foreigners in China, a Dane succeeded in packing a whole philosophy, without apparent effort, into his seven-minutes speech on *the art of making representations to officials*. When the " viking-like " Norwegian, Lars Dahle, sat down

it was amid an unusual burst of applause ; and in the
afternoon Lord Balfour, in summing up the discussion,
paid him the exceptional compliment of singling out his
address; and this in a Conference where time was hardly
ever spared for praising any speaker or any speech.
Probably every delegate had in his mind already used
almost the same expression with which Lord Balfour
characterised this address : " It seems to me, in summing
up the lessons of this Report, the words of my Norwegian
friend stand out as *the quintessence of good sense and
guidance*." The reader of this account has perhaps
more than once felt curious as to what these seven-
minute orations were really like—especially when they
were good of their kind. It would perhaps be well
to gratify his curiosity just once, and how better
than by means of an address that really exhausted
the subject of which it treated—in seven minutes !
Indeed the writer is under the impression that the full
allowance was in this case not taken. Here is this
address, then, in full : — " I shall just try," he
said,

" to make a few remarks on the question how to create and how
to conserve good relations between Missions and Governments,
and in order to be short I shall try to put what I have to say in
the form of definite rules. My first rule would be, my first advice
to missionaries would be, do not occupy yourselves too much
with trifles. It occurs very often in the course of missionary life
out in the mission field that Government officials may do something you have good reason to complain of, but if it is only small
things do not trouble about it, because if you complain every
time you have reason for complaining they would think you were
bothering them too much, and you would lose the goodwill of
the Government, and you want that for the big questions. My
next rule is, do not be too hasty in your actions. You should
bide your time : you and the time together, you know, would be
a match for anything, and would work against and prove too

much for your adversaries. There may, of course, be instances where prompt action is quite necessary, but in many cases I have found as a missionary out in Madagascar, that if you can let the Governor find out by himself that he has done wrong, he will be very thankful to you for giving him the opportunity of correcting it himself. Then if it comes to action, do try by all means to settle all difficulties with the subordinate Government representative in the district where you are, without bringing it up to higher authorities. The further you bring it, the more difficult and complicated it will be and the more ill-will you create in the mind of the Governor in the district where you are. It will be considered as a personal accusation against the official and he will find means to repay it to you if you carry your point in the first question. Then I would say, if you are to bring a matter to the higher officials, that should not be done by a single missionary but by a leader of the Mission. I have seen difficulties arising from that. The single missionary comes up to the Central Government and brings his complaint before them, and the Government after hearing the different complaints, says, " There is no unity in that mission." You should always leave this matter to the mission leader, or you will probably make a mess of it. I would say next if the leader of a Mission has to bring the matter before the central Government he should look carefully for the right season to do it. In Madagascar at least it is the case that the Government could not do two things at a time. If they are occupied in some other work you should never bring your matter before them. Again, if you bring it before them, you should always be careful to act on the supposition of goodwill on their part, that you have only to explain what you think ought to be done to have it done. Maybe you have some misgivings about its being done, but do not let them appear. It is a very polite way of telling a man what he ought to do when you really act on the supposition that he is the very man who would do it. By all means do not be too ready to go to the Consul in affairs concerning the Government. That should be a last resort. It may be necessary sometimes, but very seldom if you act wisely : and if a missionary has come to this, that it can only be done by the influence of the Consul, he is done for. He had better pack up his luggage and go home. I would mention what the Prime Minister of Madagascar once said to me. He said, ' You Norwegians have got no Consul here, but if you act up to the principles of the Bible we shall have no trouble with you.' We wish to act up to the principles of the Bible ; then let the Bible be our Consul."

6.

But graver was the tone and deeper the passion with which a greater question still was discussed :—the whole question of the relation of ruling nations to subject races. Three great national wrongs were the storm-centres of almost the only real anger manifested at this World Missionary Conference. The Hon. Seth Low had already mentioned the three together, on the Sunday evening. Public opinion, he said, had agreed to condemn the first, the *opium-traffic*. With regard to the second and third—the *liquor-traffic* and *enforced labour*—" public opinion has not moved so far yet." The Conference next day was to contemplate the marvel of a public opinion that could condemn the one and yet suspend its judgment or its action in regard to the others !

Precisely the same three wrongs were touched on by the Archbishop of York on that same Sunday afternoon in his noble and masterly exposition of the place and duty of missions towards governments, in regard to the treatment of non-Christian races. He showed how national policy is often the only expression of the public opinion of the nation, and depends directly on the ideals and activities of the citizens. The instinct, he said, which brings nations into contact with these Asian and African peoples is the trading impulse, which is necessarily based on the motive of *self-interest*. Further, since that motive, when left to itself, must almost inevitably make the all too easy transition to *selfishness*, it is absolutely necessary that a Government, at one of whose ears trade-interest has a perpetual place, should always have at its other ear a counteracting influence that acknowledges a higher law, and insists on moral ideals as well as on material advantages. Only so has the fundamental principle, to " rule for the benefit of the ruled," a fair chance of being kept alive. Memorably, too, did Dr Seth Low demonstrate the terribly urgent necessity for supplementing Man's instinct of gain by Superman's [1] principle of Benevolence. Speaking of the grave economic dislocations which China's legitimate development of her vast resources may bring about all over the world, he said :

" If those questions are going to be met in the light of natural law, so that it is to be a question of the Struggle for Existence and the Survival of the Fittest, I don't wonder that men speak of the Yellow Peril ; but if we can place side by side with that Struggle for Existence, in an effective and working force, what Henry Drummond called the Struggle for the Existence of the Other Man [2] . . . then we may escape what otherwise would be assuredly a Battle of Armageddon, and see a future ushered in wherein the Yellow Peril shall be converted into a Golden Opportunity for the cause of the truth, and the everlasting brotherhood of man."

So once again in that hall did Alberich's Gold gleam out : symbol of the great human drama of the love of Gain and the gain of Love.

7.

The Opium Wrong. — It is unnecessary to repeat or even summarise the Archbishop's account of the

---

[1] Christ's—not a certain German philosopher's.

[2] The omitted sentences indicated that, as by the Archbishop of York, so by this speaker also, *Christian Missions* were considered to be the way, perhaps the only way, by which this demonstration can be made.

" sinister and sordid story of the opium trade in China." It is well known, and the Conference was given reason to hope that the stain is soon to be removed. Bishop Brent of the Philippines, who had some share in drawing international attention to the subject, strongly maintained the absolute sincerity of all the governments —Chinese, British, and Dutch—who had manifested a desire to see the traffic checked and stopped, at loss, in every case, to themselves. He further attributed the origin of what has become a world-wide movement to the Presbyterian and Methodist Missions in the Philippines—he could say this, therefore, as an Anglican Bishop, without conceit—" I only wish I *were* Bishop of both," he added amid sympathetic laughter. This Bishop was actually on his way to preside at a Hague International Conference for considering the means towards an end about which, he said, " there is no difference of opinion — the final relegation of opium to solely medical use." Surely that end was now in sight.

The Liquor Wrong.—" The time has come," said the Hon. William Jennings Bryan on this same day, " when the Christian people in the Christian nations should ask their governments to throw their influence upon the side of temperance." He was speaking of the liquor trade at home ; but " temperance " in regard to the *African* liquor trade can only mean one thing— strict prevention. The story which Dr Charles F. Harford had to tell about the liquor question in Southern Nigeria, a British colony, drew forth a burst of wrathful amazement. Chosen by three National Committees as intermediary between Missions and governments in regard to the liquor trade among African races, he spoke with full knowledge, with the knowledge too that the law of libel (which is not sparingly used in these cases)

would be always ready to avenge inaccuracies of statement. He told of a Report of a Government Committee
of Inquiry, which reported an import of 4,000,000 gallons
of spirit into one colony *without finding any accompani-
ment of race-deterioration* ; of the methods by which
this strange finding was reached,—the *onus probandi*
cast on the missions, the Government of Southern
Nigeria setting itself to defend the trade ; of the
prejudicing of the case before ever the Committee
started its inquiry,—a Chief's subsidy suspended by
an Acting-President because he had advised his people
not to buy gin, and restored when that Chief had sent
a bellman round the town to advise his people to buy
that gin again ; a Bishop of the Diocese officially given
the lie in Parliament and flouted publicly by the Government of Southern Nigeria because he had stated that
fines imposed by government were paid in gin and
received by that government in gin in certain Southern
Nigerian Courts ; and then after that Bishop had
borne the disgraceful stigma of disseminating false
statements for a whole year, the admission by an official
of the Colonial Office that " there is no doubt that gin has
been accepted, as I say, in payment of fines and fees
in the native courts of Brass "—six in number ; further,
the discovery that a government clerk was actually
undergoing a sentence of five years' imprisonment
in Old Calabar prison for embezzling court fines *paid
in gin* ;—not one word of apology being given, then or
since then, to the despised " missionary " : and finally,
the evidence given, nevertheless, before this same Committee of Inquiry, proving that there *is* degrading
drunkenness in British South Nigeria ; that young men,
young women, and even little children are given spirits ;
that thousands of children are pawned to pay the debts
incurred by the gin-drinking of their parents, which

spells slavery for those children, and this in a British colony under the British flag. . . .

Damning statement of a damnable business. The calmer and more judicial tone of the Archbishop of York was only a grave endorsement of the graveness of the charge.

" [In that Report of the Commission] you can see (I make no comments on a difficult matter) the bias of governments to protect the interests of trade, and the bias of the missionary to protect the independent rights of self-development on the part of the natives. We can only too easily trust the bias of the government to prevail. It is for Christian citizenship to see that the bias of the missionary obtains at least fair play."

8.

The Enforced Labour Wrong.—But with even more blistering force came the inevitable reminder of the Congo horror—that supreme example, as the Archbishop justly said, of the tragedy of selfish interest and money advantage,—the nibelungish Yellow Peril,— *minus* the restraint and the activity of Christian citizenship. The Conference was reminded of the conditions under which that Congo continent—for so it is—was handed over to a European nation ; of the solemn responsibility thus incurred by the signatories of the Berlin Treaty to see those conditions kept ; and of the sickening issue of red shame. It must go down here, at least in brief—the book is unfortunately incomplete without it :—

" A stroke of the pen swept away all communal or tribal rights, which from time immemorial had been enjoyed by the people in forests and uncultivated land. Then came the demand for offensive taxes to be paid in rubber, etc., brought in from the forests which were once their own ; forced labour ; compulsory purchases at Government stores to be paid for in rubber, the amount being arbitrarily fixed by the agent of the Government, whose emoluments depended mainly on the amount of rubber he could get collected. The burden became intolerable, and then came the worst. For failure to bring in the required amount, punishment was inflicted by letting loose on the offending villages bands of savages, sometimes cannibals, armed with rifles. Mutilation, murder, rape, and unutterable outrages were inflicted on the people, often within the knowledge of European officials." (Quoted by the Archbishop of York.)

And again—from another delegate :

" No public assembly could listen without shuddering, sickening horror, to a page from this record [the diary of a Congo missionary]; but its most terrible revelations are paralleled by the implications of the Reports of the King's Commission."

.　　.　　.　　.　　.　　.

"*Arise, O Lord, O God, lift up thy hand ;*
That man which is of the earth may be terrible no
no more ! "

.　　.　　.　　.　　.　　.

But what was the practical issue before the Conference, as a deliberative assembly with moral influence, capable (if it left behind it any permanently representative body) of bringing weighty pressure to bear ? . . . For neither could that Conference—any more than all the new King of the Belgian's horses and all his men— " make reparation to the natives whose lives have been either lost or darkened."

The Churches and the Missionary Societies could at least be alert so that there might be no future parallel to this example of the ineffable Superman's work, which

" with the brightest of hell's aureoles
Doth shine supreme, incomparably crowned."

As the Archbishop pointed out, the rubber boom and other like phenomena should serve to keep Christian citizenship wide awake. Those struggling for the Existence of the Other Man must be on the look-out, for the Congo is only a type, though a supreme one. That place at the Other Ear of governments must be kept.

But, in particular, the Conference was entitled to ask if the situation in the Congo had yet been relieved ? The transfer to the Belgian Government, of course, must be judged on its merits, the responsibility of the signatories remaining wholly unaffected by that or any other internal re-arrangement effected by the trustee.

There were four speeches given on this point, and they were the closing speeches in the whole discussion. The first was by an *American* delegate, Dr Thomas S. Barbour, a member of the Commission ; the second, by a *Dutch* delegate, Professor H. Van Nes ; the third, by a *British* delegate, Rev. C. E. Wilson of the Baptist Missionary Society ; the last, by a *Belgian*, M. le Pasteur R. Mayhoffer of the Église Chrétienne Missionnaire.

The first-named advanced considerations, calculated to arouse gravest doubts as to whether any radical improvement had taken place (the new King's personal desire for reform being cordially allowed) : doubts connected with the intrinsic nature of the reforms themselves—reforms which the Primate of all England had ventured to characterise as "manifestly inadequate . . . and even at the best . . . tardy in their operation " ; doubts connected with the "almost unaltered personnel " of the new administration ; doubts connected, finally, with the unaltered system of land-tenure, which Sir Edward Grey said years ago was the mischief at the bottom of everything, and which an American Secretary of State, in a letter to the Belgian Minister, called "the deprivation of the natives of their rights to the soil," adding that the U.S. Government confidently expected to see it changed without delay.

Thus the speaker concluded that the changes that had been made were a " meagre product" of the exposure effected by the King's Commission ; and that they " played about the edges of a true reform."

The second speaker, who claimed to represent all the Dutch delegates, " in striking a somewhat discordant note," was of the opinion that the matter was entirely one of international politics, and that the Commission, and the Conference, in meddling with it were violating their own principle to have nothing to do with political questions. He pointed out that the Report was drafted before the death of King Leopold ; without, however, saying anything in reply to what the last speaker said about the actual situation at the present moment.

The third speaker, representing missions actually at work in the Congo, defended the action of the British mission societies. He endorsed the contention of the first speaker that the reforms so far are chiefly " good words." " We are still waiting for real and genuine reform : but we are *not going to give up* our divinely-appointed task to work for the emancipation and uplifting of the down-trodden and oppressed people of the Congo."

Very loud applause burst in on the speaker at this point.

The fourth speaker thought it would be " unjust to deny that great changes have already taken place " : that the change of monarch ; the translation of the responsibility and the authority from the Crown to Parliament ; the new enactments ; and the presence of reformers in the Parliament-House itself, justified the declaration that things are going on, if slowly,—" too slowly especially in what concerns forced labour," he added.

Thus inconclusively ended the debate of the World Missionary Conference on the red horror of the Congo.

9.

Neither on this nor on any other particular question was it possible for the Conference to give a formal vote or pass a resolution. And this inability, or disability, so keenly felt at that moment, was what gave the most pungent point to some of the sentences with which Lord Balfour, the Chairman of the Commission, now closed the debate. Speaking amid the growing excitement of a Conference every delegate of which saw that the speaker was coming to what he of all things desired to hear,— a Conference which was already highly strung when the speech began,—he pointed out that it would not have been of much use even if they had thrashed out the serious allegations made during the day, and then, after the debate, had passed this or that resolution. " These Conferences come " he continued, " and Conferences go, but the Governments remain. And if you are going to get the best out of the energy and the time that has been spent in organising this Conference, you will, I hope, leave behind you, as is suggested in the Report, some permanent body which will speak for you, which will hear what you have to say to it, will sift it in a sympathetic and straightforward manner, and having itself attained to the truth, if the truth is against the action of the Government, will, with one voice, leave the Government which is concerned no peace till it gets reform."

It came then—the rain of the clapping of hands, the storm of " Hears " prolonged into cheering ! There was no mistaking the meaning character of the sound. Every day since the beginning of the Conference—certainly every day except one—some such allusion or suggestion had at once been caught up by the same significant applause, but on this day the sound of it had a new, a fiercer note. It was as though a whole society of world-servants were realising its collective dumbness, its corporate impotence ; were rebelling against such stockishness, and with urgent gesticulations and strepitous clamour were demanding to be given an articulate voice : a voice with which to make known its just desires and its just complaints, and with which, if it please God, to perform more faithfully and more effectually its office of tribune to a world of men.

Was there not something else there too ? Was it not as if the unborn babe of Unity Regained had strongly stirred in the womb ? Here was a thrill of common purpose, of common will to live, of common will to do. Such stirrings surely, and only such, are worthy to be taken as premonitions of the corporate unity of the days to come, the only corporate unity that would be worth having,—the unity that is the expression of the desire of co-operation, the unity that is the Will to Live, and the Will to Act, *Together*.

CHAPTER XII

" CO-OPERATION AND THE PROMOTION OF UNITY "

AND now came the day on which all these desires and demands for some definite method and permanent organ of co-operation must be consummated. For this was the day on which the Report of the Commission on Co-operation and the Promotion of Unity was to be discussed, and on this most fitting day was to be proposed to the whole Conference a resolution which should give effect to those desires and demands. It was the 21st June, Midsummer's-day, the longest day in the year. The auspices were favourable! The sun in its course fought for Israel, uttering without speech or language a tale of achievement and fulfilment, telling of summer's genial maximum of warmth and light, the atmosphere in which everything must needs expand, and in which nothing looks forbidding or impossible.

I.

The resolution which that day saw moved, seconded, spoken to, and carried without a dissentient, was, on the face of it, merely a practical, business-like measure for promoting certain forms of co-operation between Boards and Societies working in the mission-fields of the world. It had been in the hands of the delegates for some days, and they therefore came to this day's session prepared and expectant, realising how well the

proposal tended to meet the need which had every day
been emphasised time and again. On the first day, the
work of collecting information relative to the world-wide
enterprise had been declared to be incomplete, and the
means for its definite continuance demanded. Further,
the stupendous task of world-evangelisation had been
categorically declared impossible without a far greater
measure of co-operation ; and an equally categorical demand had been made that Conference should not disperse
without taking some definite step to meet the need.
Then, on the second day, the question of co-operation in
the Church on the Mission-Field had clearly shown the
need for a practical measure of a similar kind at home.
On the third day, the Bishop of Birmingham had very
strongly appealed for some machinery for facilitating the
co-ordination of educational support abroad. On the
fourth day, Professor Cairns had urged that measures
should be taken whereby the work begun on the evangelical science of comparative religions should be continued. And yesterday the President of the Conference
had said what he had said. These issues were important enough, and were sufficiently deep to stir the
spirit of the Conference—how deeply, the significant, continued applause that punctuated each of these demands
had shown. And yet, even these things would have been
insufficient to account for the peculiar emotional intensity of the proceedings that day, the undefined sense
experienced by all that a gravely significant thing was
being enacted. There was something else behind the
immediately obvious. What this something was it is the
task of this chapter to suggest, if indeed it is possible
to suggest that which on the day itself hardly emerged
into the region of the definite.

This chapter, therefore, will best follow the lines of the
last one, and, for the same reasons, confine itself to giving

an account of the debate. For to-day, as yesterday, the discussion was the summary and the commentary of the Report. It showed the Conference at its best. And then, it was for the first time in the formal sense a debate, that is to say, the discussion of a definite motion which was to be put from the Chair and voted upon. For all these reasons it behoves to concentrate attention on the events of the day : to understand these is to master the gist of the Report.

2.

The resolution was not proposed, however, till half-way through the morning session, after the " solemn act of worship," which the Chairman with manifest sincerity had called the " most important part of the day's proceedings." Before that, a certain aspect or section of the Report itself was discussed, and the Conference listened to a number of speeches on co-operation in the mission-field itself as actually practised to-day. The object of this was manifest : it was to show how invaluable a thing co-operation is, and also how much more might be done if more definite measures were taken at the home-base towards that end. It was indeed a reminder of one of the findings of the Report,—that the progress of co-operation in the field often discovers its chief obstacle in the absence of co-operation at home. It was a reminder, too, of the belief of Bishop Wescott that, in the matter of co-operation and union, those on the circumference might often be ahead of those at the centre. The truth of this last, indeed, received a striking parenthetic endorsement by an Australian delegate, the Bishop of Gippsland, who made the surprising announcement of the serious, practical contemplation of organic union between the Anglican and Presbyterian communions of Australia, without any violation of principle on either side.

The mission-field which has gone furthest in the matter of co-operation, and has reached the most fruitful results, seemed to be China, and it was from that field that the most striking instances of co-operation were reported to them. And within the China field, the West-China province appeared to have gone furthest in this direction, —being a new field, it was one on which experiments could be tried. The Conference had already, in the discussion on the Church in the Mission Field, heard a ringing word from China, " *Hang on to co-operation like grim death!* " ; and it now listened to a succinct account of what had already been accomplished through steady adherence to that maxim in Western China. There, it was reported, was an advisory board, representative of nine organisations working in three provinces among eighty millions of people. Secondly, there was strict comity—a distinct delimitation of the territory occupied by each organisation. Thirdly, under the head of education, there was a common course of study, common examinations, and examiners and certificates, and a common Inspector of Schools for the whole union. Fourthly, there was a union university formed by the federation of four missions, comprising normal, arts, theological and medical colleges. Fifthly, there was co-operation under the head of medical missions. Sixthly, a mission press, financed by one organisation, but working for all. Seventhly, a Christian magazine for all. Eighthly, a hymn-book for all. Ninthly, constant exchange of ideas by correspondence ; and lastly, a standing committee for church union, the aim of which is definitely to work towards one church organisation for Western China. It was a striking and most encouraging recital, and it was followed by a delegate from North

China, who said that in Shantung many of the same results had been achieved. Another told of an educational union in Pekin, one Society taking the theological department, another the arts and normal departments, a third the medical. At that medical school there are one hundred students already, and the Chinese Government has undertaken to give government diplomas to those that pass the final examination of that college. A delegate from Korea followed, telling of a union university to be shortly established in the capital, Seoul. These were by no means the only instances of effective co-operation on the field that were presented that day—striking instances were reported from India, for example. But the reports from China were in themselves enough to make the Conference feel convinced by that deliberate finding of the Commission on the Carrying of the Gospel to all the World, that through co-operation the forces in the field could be *doubled, without the addition of a single man to the existing staffs.*

Then, in regard to the matter of church-federation or union, a delegate pointed out the importance of a " free interchange of full members on the recommendation of the pastor of the Church from which they come." [1] The population of China, he said, was becoming very mobile, and therefore this matter was of continual practical importance. This, again, raised the question of the two opposite principles upon which large measures of federation may take place, the one local,—among all the bodies in any area, forming a natural geographical

[1] An " Account of the World Missionary Conference " is bound to report all the different suggestions and aspirations made by delegates without pronouncing on their feasibility. It is obvious enough that Christian co-operation alone can prepare the ground for communal federation or union. The Report itself in its General Review and Conclusions shows how far from being unchallenged some of these demands from China would still be.

and linguistic unit ; the other denominational,—among similar denominations all over the Empire.   It is often impossible for a Chinese pastor to get to a distant Conference of the whole denomination, while he can with ease attend a local inter-denominational one.   As the Report tersely remarked, a Chinaman often finds he feels more warmly towards his local fellow-Christian than his distant fellow-denominationalist.

3.

It was at this point that the Conference had another vivid insight into the Oriental point of view.   This was a speech from the Chinese delegate, Ch'eng Ching-yi. As a terse seven-minutes oration, it was a serious rival to that of the Norwegian delegate on the day before. It was, in its freedom from superfluous matter, solid and lean as an athlete in training.   The Conference gasped when, with two minutes of his seven spent, the undis-turbed Celestial announced that he wished to speak on the subject under seven heads in the remaining five minutes !   And he did it easily too, and gave one of the seven heads a threefold subdivision into the bargain.

The speech was amongst other things a significant, though unconscious, commentary on two warnings given by two bishops concerning this matter of unity in the mission-field.   The first of these was by the Bishop of Hankow, who was quoted in the Report to have said that the alternative to meeting the Chinese demand for a united Church was that "we forfeit our position of leader-ship among the Christian forces of China."   In the mind of Chinamen, he said in effect, national unity has its Christian counterpart in church unity, and therefore the more ardently nationalist they become, the more they demand one Church for China.

" If the missionaries cannot supply this demand for leadership in the practical development of Christian unity, . . . that leadership will undoubtedly arise outside the ranks of the missionaries, and perhaps even outside the ranks of the duly authorised ministers of the Christian Church in China."

This was one of the warnings upon which the speech of Cheng Ching-yi constituted so illuminating a comment. And on the other hand, it equally illustrated the justice of the other warning—that of the Bishop of Birmingham, made in the discussion of the Report on the Church in the Mission-Field. His point (it will be remembered) was that it is absolutely imperative for Christians to be thinking out, to be giving closer and more earnest thought, to what are the essential constitutive elements of Church unity. The *keenness* of the speech of the Chinese delegate proclaimed the truth of the *first* warning—that the Chinese may soon be acting for themselves in this matter. And its very *artlessness* showed how completely unaware of the real difficulties and essentialities of the question they would be if they did so act ; thus unconsciously endorsing the *second*.

Here, then, is this significant speech :—

" As a representative of the Chinese Church, I speak entirely from the Chinese standpoint. We may, and we may not, all agree, but I feel it is my duty to present before you the mind of the Chinese Church as frankly as possible.

" The Christian federation movement occupies a chief place in the hearts of our leading Christian men in China, and they welcome every effort that is made towards that end. This is noticeably in the provinces of Szchuen, Honan, Shantung and Chihli. In educational work, evangelistic work, and so on, the Churches joined hand in hand, and the result of this is most encouraging.

" Since the Chinese Christians have enjoyed the sweetness of such a unity, they long for more and look for yet greater things. They are watching with keen eyes, and listening with attentive ears, for what this Conference will show and say to them concerning this all-important question. I am sure they will not be disappointed.

" Speaking plainly, we hope to see in the near future a united Christian Church without any denominational distinctions. This may seem somewhat peculiar to some of you, but, friends, do not forget to view us from *our* standpoint, and if you fail to do that, the Chinese will remain always a mysterious people to you. . . . In dealing with such a great problem, one is naturally led to consider the following points :—

" 1. Such a union is needed for these reasons :—

" (a) Things that really help the growing movement of the self-support and self-government of the Church in China are welcomed. A united effort, both spiritual and physical, is absolutely necessary [to this end].

" (b) Speaking generally, denominationalism has never interested the Chinese mind. He finds no delight in it, but sometimes he suffers for it !

" (c) Owing to the powerful force of heathenism from without, and the feebleness of the Church from within, the Christians are compelled to unite in building up a defence of the Church.

" 2. From the Chinese standpoint, there is nothing impossible about such a union. Such difficulties as may be experienced will be due to our Western friends, and not to ourselves. The difficulties are possibilities only, and must not be allowed to overshadow the advantages of the union that I speak of.

" 3. In China, and for the Chinese, such union is certainly desirable. China, with all her imperfections, is a country that loves unity both in national and family life.

" 4. There is no time more important than the present. These days are days of foundations from both political and religious standpoints. The future China will largely depend on what is done at the present time. This is a time of unspeakable responsibilities, and we have to be most careful of what we do now.

" 5. The Church of Christ is universal, not only irrespective of denominations, but also irrespective of nationalities—' All one in Christ Jesus.' ' The world is ' (to use a Chinese expression) ' one family, and China is a member of that family.'

" 6. Will such a united Church in China remain unbroken for

ever ? is a question I can only answer by saying, ' I do not know.' But what it will do itself is one thing, and what we press it to do is another. We can only deal with what is to hand to-day, and the unknown future will settle its own affairs.

" 7. I would, if you will allow me, make one suggestion, *i.e.*, that this Conference will recommend that the Continuation Committee, when appointed, make careful investigation, and will consult all the Chinese pastors and Christian leaders, and obtain from them a free and frank expression of their opinion as to the needs of such a united effort, and the best methods to bring it about. For, after all, it is not your particular denomination, nor even is it your particular mission that you are working for, but the establishment of the Church of Christ in China that you have in view.

" It is the earnest hope of your present speaker, humble as he is, that this Conference will not allow the present opportunity to pass away without taking some definite action.

" In conclusion, let us go with our Divine Master up on the top of the Mount of Olives, and there we shall obtain a wider, broader, and larger view of the needs of the Church and the World."

The Conference might well feel this challenge the best possible introduction to the debate that now followed. It was also not surprised when, on the next day, it was found that Cheng Ching-yi had been appointed the representative for China on the " Continuation Committee," the motion for establishing which was now to be discussed.

4.

And now—" We now come to our solemn act of worship," said the Chairman, with that honest impressive way of his. " We shall sing a hymn, and then let the Stewards shut the doors, that none may come in or go out. . . ."

And so for the space of half an hour there was silence in a Hall hermetically sealed, as it were, from the voices and distractions of the outside world.

Silence, indeed. For on that day, as on some of the other days, much of the half-hour was spent in united silence. Dr J. O. F. Murray, Master of Selwyn College, Cambridge, conducted the service on that day ; and when, in leading the Conference's confession of the sin involved in our unhappy divisions, he continued in the words of the General Confession, it seemed to be taken up spontaneously all over the hall, a volume of subdued sound. . . .

It was in the morning of this day, when the worship of the Conference was led by Dr Chatterji, the venerable delegate from India, that the delegates had joined in repeating together the Apostles' Creed. . . .

" I BELIEVE IN ONE GOD, THE FATHER ALMIGHTY, MAKER OF HEAVEN AND EARTH ;

AND IN JESUS CHRIST, HIS ONLY SON, OUR LORD . . . I BELIEVE IN THE HOLY GHOST, THE HOLY CATHOLIC CHURCH, THE COMMUNION OF SAINTS . . . AMEN.

5.

The Chairman of the Commission, Sir Andrew H. L. Fraser, late Lieut.-Governor of Bengal, now stood up to move the resolution relating to the formation of a Continuation Committee for the carrying on of the work of the present Conference. The scope of the proposed Committee appears from the first article of the resolution, with its seven subdivisions :—

" That a Continuation Committee of the World Missionary Conference be appointed, international and representative in character, to carry out, on the lines of the Conference itself, which are inter-denominational and do not involve the idea of organic and ecclesiastical union, the following duties :—

" (1) To maintain in prominence the idea of the World Missionary Conference as a means of co-ordinating missionary work, of laying sound lines for future development, and of generating and claiming by corporate action fresh stores of spiritual force for the evangelisation of the world.

" (2) To finish any further investigations, or any formulation of the results of investigations, which may remain after the World Missionary Conference is over, and may be referred to it.

" (3) To consider when a further World Missionary Conference is desirable, and to make the initial preparations.

" (4) To devise plans for maintaining the intercourse which the World Missionary Conference has stimulated between different bodies of workers, e.g., by literature or by a system of correspondence and mutual report, or the like.

" (5) To place its services at the disposal of the Home Boards in any steps which they may be led to take (in accordance with the recommendation of more than one Commission) towards closer mutual counsel and practical co-operation.

" (6) To confer with the Societies and Boards as to the best method of working towards the formation of such a permanent International Missionary Committee as is suggested by the Commissions of the Conference and by various missionary bodies apart from the Conference.[1]

" (7) And to take such steps as may seem desirable to carry out, by the formation of Special Committees or otherwise, any practical suggestions made in the Reports of the Commissions."

Such was the essential part of the resolution. It was now moved, seconded and discussed.

The Commission which brought forward the resolution was, as we have seen, the Commission on *Co-operation* and the promotion of *Unity*. And although the resolu-

[1] The principles on which the Commission are agreed constructive work could be built are stated in their Report as follows:—

" (a) It should from the beginning be precluded from handling matters which are concerned with the doctrinal or ecclesiastical differences of the various denominations.

" (b) This being assured, it would be desirable that it should be as widely representative as possible.

" (c) Yet it should be a purely consultative and advisory Association, exercising no authority but such as would accrue to it through the intrinsic value of the services that it may be able to render."

tion itself had more direct bearing on the former than the latter aspect, it was right and it was relevant that a good deal should be said on the wider question. The Report had distinctly paved the way for the discussion of unity. And the Chairman, in presenting that Report, had almost invited such discussion, when he said, " We in our Commission and you in this Conference have surely had before you the vision of unity, a vision fair and beautiful, far better and far higher than anything we have dreamed of before. . . ." Full justice was indeed done to both the immediate and the more remote aspects of the question. But this should not make those who were not present lose sight of the fact that the immediate question alone before the House was—the taking of a single, small, proximate step towards giving effect to the demands that had been made from all quarters for some machinery of co-operation.

6.

Much witness was heard regarding the genuine services which this Continuation Committee would render to the cause.

Dr Julius Richter, the German historian of missions, to whom the great value of the work done by the eight Commissions in the science of missions naturally appealed, emphasised strongly the usefulness of such a Committee in carrying on that " close and united study of missionary problems." Most of the Commissions, he said, were strongly under the impression that their work is not yet finished.

" Studying the history of Christian missions in different fields, I have often had the impression of a great busy municipal site, or newly started township, where it is hoped that a very big city shall be built up. But there is no underlying plan ; everybody builds where he chooses, according to his own ideas, often without regard of his neighbour and of the future development of the city. So the different missionary organisations are building more or less according to their own ideas, every one trying to incorporate as much as possible of its own peculiarities. Would it not be advisable in such cases that, by friendly consultation, the new settlers should institute some sort of central organisation, with, however, restricted powers, to bring harmony into the scattered endeavours, to concentrate effort on needy points. These days have brought us again in view of the great mission fields, of the great, overwhelming tasks lying before us, of the pressing obligations. And on the other hand they have given us a strong impression of the comparative weakness of our own forces, and of our isolated position. How useful and helpful would some sort of central organisation be ! "

The same point was urged with equal emphasis by Dr Arthur J. Brown, the Chairman of the North American Committee of that Commission. Mission work all over the world, he said, is characterised by a lack of unity, of movement, of breadth of conception, and of definiteness of plan. The state of the Church militant is the state of Israel in the Book of Judges. Yet surely we all see, he said, that liberty does not necessarily involve chaos ! And the speaker who succeeded him, a Canadian lay-man, showed how specially co-operation appealed to the lay mind. Five dollars or £1 can be got, he said, for a really efficient institution, for every dollar or 4s. which could be obtained for a weak one, appealing to denomi-national loyalty only. " To-day," he continued—

" To-day I believe you can appeal to the mind of all parties, and supply all the money that the Boards require for this advance, if you tell them that it is *the policy of the whole Church to reach the whole world*, but not if you try to maintain competing institu-tions in a non-Christian land."

The " supporting constituency " (as he phrased it) of both Canada and the United States would feel that this proposal of a Continuation Committee would be completely in line both with their own ideals and their own local organisation. For example, in 1909 there was held a very large and important convention to consider the missionary responsibility of the Canadian churches to the incoming settlers in Canada, and the responsibility of Canadians for their share in world-wide evangelisation. Through that convention a resolution favouring co-operation everywhere was submitted to the representative bodies of Anglican, Presbyterian, Congregationalist, Baptist, and Methodist bodies in Canada, and unanimously approved by each.

Nor was this the only speaker from Canada. Later on in the debate a very tall young delegate from the western plains of Canada underscored the points made by his fellow-countryman. "The longest man in the Conference," as he called himself, with eagle-like face and eyes, spoke with prodigious animation. He, too, represented the layman's point of view, and speaking of the laymen's movement in the North American Continent (of which the Conference was to hear much more on the closing day of the Conference), he said that Christian laymen were not simply talking about union, they were actually doing the work in their united relationships, and that they believed in the evangelisation of the world in this generation, *provided there was universal co-operation for the task*. Men would give, he agreed with his confrère, to a united appeal :—

"On one occasion a Presbyterian, an Anglican, and a Baptist went to a wealthy Methodist to ask him to increase his subscription. Imagine a Methodist up against that kind of combination ! . . . Only one thing could happen, and that thing happened : he gave a magnificent subscription to missions." . . .

The "longest man in the Conference" brought the prairie air into the Conference Hall, and the bell which, to their regret, rang him down found them breathless but refreshed.

And similarly, the Chairman of a federal council of churches in the United States, "with a communicant membership of 17,000,000, representing fully 50,000,000 of the population," showed with what readiness and joy the promoters of such local achievements in co-operation would welcome anything which, like this proposed Continuation Committee, made towards the universal application of the principle.

For the Continental constituencies, Dr J. Richter, in the speech already mentioned, had shown how very greatly the Societies, and specially the smaller Societies on the Continent of Europe, where the missionary movement was not yet strong, would benefit by the proposal now before the House. Twenty-five Continental Societies, he said, representing by far the greater part of the missionary energy of the Continent, had laid before the Conference a comprehensive petition to establish just such a Continuation Committee.

In the restricted sphere of the leading German missionary societies they had had a central organisation for twenty-five years, called the *Ausschuss*, and it had become an indispensable factor in the German mission life. It acted as intermediary with the German government ; it shaped " the educational policy of the missions and of the Colonial Government." And it was just because they in Germany had seen the value of the principle of concentration that they so strongly believed in and supported the international extension of the same principle ; from lack of which, he said—from lack of " effectual representation " in the world-wide movement —they had suffered much in the past. The great and leading Societies in the English-speaking world should feel their responsibility to help " their weaker brethren," and it would be worthy of a World Missionary Conference, which represented Christian missions as a world-power manifested in service, to contribute notably to helping the weaker countries and societies in their need.—Truly, the strengthening of the ties which the Edinburgh Conference effected between the Continental movement and that in the English-speaking world, is destined to strengthen the whole world-wide cause ; and the increased knowledge of the Continental missions gained by those in Britain and America is not least destined to benefit the *latter*.

7.

It was not forgotten in the discussion, however, that the present resolution was only a first, and to some extent a temporary step. The perusal of Clause (6) in the resolution was a reminder that a Continuation Committee of this Conference was not the same thing as the International Committee, the formation of which had been suggested by more than one Commission.

Naturally, such a Committee could come into existence only after much consultation with the Missionary Societies and Boards. The Continuation Committee of the Conference was only a step towards that end, though a great and important one, because of the real representativeness and intrinsic weight of the Conference itself. Lord William Gascoyne-Cecil, indeed, was able to support the resolution just because the proposed Committee would be limited (he thought) to studying the question, so that subsequent steps would only be decided on after due consideration and thought. The noble lord concluded with " a small sweet idyll," like a fragment of some georgic on bee-keeping, to illustrate his point : as an expert bee-keeper he had often had " the

N

awkward duty of taking the honey from the bees," and had learned the absolute necessity of taking away the frames very quietly and gradually. If and when the stinging begins, there is no saying when it will stop. . . . The almost equally delicate task of making the applications and identifications of his parable was left by this wary bee-keeper to the many leaders of the Societies and the Churches among his audience. Perhaps Dr Wardlaw Thompson had that idyllic simile in mind when he said that he did not think it " took much imagination to forecast some of the leading articles in some of the newspapers which would appear next week. Yes, but the leading articles would not be the only thing. There would be men on both sides. . . ."

The prophetic power which Virgil attributes to the bees had certainly communicated itself to the Secretary of the London Missionary Society that afternoon.

However these things may be, the meaning of " the honey " in the parable was clear. It was an organisation greatly needed, yet difficult to win ; something more advanced than this Continuation Committee, though less ambitious than a plan for ecclesiastical reconstruction ; something with no authority save that derived from the indispensableness of its services, yet on the other hand, truly representative of Boards and Societies all over the world. Such an International Committee would be indeed an immense step—a step, Dr Eugene Stock seemed to indicate, towards that " union " through which the " unity " that already exists might find a local habitation and a name, and a true organ of expression. Thus, too, Silas McBee, the Editor of " The Churchman," a man who has literally given his life to the cause of unity. As Vice-Chairman of this Commission, he had not only received the correspondence, but had gone about everywhere getting into touch with the leaders of the Churches, and his speech on this occasion, with its beautiful Christian spirit, showed that such labours had not been in vain.   Thus, too, another notable speaker, Dr J. Campbell Gibson, the Chairman of the Commission on the CHURCH IN THE MISSION FIELD.   We *have* unity by simply being in Christ, he insisted.   But we need organised expression of it: " a body which could speak with one voice for all the missions of the world."   He found a good omen in the name " *Continuation* Committee " :   it would *continue*, upwards in an inclined plane, to something on a far higher level. Lord William Gascoyne-Cecil's simile of the jerking off of a bee-frame was paralleled by this speaker in his own way. " If you attempt to reach a high level, a level yet beyond your reach, *per saltum* and at once, you may not manage it, but as long as we are moving up an inclined plane [we] will eventually reach the end."   When men who are expressing deep underlying principles, but in a different way, perhaps, come together, they are doing a thing it is deeply advantageous to do and to learn to do. And he concluded :—

" While I rejoice equally in co-operation, I do not believe that the minds of Christian men can ultimately rest in less than that highest level of all, the unity of the Church of God, of which we have robbed ourselves too long, and which it may cause us weary years to restore ; but it will be restored by our Lord Himself, if we seek it in humility, with infinite patience, and with an endless consideration for the difficulties of our brethren."

These words—and they did not stand alone—showed how naturally the idea of the Continuation Committee, with its expected termination in an International Committee of Missions, led the minds of the whole Conference to contemplate the vision of a higher unity still.   It was as if all seemed to be feeling, and all to be confessing, the need of a One Body to give outward and visible expres-

sion to the inward and spiritual grace of the One
Spirit.

Thus the Continuation Committee seemed to become
transmuted by some sort of spiritual alchemy into a
symbol of something greater far. Otherwise, what was
there in so modest a proposal to call forth two such
utterances as these :—

" (This Committee) could not have been launched except in such
an atmosphere as that which we find ourselves breathing in this
Conference. Ten years ago it would have been, and was, impossible ! "

Or this, from another seasoned veteran in missionary
movements and international missionary conferences :—

" My impulse in speaking just now is that I want to sing a
doxology. I have come to a point in my religious experience in
this Conference which five years ago I think I should not have
dreamed of ! "

8.

In reflecting on the significance of the resolution before
the House that day, it ought not to be forgotten that the
Edinburgh Conference had succeeded in bringing together
men of far more divergent types of Christian thought and
Christian belief than had assembled at New York in
1900 ; and *yet* was finding possible what the delegate
already quoted said had proved impossible in 1900,
at a Conference which in composition was homogeneity
itself compared with that of 1910. Thus the resolution
was a doubly notable event.

But not only were there now present men representing
schools of thought, which were oftener polemically contrasted with each other in books, pamphlets, and
church magazines than represented together on one
religious platform : but in the discussions themselves,
these differences had not by any means been concealed,

but frankly, sometimes with very great frankness, had been touched upon. Thus the resolution was a trebly notable event, since it registered a new conception of the function of a common platform—a platform on which men might learn from each others' differences, however wide, through faith in the amount of unity, which, as a matter of fact, had enabled them to come together.

Had it been otherwise—had the Conference been tamely homogeneous,—its unanimity would have been a viscous adhesiveness rather than the " definite coherent heterogeneity" in which both Herbert Spencer and Hegel, in their different ways, have taught us to see the attainment of successively higher stages of unity and of life.

It must be admitted that some of the Anglican members, to 'whom the Conference was chiefly indebted for this saving element of heterogeneity, occasionally went beyond the limitation within which all the delegates without distinction had to keep, that is to say, the bringing of individual ecclesiastical or other dogmatic views into the discussion. They were, however, listened to with very great patience, probably because the delegates realised that under the circumstances these men were morally bound to make their position clear, to themselves, to their hearers, and to their constituency ;— possibly too, because they were interested to hear what that position was :—so that the trespass was more against the letter than the spirit. The tribute to the fearless honesty of the one party ought to be balanced by a tribute to the exemplary patience of the other, under a trial which just occasionally it seemed difficult to suffer gladly. Great, however, are the miracles wrought by the light touch : the most flagrant breaker of this Conference taboo was a certain wise Bishop, who gave the Conference the joy of a great laugh in his first sentence : whom the Conference thereupon, in gratitude for that benefit,

allowed to say whatsoever he listed. He certainly took
his full allowance. ' The Chair,' his finger all the time
on the meeting's pulse, was ready to stop the *lene tor-
mentum* if the patient showed signs of "having had
enough." But all seemed well. ' The Chair' decided to
let it go, and this illegal tormentor actually retired amid
the cheers of the sufferers.

Perhaps this courageous Bishop derived advantage
from the fact that those sufferers had, a few minutes
previously, been given a welcome opportunity of relieving
their feelings in a congenial fashion. "We are not
ready," had remarked a delegate, in a parenthesis
less obviously relevant to the subject than to the
atmosphere, "we are not ready as American Christians
to apologise for the Protestant Reformation ! "—

—The moment when steam first issues from the safety-
valve is a marked one. Not otherwise the noise of the
escaping steam which burst forth at this point. . . .

And which benefited the genial torturer who followed
at least as much as those whose feelings it had
relieved.

9.

The question *how far* inclusiveness can, or should,
be carried seemed, in fact, to have been solved auto-
matically. It *should* go just exactly as far as it *can* go :—
that is to say, no differences however important need
ever be allowed, even by the most conscientious holder
of them, to count against the naked fact, that those who
hold those different views have nevertheless found it
possible to meet and to confer together on a common
work. Again, it *can* go just exactly as far as it *should*,
and cannot in the nature of things go further : therefore no fear need be entertained lest it be going too far.

In two somewhat different senses of the words, inclusiveness at interdenominational Conferences never *can* go too far. Thus the principle, Let all come who will, is a " safety " one.

A Baptist delegate from Delhi was really intending the same principle, and illustrated it humorously by a reminiscence :

" A great many years ago when my mind was first agitated on this subject, I thought that we might co-operate in industrial work, and I looked at my big ecclesiastical brother [in the Cambridge Mission to Delhi] from top to toe, to see what similarity there was between him and myself. And I found there was nothing—till we got to our boots. (Loud laughter.) You must admit that when you unite on boots you are on the road at any rate to co-operation." (Loud laughter.)

But this philosophy, which the author of " Sartor Resartus " would have appreciated, admits of extension. Baptists and High Anglicans are not the only persons who wear boots. And it was more than once pointed out during the discussion, on that and other days, that no measure of missionary co-operation could be considered complete until it included *all* who were doing mission work among non-Christians in the name of their one Master, the Lord Jesus Christ, including Greek Church Christians, with a great Japan mission under the well-known Bishop Nicolai, and Roman Catholic Christians, with missions all over Asia and Africa. " I can bear testimony," said one delegate, " to the fact that it *is* possible for us in a really practicable way to co-operate with the Roman Catholic Church,— and remember that the Roman Catholic Church does not mean the Vatican or the various hierarchies, but the great mass of devout people we are constantly in touch with. We can affect *them* ; we can so melt their minds as to affect the central body."
" It is for us to shame Rome out of her proud loneliness

. . . an aloofness which is more pathetic than it is splendid . . . ; it is for us to startle the Greek Church out of her starved orthodoxy : . . . because God is our Sufficiency!" The speaker indicated in fact—or so it seemed—that his own personal inclusion in the Conference solved *in principle* the problem of the inclusion in it of all who call themselves Christians without distinction. And,—so far as the mere inclusion of Christians from those denominations in a World Missionary Conference goes, — there were several indications that this was a conception that need by no means excessively perturb either Roman Catholics or Protestants ; and that the idea of seeing Bishop Nicolai and Monsignor Bonomelli, seated on the same bench with Anglican Bishop, Scottish Moderator, and Nonconformist President—all of them humbly obedient to the absolute and indeed infallible *ex cathedra* rulings of John R. Mott—was in no sense and by no means a visionary one. Thus, on the one hand, it was a well-known Nonconformist delegate who said :—

" I long for the time when we shall see another Conference, and when the men of the Greek Church and the Roman Church shall talk things over with us in the service of Christ. The Kingdom will not come until every branch can unite together in some common effort of service for the Lord ! "

And on the other hand, it was a Roman Catholic Monsignor and Bishop who, though not a delegate, had expressed most clearly of all his approval of the basis on which the delegates had met. Most interesting was the story told by the Editor of the " Churchman," Silas McBee, whose speech has been already mentioned, of a visit he had paid to this well-known Italian dignitary, Monsignor Bonomelli, Bishop of Cremona, reputed to be both a modernist and a personal friend of the present Pope. This old man, nearly eighty years of age, described by the speaker to be " one of the great evangelical preachers of the world " and " one of the greatest bishops," had written a letter specially to be read at the Conference. And in this letter, when it was read, was recognised a document that might almost have been taken as a charter of the principles for which the Conference and all similar Conferences stood. It is too long to quote here, but in order that the reader may not be deprived of the opportunity of reading a notable document, it has been inserted as an appendix to this chapter.

From all this will be apparent the truth of the observation, that this Conference was remarkable for having brought together, whether in person, or in spirit and sympathy, people of very widely differing positions. It was, in a word, far more representative than such Conferences had ever been in the past, and therefore its unanimous adoption of the motion then before the House, became a proportionately more significant and hopeful event.

10.

Thus an important thing that this Conference, and, especially this debate, made clear, was the necessity of trying to understand, and understand sympathetically, what are the principles for which Christians who differ with each other stand. These principles, it is true, were related to issues which were not the actual issue before the Conference that day ; but they lay behind that issue, and the knowledge that they did lie behind it, and must at some distant day be faced, was what gave to the debate its intensity, its moments of sometimes almost anxious intensity. Nothing was more remarkable than the freedom with which differing views were stated, and it was this freedom and this frankness that were such a hopeful sign for the future and that made the unanimous passing of the resolution so remarkable an event. It was discovered that without compromising these it would still be possible to co-operate, and that the principle on which the Conference had been based could still be adhered to, and proceeded on. The principle would hold. The enormous section of Christendom represented at Edinburgh, 1910, *was ready for a Continuation Committee*. Holding their differences and respecting those who differed, the men there met in Conference, and others like them, could still continue to meet for the interchange of ideas and the devising of common measures. They could thus learn to understand each other better. The enthusiasm with which the motion was passed showed that in passing it the delegates realised that they were going forward, that they were making progress, in the path along which God had evidently been leading; realised too that this was a stepping out into something which must be supernatural if it was to be anything at all.

The Report itself, in the chapter referred to, had already enunciated these principles with a truthfulness and a careful balance which could hardly fail to command universal assent. " Co-operation," it said, " is a moral problem "—the old problem of sympathy and mutual respect, faith, and love. " We cannot too often remind ourselves

" that no large progress either in the unity of the Church or in co-operative effort can be made with our present spiritual conception and capacity. The true path does not lie in treating our differences as unimportant, and impatiently brushing them aside as unworthy hindrances, but in finding through patient self-discipline a higher point of view which transcends them and in which they are reconciled. On the intellectual side this is a task that calls for strength and perseverance; and on the moral side we need the power of a mighty love, which, by the clearness of its perception and the flow of its energy, illuminates and transforms the situation and makes all things new."

Penitence, it said also, is due for the arrogance and lack of insight of the past, and for the very absence of desire for the cessation of the divisions of to-day. And prayer is needed, because human wisdom can discern no one remedy for the situation.

" Unity, when it comes, must be something richer, grander, more comprehensive than anything which we can see at present. It is something into which and up to which we must grow, something of which and for which we must become worthy. We need to have sufficient faith in God to believe that He can bring us to something higher and more Christlike than anything to which at present we see a way."

Such were the principles on which both Edinburgh, 1910, and its Continuation were broad-based. And the resolution was nothing more than a proposal to create a method of personal intercourse, with a view to the promotion of practical ends in that spiritual spirit; for it is by personal intercourse that Christendom can be drawn together far better than by an ambitious project of co-operation or church-federation: just as it is not identity of intellectual opinions, or even the pursuit of identical aims, that keeps families together and the family bond strong, " but rather personal and intimate knowledge of one another, and mutual trust." And no manner of doubt was left but that the Conference endorsed these sentiments of its Commission's Report. A well-known delegate—a Nonconformist—said, for example—

" We meet here a very remarkable body, and we have had speeches this morning from men from whom many of us have been accustomed to be quite separate; but I want to thank the

Bishop of Southwark and others who spoke for the expressions they have given of their desire for unity. I thank them especially, because it seems to me that the spirit of unity can only be obtained in being perfectly frank, by making everybody understand our position. I do look forward now with greater hopefulness than ever to a day when we shall be able to meet to consider questions which have been tabooed at this Conference—and very properly tabooed—and shall be able to talk frankly to each other about the things on which we differ as well as the things on which we agree, recognising that we are members of the Body of Christ, and seeking the guidance of the Spirit of Christ to lead us into the larger and fuller truth which comprehends the different opinions. So I rejoice in the measure of agreement we have come to to-day."

And to this utterance many parallels might be adduced from the debate.

II.

It has now been shown how the question of Unity was quite secondary to the practical question of Co-operation before the House. Still, the Commission stood, in virtue of its very title, for the "Promotion of Unity," and therefore it was as natural as it was in the highest sense useful, that many things were said on the remoter issue, which all felt with more or less keenness of con-sciousness was ultimately involved by the immediate proposal. The Report had already given a most valuable lead in regard to this ultimate problem. In the memor-able chapter, already quoted from, it had said :—

"While we may differ from one another in our conception of what unity involves and requires, we agree in believing that our Lord intended that we should be one in a visible fellow-ship. . . . The realisation of the ideal may lie in the far distance and the difficulties to be surmounted may be over-whelmingly great ; but it is something to have felt the stirring of a hope so rich and so wonderful."

And it then went on to an analysis, masterly in its sympathy and truthfulness, of the divergent conceptions entertained by Christians in this regard. It finds that these reduce themselves to two main types :—to that of those who see, in the transcending significance of the faith common to all, the fundamental and determining fact in the situation, and who therefore incline towards the formation of some sort of federation of Christian communions and the practising of free intercommunion : and the conception of those who believe that this common measure of faith is wholly imperfect because it fails to include essential parts of divine revelation or essential means of grace, and that to surrender these, or to do anything from which that surrender could be inferred, would be a culpable neglect of trust. All the denominations, according to this view, are emphasising some fragment of vital truth, and the full, rich, final unity, which is all that is worth aiming for, must include all these fragments. The pursuit of this ideal, which may be more difficult, protracted, and costly than the other, appears to such thinkers safer and more truly conducive to the health of the body than the other. It will not ignore or minimise differences in spite of (*or rather because of*) the fact that the Christian bodies on the mission field desire a satisfactory Church-union ; but rather seek, by patient and prayerful thought, to ascertain the elements of truth in them all, so that they may be embraced in a higher unity. To the first class of thinkers the resolution of this day probably commended itself as a step towards a federation of Churches in the mission field (and at home) in the comparatively near future. To the second, as a way of permanently securing a most valuable common meeting-ground whereon this indispensable personal contact and exchange of views may take place.

And so at the Edinburgh Conference both these types of thinkers, with their many variants, freely expressed their thought, and though that expression often revealed the most radical differences on fundamental aspects of the question, the sense of brotherhood, instead of suffering comminution, seemed to increase and grow stronger. This fact carried with it its own encouragement. It gave hope of victory just because it itself was victory. Thus, for example, an Australian delegate, on the " extreme left," utterly denied that " any outward organic unity " was necessary or practicable or even desirable—it would be material, mechanical, unwieldy, dangerous, inorganic, non-spiritual, external. .!. . Such an ideal was the single obstacle to progress. *" One single legion,* vast and unwieldy, may be broken and torn by disunion within itself," he said. The very next speaker, a Congregationalist like the first, after telling of a remarkable church-union movement in South India, went on, " But some of us are seeking more than that, and I believe that federation and co-operation will be valuable in proportion as they have their ultimate end in Christian union, *in a great united organisation!* " Again, Professor James Denney, in a tremendously powerful address that very evening, found that the Church was and could only be one in this—that all its members represent the same attitude of the soul to Christ. Its basis of unity was found in the common loyalty of all sinful men to Jesus Christ as their Lord and Saviour, not in any number of carefully digested theological propositions or any ecclesiastical constitution however carefully it be framed,—something that has no theological, no intellectual embarrassments about it at all. It is difficult to be sure whether the Professor meant to negate the very idea of corporate unity, or merely a corporate unity that is based on an idea of Catholicity to which Christians have given very

earnest thought. One would have liked to see the matter
threshed out between him and the Bishop of Birmingham
—another great teacher and scholar—whose utterance
on this subject, quoted at the very end of Chapter VIII.
(The Church on the Mission-Field), makes so curious a
contrast with the former's ; an utterance which, though
apparently meaning the precise converse of that of the
Scottish Professor, was delivered with equally passionate
conviction, and with quite equal intellectual incisiveness !
. . . A final contrast : one well-known delegate from
America thought that all the differences that divide the
denominations were so unutterably unimportant that
they might be made up into a mere appendix to some
handbook of common Christian teaching ; and *then*,
" I suggest we follow the example of modern science—
cut out the appendix ! " While on the other hand,
speaker after speaker, Anglican and non-Anglican, urged
the intense *importance* of denominational distinctions,
because they enshrine fragments of truth which are
necessary to the perfect whole. . . .

" We have no use for the Least Common Denominator of Christianity. We look with hope to its Greatest Common Measure some
day, a day not yet in sight. . . . One day we shall be one, but it
will be effected by a higher union than is in sight at present,
when our deepest convictions and needs are met and satisfied, not
whittled away."

So " the Lion in that enormous den of Daniels "—as
Bishop Montgomery feared he was. But as far as these
words went, he would have probably found most of the
Daniels roaring in unison with him.—These samples,
which might easily be multiplied and varied, show clearly
with what freedom men were speaking their mind that
day.

12.

And now, is it fully understood both why the debate on this so simple a resolution was attended by such excitement, and by such moments of occasional tension ; and why the unanimous carrying of that resolution called forth such an outburst of emotion ? All the livelong morning and afternoon the discords had been suffered freely to rush in, and they made the fuller, the sweeter, and above all the more significant, the harmony that issued now in the unanimous vote which crowned the debate. That was not, indeed, nor was it even imagined to be, a final cadence, a full close : but it was like some partial cadence in a complicated fugue ; a cadence which, though reached with effort and dwelt upon with delight, forms but a new starting-point, from which to weave a fresh web of the harmonies and dissonances that run out, at last, into the full close of the great Common Chord.

13.

The Chairman rose. Was the Conference ready to vote on the Resolution ? A murmur of assent, not loud, but deep—voluminous. A delegate rose. The Chairman leaned swiftly to him. . . . " Dr Wallace Williamson has the floor ! "—Dr Wallace Williamson, speaking from his place in the House, merely wished to call the attention of the Committee to the necessity of providing for the continuance of the Continuation Committee. . . . Dr Robson explained that the point had not been overlooked. . . . Bishop Roots thought that one or two verbal matters might be left in the hands of the Business Committee. The Chairman :—" Yes, matters which are merely verbal and general, involving no change of substance, may be entrusted to the Committee." . . . The brief sentences were interchanged in a weird silence that made their formality sound unnatural—as unnatural as the starter's formal directions sound to the runners in some momentous race, when, toeing the line and breathing deep, they listen for the pistol, motionless as marble, yet incarnating the very idea of motion.

Then after a pause : " *Shall the vote be now taken ?* " Again the same murmur, charged with the emotional intensity of expectation that has reached its climax. The Chairman turns to Sir Andrew Fraser, the mover of the motion. He has the right to close the discussion. Sir Andrew Fraser evidently feels that at that moment no mortal being could have said anything more without discomfiture, besides ruining a God-prepared climax. Sir Andrew Fraser signifies that he waives his right. Then—

" *The Motion has been moved and seconded : those in favour of it say Aye !* "

A roar : " *Aye !* " short as the monosyllable itself, but with a volume like a Handel chorus.

" *Contrary, No !* "

A silence, as voluminous as the former sound.

" *The motion is carried unanimously.*"

14.

Has this chapter interpreted truly the reason of the strong emotion with which all now vented their pent-up feelings, spontaneously bursting into the glorifying of God ?

> " PRAISE GOD FROM WHOM ALL BLESSINGS FLOW,
> PRAISE HIM ALL CREATURES HERE BELOW,
> PRAISE HIM ABOVE YE HEAVENLY HOST,
> PRAISE FATHER SON AND HOLY GHOST ! "

o

APPENDICES TO CHAPTER XII.

(1)

Message to the Edinburgh Conference from Monsignor Bonomelli, Roman Catholic Bishop of Cremona.

A Conference of representatives of all the Christian denominations, held with the noble aim of better making known Christ and His Church to consciences which feel and exhibit in practice all the profound and fecund beauty of religious aspirations, is a fact of such importance and significance that it cannot escape the attention of any one who may follow the Conference, however superficially, in what a degree the most profound problems are agitating and revolutionising the modern spirit. This Conference, indeed, proves that religious feeling ever exercises a supreme influence over the entire life of man, and that the religious factor in our day, as throughout all time, stimulates and urges on human activity towards new conquests in the path of civilisation. The progress of science, the various phases of philosophy, the evolution both of thought and of practical life,—these all group themselves round the religions which human history displays and classifies at different epochs. It has been well said that as the prism exhibits the various colours contained in light, so mankind displays the various forms and shades of religion.

Moreover, your Conference, which is being held in Scotland, the land of strong and noble ideals, though at one time torn asunder by religious strife, is a triumphant proof of another consoling fact ;—the most desirable and precious of human liberties, religious liberty, may now be said to be a grand conquest of contemporary humanity, and it enables men of various faiths to meet together, not for the purpose of hating and combating each other, for the supposed greater glory of God, but in order to consecrate themselves in Christian love to the pursuit of that religious truth which unites all believers in Christ. United in one faith, the various spiritual forces combine in the adoration of the one true God in spirit and in truth.

For these reasons I applaud your Conference. I know very well that some sceptical spirits, saturated in gross materialism or cold positivism, may smile at your initiative, and tax you with utopian optimism, or with being well-meaning dreamers, shutting your eyes to the realities of life. Such will not fail to say that you, being yourselves profoundly divided in your religious beliefs, of which you endeavour to be the jealous guardians, cannot have any data or principles, accepted by all, on which to base your discussions. Besides, religion is too much a matter of individual conviction and feeling for us to hope ever to see one only Church, capable of embracing all believers in Christ. But no, only a superficial observer could be deluded regarding the practicability of such efforts. Yours, gentlemen, is not an optimistic idealism, nor an ideal dream. The elements of fact in which you all agree are numerous and are common to the various Christian denominations, and they can therefore serve as a point of departure for your discussions. It is, therefore, legitimate to aspire to a unity of faith and of religious practice, and to work for its realisation by the consecration of all energies of mind and heart. This is a work in which we in our day may well co-operate. In this field, as in others, it is well to keep in mind that from the clash of opinions discussed in a free and calm spirit sparks of truth cannot fail to be elicited.

Now, on what matters and on what principles are you agreed, gentlemen? To my thinking they are as follows. Like myself, all of you are persuaded that the physical, ethical, and social developments of life do not satisfy man, because man, whether he wills it or not, is oppressed by the Infinite, and this consciousness, from which he cannot deliver himself, urges him to harmonise his physical and social conditions with the supreme Reality, which is God, the Source of all these conditions, and to which they are subordinate. Without such harmony the ethical and social life loses its significance and impresses us with its insufficiency. Faith, therefore, in God the Creator, which bestows on human life an eternal and absolute value, is for you the primary point of agreement. You all share faith in Christ the Redeemer. " Christ reveals Himself and is adored as divine ; this is a religious fact of unequalled importance. Jesus has in reality not vanished either from history

or from the life of Christianity ; He lives at all times in millions
of souls ; He is enthroned as King in all hearts. The figure
of Christ has not the cold splendour of a distant star, but the
warmth of a heart which is near us, a flame burning in the soul
of believers and keeping alive their consciences. Putting aside
certain opinions, which, honoured at the moment, may possibly
be abandoned to-morrow, criticism had hoped to effect a
complete demolition of the conception of Christ, but what
criticism really demolished was merely irrelevant matter. . . ."
The figure of Christ, after all the onslaughts of criticism, now
stands forth more pure and divine than ever, and compels our
adoration.

Thus we are united in the profound conviction that a
universal religion is necessary, and that this must be the
Christian religion ; not a cold and formal religion, a thing apart
from human life, but a living force, pervading the human soul
in its essence, and its various manifestations—a religion, in
short, which completes and crowns our life and which bears
fruition in works of love and holiness. Again, all of you feel
the need of a Church which may be the outward manifestation
of your faith and religious feeling, the vigilant custodian now
and here of Christian doctrine and tradition. It sustains and
keeps alive religious and individual activity in virtue of that
strong power of suggestion which collectively always exercises
on the individual. "Sir," exclaims Johnson, "it is a very
dangerous thing for a man not to belong to any Church!"
And this is true. How many of us would fall a thousand times
were it not for its support!

Finally, from the various Churches and religious denominations into which you Christians are divided there arises a new
unifying element, a noble aspiration, restraining too great
impulsiveness, levelling dividing barriers, and working for the
realisation of the one Holy Church though all the children of
redemption. And now, I ask, Are not these elements more
than sufficient to constitute a common ground of agreement,
and to afford a sound basis for further discussion, tending to
promote the union of all believers in Christ? On this
common ground, gentlemen, having your minds liberated from
all passions or sectarian intolerance, animated, on the contrary,
by Christian charity, bring together into one focus the results

of your studies, the teachings of experience, whether individual or collective, calmly carry on research, and promote discussion. May truth be as a shining light, illuminating your consciences, and making you all of one heart and one mind. My desire for you is but the echo of Christ's words, which have resounded through the centuries—"Let there be one flock and one Shepherd."

(2)

[The writer ventures to add to the former appendix another one, containing a few passages from a recent book, by one who probably does not " feel justified in calling himself a Christian in any sense of the term." They are an interesting comment on Chapter XII., for they show how the divisions of Christendom sometimes strike the world ; and they reveal the sort of reflections which a discussion such as that just related would probably suggest to this sort of thinker.

The whole meaning of the author has no doubt not been fully conveyed by this selection, which is somewhat arbitrary. To the author Catholicity means of course something that quite transcends Christianity. But we are only concerned here with Christianity ; and *under this aspect* the selection might be said fairly to convey the author's thought.]

" The idea of the Catholic Church is charged with synthetic suggestion ; it is in many ways an idea broader and finer than the constructive idea of any existing state. . . .

" I write here of the Catholic Church as an idea. To come from that idea to the world of present realities is to come to a tangle of difficulties. Is the Catholic Church merely the Roman Communion, or does it include the Greek and Protestant Churches ? Some of these bodies are declaredly dissentient, some claim to be integral portions of the Catholic Church which have protested against and abandoned certain errors of the central organisation. . . .

" Many people, I know, take refuge from the struggle with this tangle of controversies by refusing to recognise any institutions whatever as representing the Church. They assume a mystical Church, made up of all true believers, of all men and women of good intent, whatever their formulæ or connexion. Wherever there is worship, there, they say, is a fragment of the Church. All and none of these bodies are the true Church.

" This is no doubt profoundly true. It gives something like a working assumption for the needs of the present time. People can get along upon that. But it does not exhaust the question. We seek a real and understanding synthesis. We want a real collectivism, not a poetical idea—a means whereby men and women of all sorts, all kinds of humanity, may pray together, sing together, stand side by side, feel the same wave of emotion, develop a collective being. Doubtless right-spirited men are praying now at a thousand discrepant altars. But for the most part those who pray imagine those others who do not pray beside them are in error, they do not know their common brotherhood and salvation. Their brotherhood is marked by analysable differences ; theirs is a dispersed collectivism ; their churches are only a little more extensive than their individualities and intenser in their collective separation. . . .

" There was an attempt at a Reformation in the Catholic Church, and through a variety of causes it failed. It detached great masses from the Catholic Church, and left that organisation impoverished intellectually and spiritually ; but it achieved no reconstruction at all. It achieved no reconstruction because the movement as a whole, lacked an adequate grasp of one funda-mentally necessary idea, the idea of Catholicity. It fell into particularism and failed. It set up a vast process of fragmenta-tion among Christian associations. It drove huge fissures through the once common platform. . . .

" The Reformation, the reconstruction of the Catholic Church, lies still before us. It is a necessary work. It is a work strictly parallel to the reformation and expansion of the organised state. Together, these processes constitute the general duty before mankind."

From " First and Last Things," by H. G. WELLS.
(Bk. iii. § 13—" *The Idea of the Church.*")

CHAPTER XIII

THE PREPARATION OF MISSIONARIES

Six of the eight full days of Conference had now passed. Were an attempt to be made to sum up their collective message thus far, it would surely be :—If THIS be the task before the Church ; if the evangelisation of all the world, the Christianising of the nations by a gospel presented in its fulness and its universality, by an education as profound as spirit and as wide as life, through daughter-churches raised to the measure of the stature of the fulness of Christ :—if THIS be the task before the Church, then *what manner of men must they be who are sent to set their hands to it, and what manner of Church must that be which sends them !*

The men Sent—the Church that Sends. And so the two remaining days were now to be given to the consideration of the Reports of the two remaining Commissions on " The PREPARATION OF MISSIONARIES," and " THE HOME BASE."

And so, too, the sequence of thought from the deliberations of the previous day was carried on. For the Training of Missionaries at the Home Base was to supply one of the most obvious applications of the need and possibility of co-operation, for which the momentous resolution of yesterday had so signally prepared the way.

I.

With very great expectancy was the discussion of the
REPORT ON THE TRAINING OF MISSIONARIES approached
on this last day but one, and most of all by the missionary
members of the Conference, who felt an acutely personal
interest in the subject. Moreover, the Report to be
discussed was one of the ablest and most valuable of the
series. Now, for the first time, had this all-important
subject received a really adequate attention : since now,
for the first time, it had been considered by the collective
intelligence of Reformed Christendom. Surely this day
would leave it beyond all doubt that changes of far-reaching character were going immediately to be made in the
ideals and the methods of missionary training !

This high hope did indeed become one of the most
settled and definite convictions left by the Edinburgh
Conference, though perhaps it is not unfair to say that
it was not so much to this day's discussion that that
conviction was owed. It was owed to the Conference
itself, taken as a whole, and to the Report of this Commission. The discussion itself, though good things were
said during its course, was at a disadvantage. For one
thing, it was humanly inevitable that there should be
some reaction after the strong tension and excitement of
yesterday. Then, possibly, the subject did not lend itself
so well to discussion as some of the others. The Report
had summed up all that was to be said on the present
state of things, and on the broad principles of missionary
training. What most people wished to hear discussed
was what was immediately to be done to carry out those
principles. Yet here, of course, the Conference worked
under a radical limitation—no one of its members was
empowered to make any authoritative proposal, or proposals, which might have served as the basis of a practical

discussion. The Conference had no executive power, and the very men who were most concerned with this question at the Home Base—secretaries of societies, heads of mission colleges, chairmen of candidates' boards, and the like—probably felt they had no right to dwell on the particular defects of the institutions they re-presented, and no authority to commit, or seem to commit, those institutions to any scheme of reform.

Nevertheless, if one conviction more than another was left in the minds of the delegates to Edinburgh, 1910, it was that a profound reform of missionary training was about to take place ; and that this Report had made co-operation in effecting that reform possible. For now the Churches and Societies had in their hands a document to which they had already assented, because it was virtually written by themselves ; a document which possessed the moral authority to command consent and compel action, and gave a definite aim and a definite ideal to be worked out everywhere and by all.

2.

The Report was indeed a masterly document, a con-tribution of the first order to the philosophy and art of training, not only of missionary workers but even of workers generally. Its Committee represented the highest talent and the best experience to be found on both sides of the Atlantic ; its correspondents were the men and women engaged in the task, responsible secretaries of Boards, and experienced workers in the field ; and the time and labour which one and all had given to their task were lavish. Need more be said to prove the moral authoritativeness of this document, the study of which would have been bound to influence the whole Church, even had the Edinburgh Conference never met ? The whole Church, be it said ; for if the Report will help the missionary Societies to make the reforms of which they have long felt the need, it will also be to the rank and file of the Church a revelation of the existence of the problem, and the meaning of missionary training itself. Nay, it will do more : it will convince complacent critics that they have part and lot in this matter ; it will drive all to recognise that the problem of the men Sent is the problem of the Church that Sends.

A glance at the contents of the Report is enough to reveal the reality and the extent of the problem. The subject of missionary training is first connected with the situation on the mission field to-day, which the reader of this book also has been considering in several great aspects. Thus the Report is linked on to four of the other seven. There is then given an exhaustive account, analysis and classification, of the agencies which to-day select and prepare missionary candidates—Boards, institutions, general theological and special missionary colleges—pointing out their merits, but showing their deficiencies in relation to the task as revealed in the first chapter. It then considers the *fundamental* principles of preparation for missionary work, and their application to the training of ordained, lay, medical, and women missionaries. And then it passes to consider the *special* preparation needed to equip the missionary, of which language-study is the most outstanding aspect. It concludes with practical findings or proposals, and with a final word to the Church.

3.

No address at the presentation of the eight Reports made a deeper impression on the Conference than that now delivered by the Chairman of this Commission, Prof. Douglas Mackenzie. As he stood to present the Report, one knew instinctively that the fine presence of the tall soldierly figure was just the counterpart of a finely-tempered mind, a commanding intellect. The son of a missionary statesman, the alumnus of a great Scottish University, successively professor and principal of leading colleges in the New World, he spoke with the authority of absolute competence, and the earnestness, nay, the passion, of a man who felt that he had a most serious message to deliver. His consciousness of the defects of the present system, and the relative failures reported to the Commission from the mission field as its direct result, was clearly heavy upon him ; never before had the Conference listened to quite such plain speaking. Faithful were the wounds of this friend.

Yet he opened with a note of lofty ambition, and through all was an undertone of strongest hope. Nothing, he insisted, would draw the Church's best to give itself to the world-wide work of the Gospel so much as the conviction that that work calls for the Church's best. And nothing would create this conviction so much as the knowledge that missionary training is worthy of so great a work. Educators would read this Report, many of them men out of sympathy with mission work ; but sympathy for that work would come with the conviction that the Church is taking it seriously enough to lavish on it the pains of a commensurate preparation. " Students in our Universities," he cried, " are ready to be kindled into enthusiasm, if only we can make the avenue of the mission-field seem as large and as worthy as the avenue of any of the great professions of the world." (That it is indeed so this Edinburgh Conference had surely proved up to the hilt.) In a word, there are thoughtful and intelligent men all over these countries of the

West who are prepared to become increasingly interested in the modern forward movement—when they see that it is conducted in a way that compels respect. Not only so, there are thoughtful and intelligent men in the non-Christian world itself who will judge by this Report, and by the Church's action, of the value which Christendom sets on *them*, and on the enterprise of bringing to their nations the message of Christianity. Business men too, in the best sense of the word, men who judge of causes by those who plan and execute them and by the efficacy of the methods they employ, these men will allow their interest to be captured for missions, when they see that the Church has realised that even new efforts, resulting in whatever reinforcements of men and money, must be fruitless unless those men are trained to do also a new work. These were the high ambitions with which this Commission sent forth its Report, jealous for the glory of Christ and His world-wide cause.

And even if no effort resulting in large reinforcements of men and money is made, the *quality* of the few who may go will triumph over the absence of money, and neutralise many other obstacles and drawbacks. The whole matter on the human side of it, he said, hinges on the quality of the missionary, and therefore becomes a supreme question for this Conference.

Dr Mackenzie found that the knowledge which the missionary requires might be compressed into two clauses —the knowledge of Christianity, and the knowledge of the country to which he brings Christianity. They do not take long to repeat, these two small clauses ; but in their relation to each other how complex becomes their demand ! The foregoing chapters have surely been a sufficient commentary upon this statement. Men who all their lives long have to teach, what a knowledge of the science and art of teaching should they have ! Men who

have to preach the gospel to minds to which its initial
presuppositions are completely strange, what a knowledge should they have of those minds, with their interests, their traditions, their beliefs and their whole
ethos! And, similarly, what a knowledge should they
have of the religion of Christ, in all its universality and
spirituality! It is unnecessary to labour the matter.
It is tremendously clear when one is brought full up to it;
but the things involved by it only become clear when
one thinks it through,—just as it is only to the eyes which
gaze stedfastly and closely at some shelly beach that
there dawns, very gradually, the revelation of the
wonderful varieties crowded together there.

What, then, of our existing system and the results it
has produced? It was now that the speaker's tone
became so very grave. He made every safeguard
against exaggeration, or any foolish ignoring of the great
men that have worked and are working in the mission
field, or of the results of these men's work. Full admissions
were made as to the value of the training that had helped
to make these men what they were and are. Yet it
was from the mission field itself, from these men themselves, and from those who have most to do with missionary preparation at home, that the severest criticisms,
the bitterest complaints had come! There was no
deliberate neglect on the part of the home societies;
just as there was no deliberate neglect on the part of the
missionary, who found himself shrinking from the really
difficult tasks on the field itself, because he felt within
himself he was incompetent to face them: incompetent
to stand up to this Mohammedan Sheikh, and that
Brahmin pundit! . . . No, there was no deliberate
neglect, and it was not his fault, or anybody's fault in
particular. The blame must be shared all round, and a
united effort made to make the training of missionaries

worthy of their work,—and not the training of missionaries only, but of all workers in God's work, for it is certain that the standard of missionary training can never rise higher than that of the training, which the Church gives to all the candidates for all her ministries. The Church will get the workers she desires and the workers she deserves. In the last analysis, the state of missionary training is the state of the ambitions, of the ideals, and of the life of the CHURCH, of all Christians at home!

Such was the chairman's summing up—or this hearer's impression of his summing up—of the Report. The reader who began this chapter thinking that here at any rate was a subject that concerns the expert and the specialist, may be already convinced that it is a subject of the deepest general interest. He certainly would have been so convinced had he heard Douglas Mackenzie's presentation of the Report.

4.

In the remainder of this chapter an attempt will be made briefly to illustrate these principal aspects of a great subject.

And at the very outset let an important objection, or rather apprehension, be squarely faced and met. Is there not a danger of exaggeration in all this ? of swinging over into a disastrous extreme ? of deifying intellectual ability to the detriment of spiritual capacity ? of contemning the commonplace missionary, and putting altogether too high a premium upon cleverness ? in fact, of over-elaborating and overdoing this whole business of preparation and equipment ?

These considerations, though they were not urged as objections or even as deep apprehensions, were given a very large place in the discussion. The Candidates' Secretary of the Church Missionary Society, for example, while admitting to the full the need of reform, urged that there was a danger of missing much valuable material if we think too exclusively of leaders, not to say the danger to the morals of young men who might think to become leaders when they should still be followers. Once, as another reminded the Conference, God chose out of all the "candidates" a man whom Samuel would have passed over, and made of that man a Leader. And like those who assert that Wellington would to-day infallibly be refused a commission, so Walter B. Sloan of the China Inland Mission told of some mighty men of valour in China who would infallibly (he believed) have been refused by some Candidates' Committees. (But the speaker soon showed that the China Inland Mission spend a great deal of trouble in training their man when they have selected him.) Various delegates expressed their conviction that the principal need is for men of the Bible, men of love, men of a Christlike nature. . . . Most effectively of all, the apostolic figure of Bishop Ridley, missionary and bishop of the Indians in North-West Canada, urged with all the authority of a first-rate and first-hand experience that sympathy is the one thing of paramount importance ; the mission field needed a Bishop French, but, what of a Rowland Bateman, who, by the sheer force of sympathy and the human and divine love for men, became the prince of evangelistic missionaries in the Punjab ?

Thus powerfully did these speakers enforce once more the plea of the Conference's friar-missionary, Brother Western, a few days before, for *the commonplace missionary*.

It was made amply evident, therefore, that this plea for the commonplace missionary had been fully taken into account by those who nevertheless desiderated a far better training for missionaries. The Superior of Mirfield, for example, said that the main requirement in the mission field can be expressed in one syllable, *"Saints"*: and then showed how deeply true it is that spirituality itself, like every other thing that lives and grows, needs training; needs teachers, too, who know the laws of that training. Miss Ruth Rouse of the Student Christian Movement among women—and here let it be said, the women delegates though so late in coming to the front now made up for it by the uniform high quality of their addresses—showed strongly the need for specialised training in certain cases, and better training in all cases: and then went on to show how real the demand is for the all-round training of the soul, so that men and women might go forth with a whole, developed human capacity, and meet at every point the souls of those to whom they go. Such an ideal, of course, includes character and spirituality just as much as it includes a developed intellect. Similarly, and perhaps most strikingly of all, Fr. Kelly of Kelham, one of the most daring and original of workers in the sphere of clergy-training, gave a yet deeper application of this Christian-platonist doctrine. He spoke of the difficulty of training itself, in the absolute: the difficulty of teaching anybody anything. The teacher must be, first of all, a man who is a seer of the thing he teaches. Then he must know how to make, or leave, his disciples to see that thing for themselves. And, thirdly, Christian "knowledge," a tremendously simple thing in itself, and an equally complex thing when applied to all life, must be known and shown to be practical through and through; every point in theology must be taught as vitally connected with the common life of men, or not at all. The bank-manager must be convinced that Christian doctrine and the running of his bank are intimately connected; car-drivers and professional footballers, that theology—

the Virgin-Birth, Cross, Resurrection, and all else—
makes them understand their work better and do it with
more energy and more purpose. Theology, in short, must
be so taught that it throws light upon the life that
men, not parsons, lead. . . .

"That is the view of Christianity that we want for the
mission field, that the missionaries ask for; and I cannot help
thinking that they hardly seem to imagine how entirely new a
thing they are asking, and how little we ourselves understand
of it."

Truly, if there was a Socrates at the head of every
missionary college or theological hall, we should say that
the problem of missionary training was *ipso facto* solved;
for his disciples (like those of a Greater than Socrates)
would then be certain of learning, not things, but a
method. If each missionary who arrives on the
mission-field arrived ignorant of everything save how
to learn, but knowing that consummately, the Eight
Commissions of the Edinburgh Conference would have
numbered, not eight, but seven. The present one
would have dropped out.

5.

The Chairman of the Commission, having heard all that
had been urged in this matter, showed that it had been
by no means lost sight of, and was included in the main
position urged by the Report.

"We are all of us one about this fundamental position that
everything depends upon the quality of the missionary that is sent
out, and that that quality is not merely intellectual but spiritual,
not merely spiritual but physical, not merely physical but ethical,
and not any one of these, but all of them together. It is the
quality of a finely disciplined traveller. By this we do not mean
a genius, but someone built for the commonplace missionary.

P

Brethren, do not be afraid, you will not get too many of the other kind. It is the average man and woman who is going out, but we want every man and woman refined to that finish of power, of explicit power, which hitherto has not been possible, and we believe that if missionary education becomes a matter of anxious concern, and definite planning on a large scale, then the commonplace missionary will no longer be so-called. He will be so informed with wisdom, and with the power of the Spirit of God, that his efficiency will be multiplied tenfold."

6.

We are now in a position to understand, and not misunderstand, the emphasis placed by the Report, by scores of correspondents, and by nearly all the speakers, on the necessity for reform in definitely missionary training. The following wise words, by one of the great African missionaries, Stewart of Lovedale, carry entire conviction :—

"Complete and thoroughly trained fitness for work, whatever that may be, is not merely *the tendency, but the absolute demand of the present day,* and the man who possesses that fitness and the capacity to use it is the man who is preferred for any position. Without special knowledge, he has little chance of success either as an applicant or worker. It is this very training that the missionary does not get ; the purely theological training he receives in common with the minister whose life is to be spent in a country parish is good as far as it goes, but for him as a missionary it is wholly defective, because incomplete."

"'The Dawn,'" this great African goes on to exclaim, in the words of a proverb of his adopted land, "'*The Dawn does not come twice to awake a man.*'" We have one life and one opportunity of definite preparation for it. "If men are not sent to India, even to plant trees there, without a course of instruction at Cooper's Hill, they should not be sent to plant Christianity in India, Africa and elsewhere without some training to fit them for such work."

And—in passing it may be said—an African delegate bore out completely the words of the South African missionary when he vigorously denied that a less highly-trained missionary was good enough for Africa, as contrasted with the countries of the Orient. The highest gifts, he maintained, and the highest training, were called for in African missionaries as much as any other, and the non-recognition of this truth had been fraught with deplorable results.

The memory of names like Mackenzie, Livingstone, Steere, Krapf, Stewart, Mackay, Pilkington, Coillard, Scott, Bentley, Grenfell, Lawes, and many another, surely are enough to clinch the argument.

So many-sided is the missionary's life, so numerous the calls made upon him, that it would be easy to multiply out of all reason the subjects which it would be advisable to study. One delegate said that he had added up the subjects which he could have desired to study before reaching the field, and found that had he given them all their due he would have started work at the age of seventy! (much about the age, by the way, at which Raymund Lull actually did begin his work in North Africa!) A member of the Commission had made a list of twenty-four different subjects, suggested by various correspondents as likely to be profitable, exclusive of "extras." A correspondent from China suggested eight groups of subjects. At Yale University the "Courses of Study of the Missionary Department" number one hundred-and-three items under thirteen heads!

The Report, however, had reduced the essential groups to five. The demand for such teaching, said a member of the Commission, had come not from themselves but from the missionaries in the field. And it was on the strength of the correspondence, not from a *priori* considerations, that these essential five headings had been suggested.

7.

1. *The Study of Comparative Religion.*—The reader, when he recalls for a moment the chapter on " the Gospel Message in relation to the Non-Christian Religions," will hardly ask for this point to be laboured. He will remember the solemn impression made by that Commission ; the conviction that this deeper study of Christianity, in its reciprocal relation to other religions, is fraught with the most profound significance and importance, not only for the missionary but even for the Church itself. The present Report and to-day's discussion assumed that the lesson of that Commission had been laid to heart.

2. *The Science and History of Missions.*—In spite of the infinite variety of the conditions of mission work in the different countries, from Esquimaux lands to the South Sea Islands, from Indian territories in the Americas to Japan, from Siberia to the Land of the Kaffirs, there is such a thing as a Science of Missions. And as for the " History of Missions," it begins with the Gospels and the Acts ; there are vivid lights upon it in the Epistles and a lightning-flash from the Apocalypse ; it is continued in the story of the Apologists and the Gnostics of the second century, of the persecutions in the second and third, of the rapid break down of heathenism in the fourth, of the mass movements in the fifth and following ; of the Christianising of Ireland and Scotland—Patrick in Erin, Columba of fragrant Iona in Alba ; of the Christianising of England and Europe by those mediæval missions, which, as Fr. Frere so clearly showed at one of the evening meetings, are so richly suggestive in their

comparison and contrasts with the missions of to-day ; the history of Islam, its reproach, and the tardy lifting of that reproach away, beginning with the meteoric figure of Lull ; the history of Jesuit missions with Xavier, and of all Roman missions with their mixed gold and dross ; down to the crowded history of the modern period, from beautiful Zinzendorf down to the heroes of yesterday and to-day, a history perhaps best read in many a noble biography :—surely *there* is a course, which, properly taught, would be as passionately interesting as a romance, and would of itself distil a science of missions from its rich secretions of missionary ideals and methods, circumstances and experiences, doings and sufferings ?

3. *Sociology.*—Again the reader will recal how those two days on which the Church in the Mission Field, and Education in relation to National Life were discussed emphasised the way missions are moulding the history of great nations : while many African races would never even have had the beginnings of a history but for missions. " The missionary should be recognised," says the Report, " as having a relation to the whole development of the East, which is social in its widest sense." These men and women who are being trained in missionary colleges are going to be leaders, some of them, participants all of them, in movements which are transforming the very fibre of ancient civilisations, discarding the old and introducing the new. Thus Dr Edward W. Capen of Boston, a member of the Commission, in his speech at the debate. The missionary must appreciate the significance of these movements, note their similarity with world-wide social movements in the historic past, and their place in social evolution. These were no empty words. At that very Conference it had been shown how Japan is looking in vain for help in the terribly

novel problem created by the industrial and economic forces which she has suffered to be let loose in her midst. China, too, is summoning up spirits which she will find it was easier to summon up than it will be to control. From whence shall she find guidance and counsel ? No delegate could forget Dr Coffin's striking address on the night of the first full day of Conference, in which he appealed for a Christian sociology in the West so that we may give a Christian sociology to the East. The social work and the missionary work of the Church are two fruits of the same passion, and both must be kept equally prominent, equally dear to her heart.

All these things constituted one single argument for the study of a science of missionary sociology. This, of course, includes the indispensable study of the social life and traditions and customs in the different mission lands to which the candidates are to go.

" Much has been said in this Conference about the need of naturalising Christianity, and of the danger and folly of westernising the nations of the East. If this danger is to be avoided, it is necessary that the body of missionaries should be prepared by a study of sociology, both general and particular, to work for a Christian community which shall be both Oriental and Christian."

4. *The Teaching of How to Teach.*—The Chairman of the Commission had complained that so many preachers and ordained men are without any educational training, and so many educationalists have been given no training in theology : he might have added a third class, educationalists who have had no training in education ! As, however, these abound in the most expensive schools of the West, it would hardly be fair to blame missions too severely. The writer remembers the late Bishop Creighton, at an ordination address, impressing on the ordinands, in a peculiar, almost awestruck tone, what it

meant to be setting their hand to a work in which they would be always and everywhere—*teachers* What shall be said of the missionary, every moment of whose life is spent in some form of direct or indirect teaching; who is always like one speaking to children?—for even the educated non-Christian mind is as blank as a child's in regard to the preacher's message, while the uneducated or barbarous mind is ever a child's indeed. Surely then every missionary, and not only the educationalist so-called, should receive some training in psychology, some practical knowledge of how to present truth, in fact of how to teach? Yet it is a strange thing, but true, that even to-day, or certainly till yesterday, men, themselves indifferently taught and knowing nothing of teaching, have been put down in mission schools to learn from their own failures, if they ever do learn, how not to teach. Besides, as Miss Jane Latham—till lately a Principal of a training college in London—reminded the Conference, nearly every missionary has at some time in his life not merely to teach in his general evangelistic work, not merely to teach in his particular educational work, but he has also to *teach teachers to teach*. . . . Enough! It was the greatest Teacher of all who taught the impossibility of the blind leading the blind.

5. *Language Study*.—As every food but bread may, in starvation times, be economised, so language study remains the irreducible minimum of the missionary's special equipment. Yet even on this point the Chairman of the Commission had grave words to speak. The Report merely voiced numerous testimonies from the missionaries themselves and from competent observers, when he affirmed that all was not well even here; that the Societies at home did not seem to be quite aware of the true state of things; that language syllabuses were often absurdly imperfect, the instruction unsuperin-

tended, utterly antiquated and unsound. Here, also, of course, the assertions were safeguarded. No class has produced finer linguists than the class of missionaries ; some speakers claimed that practically all do reach a respectable facility in their language. . . . Terms like these are, it need hardly be pointed out, relative. It entirely depends on what the standard is taken to be. One critic will regard as deplorable results on which another will look with equanimity or even complacency.

But absolutely no doubt was left on the mind of the Conference that vast improvements should be made, could be made, and also would be made, in language-training. A spirit of intense hopefulness prevailed. A brisk debate developed on interesting technical questions as to where and how the training in language should be given. Doctors disagreed with refreshing completeness. The greatest authority on African languages in Germany, or the world, Professor Meinhof,—no arm-chair philologist for all his phonetics and syllabaries, but a practical linguist and teacher of languages,—was emphatic for a through grounding at home before going to the field. Professor Harlan P. Beach of Yale, a man of rich experience both at home and abroad, vigorously supported the same view. Yet the Home Director of the China Inland Mission, which has been, as a Society, perhaps most successful of all in language-training, was equally emphatic against this course ! And his views also met with loud approval. Others were for combining the two methods. Training-centres at home were talked of, Government Oriental Colleges, training-centres in the field—Cairo for the Arabic language, and similar centres for the languages of India, China, Japan. . . .

Probably a reconciliation of all these views will very soon be arrived at. Probably the study at home, if superintended by men who have a practical knowledge of the language, and taught by natives of that language, will always have its own place and value. This, as was pointed out, may, and must, be effected by co-operation. It can never annul the equal necessity of co-operating in language-training on the field, whether by common training-centres or by co-ordinated and unified language-syllabuses and examinations.

8.

Co-operation, in fact, became the victorious note of the day. It was struck resolutely and resonantly by Mrs Creighton at the very beginning of the session. She spoke of the founding of a United Board of Missionary Study which should carry on the work of this Commission, applying its conclusions, and assisting the Societies to carry them out. In each country where missionary interest is alive should be a Board like this, and in each case it might develop into a central missionary training-centre. Miss Belle Bennett, a delegate from a Mission Board in America, showed that some such common plan was already being practised there. And Miss Humphrey, a member of an Anglican Candidates' Committee, warmly welcomed the idea of co-operation :—

" Why should each society go on throwing up its little molehill of knowledge and experience in such things, when we might all contribute to raise one great mountain of wisdom—for the benefit of all, as well as of each ? And in the meantime, I, for one, go away from this Conference, fully purposing to try whether those of us in Great Britain, who are interested in the selection and training of women-missionaries, cannot meet informally in the autumn to confer as to the possibility of common action in certain matters as a beginning."

And, finally, the same note was struck by the Chairman of the Commission in his reply on the whole debate.

He hopèd and believed that the Continuation Committee appointed yesterday would take notice of this universal demand for co-operation in missionary study, and would make it one of their earliest actions to enquire into the possibility of forming these Central Boards of Missionary Study.

All this special missionary training, however, is *general,* as being indispensable for all missionaries. There is, in addition, the *specialised* training for those who are going to take up some more highly specialised form of mission work. Obviously this last is only needed by comparatively few. The Report has a full section on it, but it is unnecessary to say anything about it here. Two remarks gave the true principles which should regulate such training. " This specialised training is right if the specialised demand is right " was one. And the other was the golden word of the Nestor of the Conference, Dr Miller, when he was led to the dais.—The Conference and the Church seemed to be learning now, he said, that it is not one form but many forms of activity that are needed for the Christianisation of national life. " Nothing had rejoiced him more than to perceive how fully that lesson has been learned." And he pointed out how the danger of attempting too much would be obviated by the distribution of this specialised labour among the many members and organisations which make up the whole missionary body. And thus, too, the Christian ideal, the co-operation of all in the one work, would be realised.

9.

And so the discussion on this Commission linked itself with the great event of yesterday. But it also pointed forward to that of the morrow ; the missionary is, etymologically and actually, only the Sent : he represents a Sender. The Church is that Sender. " The Boards are hindered by the Churches themselves," cried a delegate from America : the Churches should desire " that their very best life be put into this enterprise." As it is, if mediocre men are sent out, there are protests, and if the best men are sent out there are protests. By the Church, says the Report in its summing-up, by the Christian consciousness of the whole community, is exercised the decisive power, controlling the supply of candidates and dominating each stage of their training.

Thus the concluding passages of this Report, as of several of the others, are the most impressive and far-appealing of all. The significant title of the chapter in which they occur is, a Last Word to the Church.

The attitude of the community is seen in the smallest things as well as the greatest; the Bible-teaching[1] it gives, or does not give, in family, day school, Sunday School, and parish ; in the missionary books it does or does not supply to its children to read; the missionary ideals it does or does not hold up before its sons and daughters ; the self-sacrifice, the tradition of giving and of serving, that are or are not seen in its families ; the missionary information through magazine or study-circle, amongst children, amongst boys and girls, among young men and women, in colleges and in parishes ; the missionary fire burning, or extinct—frankly or otherwise—in the Minister of religion, in the Teachers of the theological colleges, and the Disciples that sit at their feet :—*these* are the things that determine the supply of candidates for the mission field, its rise and fall, its quantity and quality.

---

[1] It ought to be a matter of general concern that candidates " are frequently rejected for lack of this rudimentary knowledge," and that " years of missionary purpose are frequently wasted without any intelligent attempt at self-preparation."

" If the Church were fully alive, every member would be awake to the obligation of personal service " ; and, " If the missionaries are to be more fully prepared it is not too much to say that this can only be done by raising the standard even of the home ministry. . . ."

But not only so. A few exceptional individuals will always, no doubt, soar away from all the standards familiarised to them by their environment, whether it be their family, their congregation, their Church, or their country; and these, whether they go abroad or stay at home, will always in an exceptional way directly reflect and show forth the image of the Lord Christ. But it remains true that the great mass of candidates for service abroad, or service at home, are profoundly and permanently affected by the environment in which they have been brought up, and from which they have caught their ideas and ideals of the Christian life. If these are mediocre, then those youths and maidens will start from mediocrity ; their higher will be but a little higher than the tame general level. Thus the Gospel goes forth on its quest " weighted with a fatal disparagement," and it is to the easy tolerance of a beggarly standard of Christian living and Christian giving and Christian character at home, it is to *this* that that fatal disparagement is due. The World is One now. But does the Church stand as One behind this enterprise to win that world, to lose herself that she may save herself and the world too ? The World is one, and year by year the tides of spiritual influence between East and West ebb and flow with an ever-increasing unimpededness : a tremendous fact, that is " a deep and solemn challenge to us to prove that our faith is life indeed to us, and that the Kingdom of God is for us the supreme reality and the final fact." If the Spirit of Jesus holds sway in the bosom of the Church from which these Sent ones go into all the world to preach the

Gospel, they will go forth after a Missionary Training received even from their mother's womb. And *then* will they have power to baptise all nations into the fulness of the Name, and to teach them to observe all things which He commanded, and which they learned from Him in successive classes of one great School—the Church at the Home Base.

CHAPTER XIV

" THE HOME BASE OF MISSIONS "

THE last day of the Edinburgh Conference had now arrived, and with it the subject which was logically not last but first. The deliberations of the Conference had begun, as it were, with the apex, and now, as the very title of the Commission presenting its Report to-day announced, it had worked its way down to the foundation. Was that foundation laid deep and broad enough to support the Building it was proposed to build ? Had the Church of God resources great enough, organisation strong enough, spirit keen enough, to carry through her proper task ?

It was possible of course to have proceeded by the opposite way. But such a course, though eminently logical, would have been eminently ineffective. It was the overwhelming sense of the task to be accomplished that gave reality and desperate earnestness to the reckoning of the resources which are at the present disposal of the Church for that task.

The individual child, it is true, begins by learning about that which is nearest to hand, and gradually advances towards the most remote. But with the race-child it was not so ; astronomy, the remotest science, was also its earliest, and geology, the nearest of all, its latest ; mankind was overwhelmed with the significance of the stars seven millenniums before he gave a thought to the significance of the fossils, upon which his foot struck every time he walked abroad. And somewhat similarly, though the individual Christian extends his interest from his parish outward to the round world itself, the Christian Church as a body seems to have arrived at the science of the Home Base almost last of all.

But the question of his foundations drives the builder to examine in its turn the sub-soil in which they are to be laid. And thus his thought passes from the building that man makes to the great earth that God made. So also was the Conference driven by the consideration of her Home Base to take thought concerning that on which that base was based:—GOD. The ultimate problem presented to the Conference was the problem of the Church's faith in GOD.

I.

With how little of system the science of the Home Base of Missions has been studied as a whole may be concluded from the modest claim of the Chairman of the Commission in presenting the Report, that after all their labours they had not perhaps attained to a science of the Home Base, but they had at least cleared their way to a position from which a true science might now begin, and increasingly continue. The Report, therefore, marks an epoch in the history of missions no less than the others. The number of those who had been consulted and corresponded with was too many even to be acknowledged by name. The mass of the material accumulated could not this time have been well ranged on the Conference table at all. To throw light upon one aspect of the subject alone—that of missionary knowledge in schools and colleges—nearly six hundred schools and colleges were corresponded with, and yet the result of all that mass of correspondence is compressed into seven columns out of the hundred and eleven which constituted the Report! This gives an idea of the thoroughness with which the work was done.

The task of the Commission was thus defined by the Chairman, Dr J. L. Barton of Boston, in his opening address, " to discover how to develop and employ the entire resources of the Church." These resources, he said, are spiritual and material, and if the former were realised there would be no further difficulty about the former. But what do we find ?—for it is well to face the salient fact at the outset :—one of the first discoveries of the Commission was the existence of *a non-contributing Church*. In America, for example, one-tenth of the communicants (said the speaker) furnish nineteen-twentieths of the total sum given ; and twenty of the leading communions give to " Foreign Missions " but one-eighteenth of their total contributions to all objects. This could hardly be called self-impoverishment for the work abroad, remarked the Chairman. The consequence is that the Commission was at every point of its investigation " confronted by this stupendous fact, that in all the world there is not a missionary society that is properly supported to-day for the conduct of its work ! " " All the societies are organised for a far larger work than they are able to conduct because of the lack of support." Christendom is not yet missionary. All Christians have not set their hand to the Christian enterprise. " They do not," said the Chairman in one arresting remark, " *they do not love the work.*"

And yet nothing short of this can be the ideal at which to aim—that the Church should set its hand to this, its most distinctive task, as *one*. As the delegate who spoke first said, the Church of the living God must arise as a great Missionary Society. How to realise this ideal is the grand problem, the problem which was considered on this last day. It is, indeed, a sign of an unnatural state of things that it should be called an "ideal" at all: in the very nature of the case, it should be an essential part not of the ideal but of the actual definition of the Church. And the Conference was reminded that there is one communion among all the existing communions of to-day which has in actual truth made worldwide evangelisation the first of its ordinary recognised duties, involved in church-membership itself. The Moravian Church is a church without a missionary Society, for it is a missionary society with an active membership co-extensive, and necessarily co-extensive, with the membership of the Church!

And this Report, with the discussion upon it, made it clear that the problem of the Home Base will not be solved until this principle of the Moravian communion becomes extended to all the other communions of Christendom. The missionary enterprise is perhaps no longer considered as belonging to the faddist. But there is a further stage to be won. It must cease to be considered a matter for the specialist.

2.

To restore to the whole Church this sense of her proper function amounts to nothing short of the re-creation of the Church—a work which only God Himself can work, yet a work in which man can join by the almost forgotten secret of prayer. This supreme consideration, which takes us to the highest altitude of all, had been brought home to the Conference again and again from the first day, and increasingly as its climax was approached. Yet it did not negate, but rather involved, the practical question which was now before the Conference, how to

Q

take every phase of western Christian life in detail, and bring home to it what we might call for short *the Moravian ideal;* how to make the passion for taking the Gospel to all the World permeate every rank and class and definable section of Christendom ; how to get it appropriated by the individual in every stage of his growth from childhood to maturity ; how to lodge it in the heart of the family, as part of family life, and similarly into the heart of the congregation, the parish, the diocese or other major division of Church organisation, as part of its being; how to bring it into the school, the college, the theological hall, the ministry of the Church ; how to make laymen, business-men and professional men, adopt it as their own ; how to familiarise the press with it ; how to bring it about that those who leave home, emigrants, clerks, merchants, officers and men of the civil and military services, shall take it abroad with them :—such in detail are the several aspects of the one grand problem, and into every one of these does the Report of this Commission inquire. And to these also was the attention of the Edinburgh Conference directed in the crowning day of its days.

Such is what the Chairman neatly termed " the Training of the Home Base "—a training which, as we saw in the conclusion of last chapter, is prior to the Training of Missionaries. It need hardly be said that technical details fall outside the scope of the present work. These must be left to the many ministries charged with working them out. And though the Conference itself was concerned with the technique as well as the principles of mission, much of what was said in regard to these details may be passed over in this account. It will suffice simply to indicate the many-sidedness of the great problem, of making the whole Church one Society for the carrying of the one Gospel to one whole world.

3.

The work among the youth of the Church was truly described as the Hope of the Future. And at this Conference, so the writer of this account was informed by one who had taken a great part in organising the Conference, nothing was more remarkable and more full of encouragement, nothing gave a greater impression of enormous potential energy, than the meetings for young people which were organised in the city of Edinburgh in connection with the Conference, and other meetings at which the principles of work among the young were discussed. It was there most of all that the prospect could be contemplated with hope. And some of the most notable utterances of the whole Conference were delivered upon this subject in its several aspects,— work among the very young, among children and young people, among school-boys and school-girls, and so up to the men and women in the universities and colleges of the West.

The very enumeration of these stages brings out a truth of which the Conference was most emphatically reminded, that the education of these several classes must be undertaken in a scientific spirit in order to yield any result. Otherwise, as one delegate who was devoting all his time to the subject put it, a vast amount of the work done may be rather the Despair than the Hope of the Future. " This is the first time," he continued, " that it has ever been possible for a new generation of the Church to be trained from infancy for the Church's great task along the lines of an assured science." And he went on to show how this opportunity made it inevitably necessary that new methods, in harmony with modern educational science, should be thought out ; that workers should be specially trained for the work ;

that the knowledge and experience of all should be combined (here was co-operation yet once more !) ; and that the attainment of a limited quantity of good results should be aimed at, rather than an unlimited quantity of bad ones. And this warning was repeated in the most unmeasured terms by an educationist delegate, the Principal of a training college in London.[1] Speaking with almost savage earnestness, as a critic who only desired the good of the object of his criticism, he commented on the hopelessly unscientific methods too often employed by the Church among her young, with the result, too often, of disgusting them with the whole subject instead of attracting to it. The psychology of children must be taken into account by those who seek to train them in missions, just as much as in any other subject. And this all the more because the very ambitiousness of the Church's present aim

" is tending to carry the missionary impulse back into childhood or early adolescence, and [so] is removing it from the atmosphere of home to the hard seats, the bare floors, and the often unwelcome associations of a school-room or a meeting-house."

Thus the old haphazard methods which were sweetened by the loving associations of the home, and were excusable at a time when the missionary impulse generally came in late adolescence, will no longer serve : they must be subjected to changes as radical as the situation demands. The work and the worker must both be skilled. Otherwise the worker had best let it alone altogether. The leaders of the world-wide enterprise owe it to the child himself, to the greatness of the enterprise itself, and to the reputation of the Church herself, to think out not one scheme only, but as many graduated schemes as there are classes to be reached ; schemes which will

[1] Rev. W. L. Hume Campbell.

recognise the personality of the child with his trinity of intellect, emotion, will ; and which will therefore make real demands upon the voluntary teachers to show their good will, by themselves undergoing a training worthy of the dignity of their work.

Such were some of the demands made at the Conference, and made not by cynical outsiders, but by those who are trying to carry out their precepts into practice. And here was the element of hope : that in recent years very great strides had indeed been made by the Societies both in America and Britain in the direction of these ideals. A series of text-books written on a thought-out plan ; schemes of study, worked co-operatively, for students of the universities and colleges, and for members, especially the younger members, of the Churches : such were some of the tangible results reported to the Conference. Here was a territorial system which needed development indeed, but which at least was in being, capable now of being wrought and fashioned by the hand of the educational enthusiast. The resolution of the Conference was unmistakable, and from it could be discerned the resolution of the Societies and Boards to move forward at all costs. If this is so, the words with which the educationist who has already been quoted, though uttered in the tone of warning, may be taken as a message of splendid hope.

" There never was a day when the educational possibilities were so full of promise; never a day when the future of the world trembled in the balance as it does to-day, while you make choice between the old education and the new; never a day when the childhood and adolescence of Christendom lay so unreservedly at your feet, ready to respond with its irresistible enthusiasms to a really skilled training in knowledge, in devotion, in expression,—a training which alone will enable the scholars, as they come to maturity, to claim and to win the allegiance of East and West alike to the Faith and the Obedience of the Living Christ."

And this opinion, advanced by an educationist, was strikingly though unconsciously endorsed by one who had practical knowledge both of work in a parish and in a theological college, Professor D. S. Cairns. This Chairman of a Commission which had dealt with the most (apparently) remote, most inner subject of all, had had the privilege, he said, of seeing these new schemes of missionary study in the working, and from practical experience wished to endorse " with all his force " what had been said as to the value of this method and the hopefulness of it. He could see, he said emphatically, no better way of bringing the great untouched, unmoved, uninstructed public in our Churches into devoted interest in the missionary enterprise.

And this missionary study work, too, like everything else, was found to lead the mind of the Conference to the higher problem indicated at the beginning of the chapter. " We need," said one of those most actively concerned in this great work,

" we need to face what this [work] means and what are its demands. It is the hope of the future only inasmuch as it is making for a new standard of Christian living, a truer understanding of discipleship, and a new experience of the power of the Holy Spirit of God. Into this we, who are workers among the young, must lead them. The Church's workers among children and young people must be ahead of all in the experience and discipline of the Christian life."

4.

The movement in the universities and colleges was, it is hardly necessary to say, emphasised both in the Report and in the discussion. For a quarter of a century its importance has been recognised by those who were in a position to study its quiet working. Its missionary aim is only one aspect of its aim to make the universities and colleges centres of distinctively Christian influence. And its plan of missionary study, which was nearly a decade ahead of the parallel work among the Churches and congregations, is one aspect of that missionary work which is of equal importance with its main work of securing actual candidates for the foreign service of the several Churches. The consideration of this branch of the Home Base of Missions once again directed the minds of the delegates to the high, ultimate, unescapable question—the standard of Christian life in the Church. It is surely the lowness of that standard which, in the last analysis, is accountable for the mass of intellectual unsettlement that exists among the students of the West. This matter was pointedly alluded to by the General Secretary of the Student Christian Movement in Britain. " I do not say," he said,

"that are there fewer students committed to the Christian position, —there is a large number,—but I do say that the majority of those come with great difficulty to an assurance of belief, and one result of that is, that at the time when men might, and perhaps ought to, be facing a missionary vocation they are not ready to do so. They are not sure enough of their own position viewed especially on the intellectual side, and when they reach a position of assurance, it is then too late for them to offer. I believe if you knew the facts as some others know them, there is nothing you would pray for more than the work of the Student Movement in all our colleges."

And just as the standard of the parent's consecration has an important bearing on the attitude of the child, the boy and the girl, towards the Christian enterprise, so it often has a great influence upon the son and the daughter in those years just before they leave the home. Indeed, as the same speaker pointed out, speaking from many bitter experiences as the Secretary of a Student Volunteer Movement, the parent's low standard may bear critically and injuriously upon the life-decision of his son or of his

daughter.   On this point he spoke words that startled
and hurt.   " The power of the Christian Church is
against us," he cried.   The next sentences showed what
he meant.

" It is very difficult for a man to decide to break home ties and
to go to the mission field.   Those of us who spend a great part of
our lives talking with men who are facing a missionary vocation,
realise the agony of spirit through which the greater number of
those who decide to be missionaries pass before their decision is
reached.   That decision is greatly complicated for them, and
aborted for them, by the fact that the pressure of their own home
and the pressure of their own friends is, in the majority of cases,
brought to bear against their deciding to go abroad.   I am sorry
if that remark is painful to some people here, but I believe that
from a somewhat wide experience of the colleges of this country
it can be justified.   Cannot you help us ?, and cannot you help us
by beginning reformation here in this audience ?   I say that for
this reason, that I know that Mission Board members and ministers
are often offenders in their own families."

And he backed his assertion by some lurid examples
which only showed how far harder it is for parents to
lay their children on the altar of God than it is to lay
their substance or even their own selves.

But the movement in the universities has an importance that is independent of its enlistment of actual
candidates for the missionary calling.   From the
universities and colleges go the leaders in all the walks
of life.   Again, students of to-day will soon be the parents
of the children who, in the next generation, will in their
turn take the lead.   And yet again, as the Master of
Magdalene College, Cambridge, reminded the Conference,
it is they who supply the masters in the schools, on whom
far more than on the casual preacher or lecturer the
missionary enthusiasm of the schools depend.   Dr
Donaldson had the right to speak on this subject, for, as
he told the Conference, he had been for a quarter of a

century on the staff at Eton, and for the last six years had been Head of a Cambridge college. "I think," he said,

" that too much stress is laid on trying to reach the boys. What you want to do in the Public Schools is to reach the *masters*, and I would like that point brought out. If we could only get on the staff of every public school in this country—I suppose it is true also of America—one man thoroughly keen about mission work, it would make the whole difference to the younger generation."

It is hardly necessary to say that these words apply equally to all national schools, whether " provided " or " non-provided," and prove the immense importance of strengthening the movement among students of all normal schools and training colleges.

5.

Parallel to the influences exerted in the home, the school, the college, is the church influence that embraces all. How shall all the congregations be inspired with the Moravian ideal ? The answer to the question seemed clearly to point to *the ministry of the Church*. Here was a principle which had been known as far back as the time of the prophetess Deborah . . .

> " For that the leaders took the lead in Israel,
> For that the people offered themselves willingly,
> Bless ye the Lord."

There was a clearly causal connection between the two facts which made Deborah bless God. And when shall all the leaders in our Israel be found taking the lead in this world-wide enterprise ? When they shall have all been inspired with the Moravian ideal *in their theological colleges*, where their ministerial ideal is being formed and their instruction in practical work is being elaborated. And how shall this be ? The answer given at the

Conference was threefold ; first, by inspiring students with that ideal before they reach the theological college ; secondly, by organising missionary study in those colleges themselves ; and thirdly, by ensuring that the men on the staffs of theological colleges have that ideal in their hearts. In regard to these methods some excellent things were said by a professor at an American university, himself a man intimately acquainted with the working of a school of divinity. He said how much these colleges owed to the Student Christian Movement. The missionary interest of the students has often been quite in advance of that of their teachers. But, he went on to say, what is shown in the curricula to-day does not show all that is being done for the instilling of the missionary idea, though at the same time he desiderated the addition of a course on missions even to an already over-crowded programme :

" You will find to-day that those who are teaching the whole scope of missions, and in apologetics and in theology as well, are teaching those larger lines of comparative religion, of comparative theology, of comparative ethics, so that the whole atmosphere . . . is charged with the missionary idea."

And Professor C. E. Brown concluded his well-spent five minutes by showing how theological colleges, where the Moravian ideal is alive, are bringing men to face the call of the work abroad ; are training missionary leaders for the Churches ; and are raising up a body of men who will contribute to the missionary literature of the future. In fact it is largely true that the theological halls of to-day are a master-key to the problem.

6.

The last afternoon of the Conference was drawing to a close, and there was yet one more great movement to be brought before the notice of Conference—the missionary movement organised by laymen among laymen.

As in a long race the pace quickens at the last lap; as the last and greatest spurt takes place up the straight that leads to the finish; so was it now at the Edinburgh Conference. The American layman is to these great conventions trained and seasoned. Nothing tires him. And now the close of the long Conference found him still bursting with energy. He had waited long for his opportunity, and now he was given it. An unbroken sequence of laymen speakers, almost all from the North American continent, kept the interest and the enthusiasm of the Conference on the increase till the end. Each orator seemed more animated than the one before. Breathless, the Conference was swept along in one accelerando, up to the very close of this closing session of the Committee of the whole House.

We have said lay*men*. Among these last speakers, however, was one woman speaker—Mrs Gladding, the Chairwoman of the Foreign Department of the Young Women's Christian Association of the U.S.A. Her intervention reminded the Conference of the essential importance of women's work. The fact that before her and after her were a whole company of laymen speakers only emphasised, in reality, the backwardness of men as compared with women in the world-wide enterprise, and the need for special effort on their behalf. The Chairman, Dr Barton, had at the very beginning of the day hit off the situation by the satirical stanza :—

> " In the field of Christian battle,
> In the bivouac of life,
> You will find the Christian soldier—
> Represented by his wife " . . .

and " I can assure you he is well represented," continued the Chairman of the Commission on the Home Base,

" but the Church cannot afford to rest on that representation alone." *Place aux dames* is a maxim that
there is no need to press in an enterprise where the services
of the all are indispensable. And if but few women-
speakers were heard at this Conference, and special work
for or by women was seldom mentioned, it was certainly
not because of their backwardness in this enterprise of
the world-mission. The work done by women for this
Conference, and especially on some of the Commissions,
was a sufficient proof to the contrary. The reason
was, rather, because the great leading problems
of the work at home or abroad concerned the Church
as a whole, without distinction of sex ; because in
many forms of specialised work—such as that among
children, young people, students—most of what was
said applied equally to both the sexes ; because so much
of women's work is in connection with the ordinary
parochial organisation, and stands in less need of special
treatment and special mention at a general Conference.

7.

Certain it is that there are functions in this enterprise
of world evangelisation which can best, perhaps can only,
be performed by laymen. The utilisation of the great
existing agency of the press ; the capturing of the
sympathy of the great firms that have business abroad,
representatives and agents of which are found all over
the mission field ; the animating of men in the civil
and military services with the Christian ideal in its
fulness ; and the bringing of business experience to
bear on organisation of missions and the conduct of
their work abroad—these are all matters in which it is
indispensable that laymen should take the leading part.
In Britain, indeed, he has for a very long time taken a

leading and essential part in the whole missionary enterprise, and possibly the enormous prominence which laymen's work is assuming in the United States and Canada to-day, as these speeches at the Conference showed, is to some extent the catching-up of a long lead. But even if this be so, there could have been no British or Continental delegate who did not feel uplifted by the enthusiasm of these men from the west of the Atlantic, or failed to receive instruction from the reports they now made.

For the Continent spoke M. le Capt. Bertrand. As a well-known explorer and convert to missions—possibly to the religion of Christ itself—by what he had himself seen in Africa, the weight of his remarks was in inverse proportion to their length. They must certainly be quoted here. After mentioning the German and the French missions which he had himself studied in Central and South-Central Africa, he went on :—

" I must say I was struck by that Christian work. The opposer of missions is not so much the heathen as the white man. Briefly, the missionaries in Africa, and other countries too, have to-day a great battle to fight, not only against heathenism, but against the vices of our civilisation. It is a pity that in our civilised country so many people, especially young men, do not take the trouble to study missionary work as it is, and too often oppose it through ignorance. In Europe to-day laymen have to come to the front and help missionary work. May I ask, as one of the practical results of this Conference and as a practical help to missions, that a scheme of co-operation of the various national laymen in Europe might be studied, that this movement might become a European one too."

Thus the Continent. Britain, represented by Sir Andrew Fraser, confined itself to telling of the wonderful things it had seen among the business men of Canada, —" some of them with hard hands, and all of them with hard heads " : how these men had met together in a great convention and asked two questions : " What is required so that no one in Canada shall be able to say, ' I have not heard the Gospel because there was no man to tell me it,' " and " What is required for us to meet the obligations that rest on us in regard to that portion of the heathen world that lies to our hand ? " As business men, whose first function is, in the nature of the case, to recognise their stewardship of the silver and the gold, they fixed their responsibility for the practical answering of those two questions at £900,000 a year, and they said, " That sum must be raised." And they are going to raise it.

Sir Andrew Fraser proceeded to expound the real lesson of this experience, and what he said was the burden of all the speeches from the American delegates. It also brought the Conference very near two of the grand lessons of Edinburgh 1910—the unity of the world as the scene of the Christian enterprise—" THE FIELD IS THE WORLD," said One, nearly two milleniums ago ;— and the necessity for conceiving and viewing and planning for that work as one. Unification in the conception will bring co-operation in the execution as surely as night follows day. " The great points," said Sir Andrew, " that seem to me of immense importance are these,

the consecration to the Lord Jesus Christ of the business capacity of the great business community. Secondly, the distribution of responsibility for this work that has got to be done. Thirdly, the systematic giving ; no temporary enthusiasm, no mere sporadic effort, but a steady business determination, week by week to give what can be given, of money and energy and labour, to the cause of our Lord Jesus Christ at home and abroad, for the evangelisation of the world and the winning of His world for Him."

Compare these points with those in which a well-known American delegate, J. Campbell White, who had given seven years to working out this question, sums up his experiences and his convictions. " Define your task ! " he exclaimed. It has strangely taken the Churches of N. America a hundred years of missionary effort to ask the question what force of mission-workers was really needed in order to meet the opportunity that confronted them in the mission field. The result is that the laymen who asked that question have been able to go to their constituencies and tell them that they must quadruple their efforts if the work is to be overtaken. Australia, too, is asking the same question, and promises to return a like practical answer. " Undertake the whole task ! " he continued. Only thus will a business man undertake any part of that task. " Men are willing to have the whole burden laid upon them of the Church's duty to evangelise the whole world " ;—therefore make your appeal for the world rather than for the society in which you are interested. Then again, in each great city or district, show the churches of that city or district what they are doing as a whole, and what they ought to be doing if they did their full share. And to this end have a committee " that will sit from year's end to year's end " to organise and carry through the work of visiting and informing and soliciting which it is as indispensable as it is encouraging. . . . So flowed on the torrent of rapid speech, desperate tides of enthusiasm, exhortation, information forced through the channel of five-minute addresses : . . . budgets doubled and trebled ; business men first won for the Church of God by being interested in the enterprise of her work for God ; laymen giving not only money but time and leadership ; rich men no longer insulted by a demand from these highwaymen of to-day for their spare pence, but captured by the round challenge to surrender both money and life ; movements which, for all their immense scope, mean individual effort among individuals from beginning to end of them ; estimates, budgets, statistics, facts, figures, ways and means.

8.

Yet not for one moment did the Conference forget, could it forget, what in Report and discussion and address had been borne in upon its very soul, that these things could not fully represent the ultimate problem of all,—the problem of the Church's faith in God.

They could not fully represent that problem. But they represented phases of it, and rightly understood they partook of its essential spirituality. The Kingdom of God indeed cannot be reckoned or measured by figures ; but it has a place for those who deal in figures. Among the charisms of the One Spirit are " helps, governments." Among His instructions is the one to " him that giveth " to " do it with liberality."

Several touches served to show that these enthusiasts themselves had no need to be reminded of this great matter. Early in the day a leader in the work of the American home base, Dr C. R. Watson, had justified these enterprises as a method " of making more definite and clear to the Church the vastness of the problem, and of bringing it into terms which some men who cannot comprehend other terms will understand." Further, it was a method that had at its heart a desire to have a comprehensive vision of the whole world ; a desire for definiteness ; a desire for self-sacrifice—he had seen men's faces light gloriously as their imaginations caught the vision and their will addressed itself to the revealed task. . . . His father's son was above suspicion of unspirituality ;—but even had he not spoken, the Conference could hardly fail to be convinced by what it actually heard and saw. Work of this sort deals first and fore-

most with persons, and the work that touches persons
is holy because it touches the whole man,—thus judged
the member of the Commission who summed up the
results of the session, himself a clergyman and an English-
man. Only the Holy Spirit of God can touch the whole
spirit of man. And as for gold, that essential accident
of the enterprise of the kingdom, and more particularly
of the task of the Home Base, it was a business man that
thereon spoke a golden word. There was something
noteworthy in the chance fact that the very last of the
unofficial speakers of the day, and of all the days of the
Conference, should have been a layman, a business
man, a rich man, who, like a certain rich man of Judæa,
had been shown that in his riches lay his opportunity
for the consecration of his self, but, unlike him, had
decided to seize the opportunity. He spoke but a few
words, the speech of a layman who does not pretend
to know how to speak. Perhaps it was more colloquial
than suited most tastes ; but—it came evidently from an
experience, and its simple sincerity impressed. " Are
we letting down the tone of this Conference at this last
meeting," he asked,

" because we are needing money ? Not a bit ! Last night we
were led up on to the Mount of Privilege and told that *God was
sufficient* for us. We subscribe to that to-day. . . . We think
that this question of money is a sordid, lustful thing, but it is not.
It can be transmuted and made just as sacred as any other part
of our duty, and I do not know anyone who would say to me,
as a business man, that necessarily because I am after the money,
that the money is my master. I admit that in the past it was,
but I am now trying to become master of my money. Take my
money and my wealth ; it is just part of me. When I am giving
my money, I am just giving so much of myself. It is what we do
with our money that translates our attitude towards the money,
and our attitude towards Jesus Christ ; and so I say we have not
come down from last night. I want this question of money to be

R

just as real and just as helpful a thing in our life as any other point . . ."

—words recalling those of the Rabbi whom Browning's imagination created,

"Let us cry, 'All good things
Are ours, nor soul helps flesh more, now, than flesh helps soul!'"

Thus it was a plain business man who, at the close of a day given necessarily to matters of detail and method, work and planning for work, brought the Conference to remember once more that consecration must take as many forms as life, and that the soul's self-consecration, which is the real problem of the Home Base of Missions, depends not only ultimately but immediately on the soul's vision of GOD.

.   .   .   .   .   .

CHAPTER XIV CONCLUDED

" THE HOME BASE OF MISSIONS "

GOD is the ultimate Home Base of Missions.

Sent and Sender alike fly homing to GOD. And the base, where alone the resources necessary for the super-human enterprise are stored, is GOD.

Words !—Yet the Edinburgh Conference, if it had done anything, had shown that the whole crisis of missions just turns upon whether the Church of Christ can get behind these words, discover there a palpable reality, and then demonstrate her discovery to the world. Is this possible ?

The New Testament, at least, is a standing monument to the fact that the Church of Christ has in times past discovered behind these words a palpable reality, and has demonstrated its discovery to the world.

And God-reality is independent of time. What was once true and possible is at any moment true and possible.

Therefore it *is* true that GOD is to-day the ultimate Home Base of Missions, the available and sufficient source and resource. And it *is* possible for the Church to realise that truth and prove it upon her life to the world of to-day.

And therefore " the Sufficiency of God " is not a word only, but a fact. As much of a working fact and as full of personal significance as it was for the man, and his correspondents, who in 56 A.D. received these words from GOD in CHRIST—

MY · GRACE · IS · SUFFICIENT · FOR · THEE.

" The Sufficiency of God," it was said at one of the striking evening addresses,

" is so obviously the soul of the Christian enterprise that the work of missions would be the most consummate folly without it. For there is no task in the history of the world so stupendous as the endeavour to bring the Message of Christ to the heart of all nations. Almost every phase of difficulty is represented to such an extent that the presence of the Power of GOD alone makes the work rational. Without it, the disparity between the undertaking and the means of achievement would make the problem incomparably foolish. But the sufficiency of GOD makes the difference between folly and sublimity."

We have seen that the Report and the discussion on the Home Base of Missions suggested, though perhaps unintentionally, a situation which seemed to be bright with hope, or at least to inspire hopefulness. That might be called the positive aspect of the present situation. And we have seen how the contemplation of it led the Conference at every turn to the thought of the Sufficiency of GOD.

But there was another side to this :—beside the hope-inspiring positive aspect the Conference had also to contemplate a more negative, a more ominous one. The contemplation of this, no less, led to the thought of the Sufficiency of God; only, while the first led hopefully, the second drove desperately to that thought.

This deep note was sounded at Edinburgh, not often, but sufficiently. It was touched on the evening of the very first full day of Conference, when he who then spoke deplored the present failure of Christendom to give a Christian sociology to the New East, to help her to settle the perplexities that are beginning to trouble her soul. But towards the end of the Conference the note was struck, hard and startlingly vibrant, by another speaker. His address was one of power. It impressed because it hurt.

Professor James Denney fully acknowledged the large amount of interest which the Church is taking in missions to-day. The World Missionary Conference was a sufficient testimony to that. Further, the Christian enterprise has attained to such dimensions and entered so largely into the general movement of human things that it is impossible for an intelligent man not to take some sort of interest in missions. But it was very often a disinterested interest, the interest of the intelligent bystander who cannot afford to be utterly ignorant of what is going on in his world; but very, very little of it was the conscientious and responsible interest of people who feel that the work of missions is their work, and still less was it the enthusiastic interest of those who feel the work laid upon their hearts through the consciousness of what they themselves owe to Christ.

Members of Conference who had endorsed the finding that the problems of the mission field resolve themselves into the problem of the Home Base, were hardly, he thought, fully aware how true their analysis was. The communion to which he belonged, and he merely took it as a typical example, had increased its membership by one person for every two congregations in five years! and the number of candidates for the ministry was much smaller to-day than it was a good many years ago! . . . And then, very bluntly:—the ultimate explanation of it which deeply concerns the Church abroad and the work of missions is just this, " that men are not coming forward as ministers, nor coming forward as missionaries, *because they are not coming forward into the membership of the Christian Church at all.*"

" There is no use calling for reinforcements at the front while the recruiting is stopped at home, and that is, to a large extent, the grave situation with which we are comfronted. . . . *Something must happen to the Church at home if it is going even to look at the work which has been put on it by this Conference.*"

What that something was the speaker made plain in the remainder of his address. And what he said just amounted once more to this—the realisation of the Fact of GOD as revealed in CHRIST, and the sufficiency of God when that Fact is grasped by the faith which wills to know it at any price. The vision that will inspire the Church is not that of a billion men who do not know the One God, but of the One God who gave His Son for the billion men. For " love like that can only be answered by a love in kind ; and for a Saviour who came, not only in water but in blood, there can be no adequate faith, no adequate response which is bloodless." The Church has gained nothing whatever by cheapening the terms of the Gospel. Garabaldi would have got nothing had he not demanded all. What did Garabaldi offer to Young Italy in 1849 ? " I do not offer pay, provisions, or quarters : I offer hunger, thirst, forced marches, battles, and death." And that was the cry, concluded the speaker, to which the deep heart of his people responded ; " and when a voice like that is uttered in the Church by men who have the right to utter it, then we can be sure that the thin ranks will fill up again, and our King go forth conquering and to conquer."

Such was the sternest word spoken at Edinburgh. The Church's need of consecrated men points her back to a GOD who Himself consecrated His own Self for the redemption of the world.

Thus every aspect of the Home Base of Missions, dark or bright, hopeful or desperate, pointed the Conference to the one solution of the problem of the Home Base of Missions, GOD.

.   .   .   .

That way, we saw, had pointed each of the eight full days of Conference. The eight Reports which had been presented on those eight days, like an octave of notes, had sounded with their first and last the keynote of the scale ; and of the rest each stood in clear, definite relation to the master-tone.

For the Commission to which was assigned that first day surveyed the superhuman task, and after taking stock of all ways and all means, could only end thus— " We are frank to concede that it is futile to talk about making Christ known to the world in this or any generation unless there be a great expansion of vitality in the members of the Churches of Christendom." And in so saying they indicated the one thing so vitally needed by theseChurches, the deeper life in a more deeply-known God. The words clearly intimated, further, that the Commission that reported on the last day would arrive at the same finding. And this chapter on the Home Base of Missions has shown us how true that intimation was. And between that first and that last, six other Commissions had written six countersignatures to the same message. One revealed a Church on the Mission Field bound to that at home by the law of organism, which ordained that weakness in the one must spell weakness in the other, and that the re-baptism of the Churches of the West would assuredly be life to the Churches of the East. Another revealed an educational crisis which could only be met by a church which is willing and able immediately to reinforce and *co-operate* : and what did these two conditions imply ? One Commission showed that this co-operation in itself, if it is going to make any appreciable advance towards unity, necessitates a spiritual revival which must be in its very nature supernatural. And another showed that that reinforcement depends, both for its quantity and its quality, on the spiritual state of the churches which have to supply, equip, and train the reinforcements demanded. Another looked out at the so-called Christian nations and found them harbouring churches whose hold on God was not sufficient to influence the foreign policies of those nations, nor to Christianise their dealings with each other, with non-Christian powers, or with the weaker races they dominated. Another, finally—the one in charge of an enquiry which was by the very nature of its subject the most searching and intimate of all— found that the very religions which Christianity is called upon to antiquate and replace teach her that her own theology must first pervade all life, and that her own life must first be lived on the supernatural plane, the power of a living faith in a living GOD.

  .   .   .   .   .   .

And now we have fully seen that the Edinburgh Conference, in all its Commissions, Reports, Discussions, and Addresses, resolved that the problem of missions is the problem of the Church's faith in GOD : that the only solution of the problem of missions is the Sufficiency of GOD.

  .   .   .   .   .   .

Some might perhaps say, the thought of the Conference moved in a vicious circle. It now asseverated that, apart from world-wide evangelisation, Christendom would not be given a fuller vision and a stronger grip of her Divine Lord ; and now, that without a fuller vision and a stronger grip of her Divine Lord Christendom would not be strong enough for world-wide evangelisation.

But it is only formal logic that calls such circles vicious. Nature and life appear to work in such circles : but they are then called cycles, not vicious circles. It is actually the closing of a circuit that makes electricity available, and captures its current to be a motive-power for man. So perhaps in the world of supernature. It may be that these conclusions of the Conference reveal a supernatural cycle. It may be that obedience to the spiritual law of this particular circuit, the deliberate closing of its two ends, is going to make available a spiritual current, is going to capture for the Church a dynamic and a motive-power that will be literally inexhaustible *so long as she keeps the two ends closed*. Would not the Church's use of all the light she has, her consecration of all her present strength to fulfilling her Lord's command—would this not mean the continuous solution of both problems at once ? Would not each react upon the other ? Obedience to the full extent of her present power would increase her vision, and the increase of the vision would increase the power. She will pray for her own revival, —but she will wait for the answer at her post of duty.

.   .   .   .   .   .

But how will this revival, this new intensity of knowledge and power, light and heat, come to the Church at the Home Base ? Will it come as the wind, sweeping over whole Churches in many countries at once ? *Allahu akbar !* Who shall limit the power of God, or set bounds to what the increased practice of all-powerful intercession is going to achieve in those coming years? Christ always seemed to be thinking of the possibilities of prayer. Man always thinks of its limitations. But Edinburgh 1910 has taught again the old lesson, and from henceforth increasingly many are going to think the thoughts of Jesus Christ about prayer, and to look away to God with His eyes.

But a sudden mass-movement of the whole Church towards God and the world-mission is not the only way in which the fulfilment of the hope kindled at Edinburgh may be looked for. May it not also come like an Alpine sunrise? . . . The high clouds kindle with their prophecy of the dayspring or ever the sun is up.—Suddenly the topmost peaks are smitten with a wondrous light! The glory seizes on others, and still others. . . . See where it runs along the ridges! It seems to flash from ridge to ridge! . . . Lower and lower it comes, invading the mountain-sides, penetrating the valleys. . . . And lo, the world is light!—Will not this New Theology of our desires and our dreams, the faith which penetrates all life and has victory over all the world, first take possession of its apostles and prophets, perhaps its martyrs also, and from them, with a rapidity as great as the Sun of Righteousness wills, communicate itself to this one and to that one, from congregation to congregation, one from another catching the new impulse, till Christendom find herself strong in unity and in spirit as in the days of old?

" *O Lord, arise and help us, and deliver us for Thine honour!* "

.   .   .   .   .   .

Some such thoughts as these, at least, seemed to be in the mind of the man who in the still, solemn closing meeting of the Conference, on the evening of the day of the Home Base of Missions, delivered the closing address. The man who had watched from the chair of the Conference, and recorded in his heart all that had been said in those eight sessions, was now permitted to open his lips. The Speaker now spoke for the first and last time. And in that hour he did not seem to be thinking so much of the Church at the Home Base, as of that bowed worshipping company of twelve hundred. Would *they*, each one of them, perceive and believe the availability of God ? Would they, so perceiving and so believing, become available for God ? If *they* did, then there was good hope that the Churches which they represented would soon follow.

It was with some such thoughts as these that he spoke the memorable sentences, uttered in unforgetable tones, with which he opened that closing address—

" *The end of the Conference is the beginning of the Conquest* " :

" *The end of the Planning is the beginning of the Doing !* "

   .   .   .   .   .   .

And later :

" *God has been silently and peacefully doing His work, but He has infinitely greater designs than these. It is not in His will that the influences set forth by Him shall cease this night. Rather shall they course out through us to the very ends of the earth.*"

   .   .   .   .   .   .

Also—

" *Our best days are ahead of us, and not in these ten days that we have spent together, still less in the days that lie behind them. Without question this is proved . . . .*"

The mere facts of this Conference (he said) were so many clear pledges that *our best days are ahead of us*, that the Church's best days are likewise still ahead.

   .   .   .   .   .   .

And then, and in a final sentence which linked the last words of this the very last address at Edinburgh 1910 to the last words of the very first one, thereby closing the circuit, so that same prophetic word once more flashed dazzlingly forth—

" God grant that we, all of us . . . may in these next moments solemnly resolve henceforth so to plan and so to act, so to live and so to sacrifice, that our spirit of reality may become contagious among those to whom we go ; and it may be that the words of the Archbishop shall prove to be a splendid prophecy. . . ."

And these words, what were they ? Christ Himself was their Author and Giver.

" VERILY I SAY UNTO YOU, THERE BE SOME HERE OF THEM THAT STAND BY WHICH SHALL IN NO WISE TASTE OF DEATH TILL THEY SEE THE KINGDOM OF GOD COME WITH POWER " !

The Conference closed with prayer.

FINIS . . . ?

"'Yea, I come quickly.' Amen; come, Lord Jesus."

ANALYSIS

IN LIEU OF

INDEX

The Roman numerals refer to the Chapters.
The Arabic to the Sections.

S

s*

L'ENVOI

TO

THE READERS OF "EDINBURGH 1910"

*The Official Message from the Conference
To the Members of the Church in Christian Lands.*

DEAR BRETHREN OF THE CHRISTIAN CHURCH,

We members of the World Missionary Conference assembled in Edinburgh desire to send you a message which lies very near to our hearts. During the past ten days we have been engaged in a close and continuous study of the position of Christianity in non-Christian lands. In this study we have surveyed the field of missionary operation and the forces that are available for its occupation. For two years we have been gathering expert testimony about every department of Christian Missions, and this testimony has brought home to our entire Conference certain conclusions which we desire to set forth.

Our survey has impressed upon us the momentous character of the present hour. We have heard from many quarters of the awakening of great nations, of the opening of long-closed doors, and of movements which are placing all at once before the Church a new world to be won for Christ. The next ten years will in all probability constitute a turning-point in human history, and may be of more critical importance in determining the spiritual evolution of mankind than many centuries of ordinary experience. If those years are wasted, havoc may be wrought that centuries are not able to repair. On the other hand, if they are rightly used they may be among the most glorious in Christian history.

We have therefore devoted much time to a close scrutiny of the ways in which we may best utilize the existing forces of missionary enterprise by unifying and consolidating existing agencies, by improving their administration and the training of their agents. We have done everything within our power in the interest of economy and efficiency; and in this endeavour we have reached a greater unity of common action than has been attained in the Christian Church for centuries.

But it has become increasingly clear to us that we need something far greater than can be reached by any economy or reorganisation of the existing forces. We need supremely a deeper sense of responsibility to Almighty God for the great trust which He has committed to us in the evangelisation of the world. That trust is not committed in any peculiar way to our missionaries, or to Societies, or to us as members of this Conference. It is committed to all and each within the Christian family; and it is as incumbent on every member of the Church, as are the elementary virtues of the Christian life—faith, hope and love. That which makes a man a Christian makes him also a sharer in this trust. This principle is admitted by us all, but we need to be aroused to carry it out in quite a new degree. Just as a great national danger demands a new standard of patriotism and service from every citizen, so the present condition of the world and the missionary task demands from every Christian, and from every congregation, a change in the existing scale of missionary zeal and service, and the elevation of our spiritual ideal.

The old scale and the old ideal were framed in view of a state of the world which has ceased to exist. They are no longer adequate for the new world which is arising out of the ruins of the old.

It is not only of the individual or the congregation that this new spirit is demanded. There is an imperative spiritual demand that national life and influence as a whole be Christianized : so that the entire impact, commercial and political, now of the West upon the East, and now of the stronger races upon the weaker, may confirm, and not impair, the message of the missionary enterprise.

The providence of God has led us all into a new world of opportunity, of danger, and of duty.

God is demanding of us all a new order of life, of a more arduous and self-sacrificing nature than the old. But if, as we believe, the way of duty is the way of revelation, there is certainly implied, in this imperative call of duty, a latent assurance that God is greater, more loving, nearer and more available for our help and comfort than any man has dreamed. Assuredly, then, we are called to make new discoveries of the grace and power of God, for ourselves, for the Church, and for the world ; and, in the strength of that firmer and bolder faith in Him, to face the new age and the new task with a new consecration.

The Official Message from the Conference.

To the Members of the Christian Church in non-Christian Lands.

DEAR BRETHREN IN CHRIST,

We desire to send you greeting in the Lord from the World Missionary Conference gathered in Edinburgh. For ten days we have been associated in prayer, deliberation, and the study of missionary problems, with the supreme purpose of making the work of Christ in non-Christian lands more effective, and throughout the discussions our hearts have gone forth to you in fellowship and love.

Many cases of thanksgiving have arisen as we have consulted together, with the whole of the Mission Field clear in view. But nothing has caused more joy than the witness borne from all quarters as to the steady growth in numbers, zeal, and power of the rising Christian Church in newly-awakening lands. None have been more helpful in our deliberations than members from your own Churches. We thank God for the spirit of evangelistic energy which you are showing, and for the victories that are being won thereby. We thank God for the longing after unity which is so prominent among you and is one of our own deepest longings to-day. Our hearts are filled with gratitude for all the inspiration that your example has brought to us in our home-lands. This example is all the more inspiring because of the special difficulties that beset the glorious position which you hold in the hottest part of the furnace wherein the Christian Church is being tried.

Accept our profound and loving sympathy, and be assured of our confident hope that God will bring you out of your fiery trial as a finely-tempered weapon which can accomplish His work in the conversion of your fellow-countrymen. It is you alone who can ultimately finish this work : the word that under God convinces your own people must be your word ; and the life which will win them for Christ must be the life of holiness and moral power, as set forth by you who are men of their own race. But we rejoice to be fellow-helpers with you in the work, and to know that you are being more and more empowered by God's grace to take the burden of it upon your own shoulders. Take up that responsibility with increasing eagerness, dear brethren, and secure from God the power to carry through the task ; then we may see great marvels wrought beneath our own eyes.

Meanwhile we rejoice also to be learning much ourselves from the great peoples whom our Lord is now drawing to Himself ; and we look for a richer faith to result for all from the gathering of the nations in Him.

There is much else in our hearts that we should be glad to say, but we must confine ourselves to one further matter, and that the most vital of all.

A strong co-operation in prayer binds together in one all the Empire of Christ. Pray, therefore, for us, the Christian communities in home-lands, as we pray for you : remember our difficulties before God as we remember yours, that He may grant to each of us the help that we need, and to both of us together that fellowship in the Body of Christ which is according to His blessed Will.

JULIUS RICHTER

A History of Protestant Missions in the Near East 8vo, cloth, net $2.50.

A companion volume to "A History of Missions in India," by this great authority. The progress of the gospel is traced in Asia Minor, Persia, Arabia, Syria, and Egypt. Non-sectarian in spirit, thoroughly comprehensive in scope.

JOHN P. JONES, D.D.

The Modern Missionary Challenge

Yale Lectures, 1910. 12mo, cloth, net $1.50.

These lectures, by the author of "India's Problem, Krisha or Christ?" are a re-survey of the demand of missions in the light of progress made, in their relation to human thought. The new difficulties, the new incentives, are considered by one whose experience in the field and as a writer, entitle him to consideration.

ALONZO BUNKER, D.D.

Sketches from the Karen Hills

Illustrated, 12mo, Cloth, net $1.00.

These descriptive chapters from a missionary's life in Burma are of exceptional vividness and rich in an appreciation for color. His pen pictures give not only a splendid insight into native life, missionary work, but have a distinctive literary charm which characterizes his "Soo Thah."

JAMES F. LOVE

The Unique Message and Universal Mission of Christianity

12mo, cloth, net $1.25.

A volume dealing with the philosophy of missions at once penetrating and unusual. It is perhaps one of the most original and valuable contributions to the subject yet made.

WILLIAM EDWARD GARDNER

Winners of the World During Twenty Centuries Adapted for Boys and Girls.

A Story and a Study of Missionary Effort from the Time of Paul to the Present Day. Cloth, net 60c; paper, net 30c.

Children's Missionary Series

Illustrated in Colors, Cloth, Decorated, each, net 60c.

Children of Africa. James B. Baird.
Children of Arabia. John C. Young.
Children of China. C. Campbell Brown.
Children of India. Janet Harvey Kelman.

In the Valley of the Nile

A Record of Missionary Enterprise in Egypt.
Princeton Lectures.

Net, $1.00.   CHARLES R. WATSON

"The author carefully traces the early rapid spread of Christian faith into ancient Egypt and the development of the Coptic church, and the spread of the Moslem faith over Christianized Egypt. The earlier and more transient Moravian missionary efforts are described and then the American Presbyterian work which has achieved such success. A map, index and bibliography are appended. This is an excellent reference book as well as informing traveler's handbook."—*Watchman.*

The Missionary Enterprise

A Concise History of Its Objects, Methods and Extension.

Net, $1.25.   EDWIN MUNSELL BLISS

As compiler of The Encyclopædia of Missions and in his work as editor and writer of special articles, the author stored up an immense amount of valuable knowledge on the subject of Missions. The present work is not merely a revision of the author's earlier work, "The Concise History of Missions," but a thoroughly re-written work, considerably extended as to scope and method of analysis, and including the latest data obtainable.

Missionary Experiences During Nineteen Centuries   *Gay Lectures, 1907.*

In press.   W. T. WHITLEY

The story of missions in five continents, differs from previous works of this character in that it is written from a view point entirely historical. The defeats are considered as fully as the victories; pitfalls to be avoided as well as examples to be followed.

Adventures With Four-Footed Folk

and Other Creatures of the Animal World.

Illustrated, $1.00.   BELLE M. BRAIN

The author has established a reputation through her popular missionary readings. No one is able to detect an interesting story more quickly. In her latest work she has selected some of the most thrilling stories from the mission field, dealing with animals of all sort, from Egerton R. Young's sledge dogs in the North West to the man-eating tiger in India.

The Foreign Missionary An Incarnation of the World Movement

12mo, Cloth, $1.50 net. **ARTHUR J. BROWN**

Dr. Brown, out of a long and intimate experience deals with such questions as, Who is the Missionary? What are his motives, aims and methods? His dealings with proud and ancient peoples. His relation to his own and other governments? His real difficulties. Do results justify the expenditures? How are the Mission Boards conducted? etc., etc. The book is most intelligently informing.

The Conquest of the Cross in China

JACOB SPEICHER

With Chart and Illustrations, 12mo, Cloth, $1.50 net.

The contents of this book were first delivered as lectures to the students at Colgate University. Mr. Speicher has the true instinct of the news bringer. He has lived in South China long enough to know it thoroughly. He is distinguished by common sense in his judgments, made palatable by a free literary style.

China in Legend and Story

12mo, Cloth, $1.25 net. **C. CAMPBELL BROWN**

By one of the C. M. S. best known missionaries. It consists of seventeen stories, true to legend or to fact, ten of them studies of the Chinese people as they are when heathen, and seven of them of the same people when they become Christians. The stories cover a wide range of social life, representing every class in the community, from mandarins to thieves and beggars. As Mr. Campbell Brown is a keen observer, and wields a graceful pen, the book is unusually interesting and valuable.

A Typical Mission in China

12mo, Cloth, $1.50 net. **W. E. SOOTHILL**

"The book is comprehensive, instructive, well written, interesting and valuable in every way. Those who read it will get such a glimpse into Chinese life and methods as they may never have had, and will certainly be edified and stimulated to a new zeal in the work of missions."—*Herald and Presbyter.*

Robert Clark of the Panjab Pioneer and Missionary Statesman

8vo, Cloth, $1.75 net **HENRY MARTYN CLARK**

"The record of one of the makers of Christian India: as fascinating as a novel, and immensely more profitable. The more widely this book is circulated and read, the better it will be for the missionary enterprise. A book of this character is the best apologetic that can be written."—*Missionary Intelligencer.*

OTIS CARY

A History of Christianity in Japan

Vo. I. A History of Roman Catholic and Greek Orthodox Missions in Japan.
Vol. II. A History of Protestant Missions in Japan.

Each 8vo, Cloth, $2.50 net; 2 vols. boxed $5.00 net.

Prof. Harlan P. Beach, of Yale University, says "This work will be recognized as a standard. Dr. Cary is one of the most scholarly among the entire Japanese Missionary force and his thoroughness and intimate knowledge are derived from more than thirty years' residence in Japan."

JULIUS RICHTER

The History of Protestant Missions in India   8vo, Cloth, net $2.50.

"There is hardly a single matter connected with missions in India upon which Dr. Richter's book may not be consulted with the certainty of finding reliable and accurate information and sound and wise judgment.—*Chronicle of the London Missionary Society*.

G. CAMPBELL MORGAN

The Missionary Manifesto

Being a Study of the Great Commission.
16mo, Cloth, net 75c.

Dr. Morgan's forceful and illuminating studies find ready welcome among thoughtful readers and students. His work emphasizes the imperative character of our Lord's commands and its accompanying equipment for the service.

ROBERT SLOAN LATIMER

Liberty of Conscience Under Three Tsars

A Study of Evangelical Effort in Russia 1856-1909. 12mo, Cloth, net $1.50.

This struggle for liberty of conscience, marked by intense devotion and sacrifice, during which men, women and children have suffered the keenest persecution, counting not their lives dear unto themselves, is replete with incidents that awaken the largest sympathy and admiration of those who have sought to be true to conscience. The record is often most tragic, and can but awaken sympathy for the new movement now in progress in that land so long barred against the light of the open Bible.

H. G. UNDERWOOD

The Call of Korea

New Popular Edition. Paper, net 35c. Regular Edition, 12mo, cloth, net 75c.

"As attractive as a novel—packed with information. Dr. Underwood knows Korea, its territory, its people, and its needs, and his book has special value which attaches to expert judgment. Particularly well suited to serve as a guide to young people in the study of missions."—*Examiner*.

WILLIAM O. CARVER

Missions in the Plan of the Ages

Bible Studies and Missions. 12mo, cloth, net $1.25.

As Professor of Comparative Religion and Missions in the Southern Baptist Theological Seminary at Louisville, Dr. Carver has prepared in these chapters the fruit of many years' study. His aim is to show that the foundation principles of the Christian task of world conquest are found in the Bible not so much in the guise of a commanded duty as in the very life of the Christian faith.

ANNIE L. A. BAIRD

Daybreak in Korea

Illustrated, 16mo, cloth, net 60c.

There can never be too many missionary books like this. A story written with literary skill, the story of a girl's life in Korea, her unhappy marriage and how the old, old story transformed her home. It reads like a novel and most of all teaches one, on every page, just what the Gospel means to the far eastern homes.

ISABELLA RIGGS WILLIAMS

By the Great Wall

Selected Correspondence of Isabella Riggs Williams, Missionary of the American Board to China, 1866-1897. With an introduction by Arthur H. Smith. Illustrated, 12mo, cloth, net $1.50.

"This volume is a little window opened into the life and work of an exceptionally equipped missionary. It was at Kalgan, the northern gateway of China, that a misssion station was begun amid a people hard and unimpressible. It was here that Mrs. Williams won the hearts of Chinese women and girls; here that she showed what a Christian home may be, and how the children of such a home can be trained for wide and unselfish usefulness wherever their lot is cast. No object-lesson is more needed in the Celestial Empire than this. Many glimpses of that patient and tireless missionary activity which makes itself all things to all men are given."—*Arthur H. Smith, Author of Chinese Characteristics, Etc.*

DR. GEORGE BROWN

The Life of Dr. George Brown

Pioneer, Explorer and Missionary. An Autobiography, with 111 illustrations and map. 8vo, Cloth, net $3.50.

"Since the appearance of John G. Paton's Autobiography we have read no work of such entrancing interest. It is a narrative of this pioneer missionary's forty-eight years of residence and travel in Samoa, New Britain, New Ireland, New Guinea, and the Solomon Islands."—*British Weekly*.

JESSE PAGE, F. R. G. S.

The Black Bishop
The Life of Samuel Adjai Crowther.

Preface by Eugene Stock, D. C. L., with frontispiece, sixteen illustrations and map. 8vo, Cloth, net $2.00.

"The simple life-story, told mainly by himself, of a West African who was a kidnapped slave when a boy of fifteen and forty-three years later became the first negro bishop of the Church of England. Much information is given beside the biographical details, about the problems presented by the Nigerian peoples to their white rulers and particularly of the extent, influence and probable future of the Mohammedan invasion."—*Nation*.

W. H. T. GAIRDNER, B. A.

D. M. Thornton
A Study in Missionary Ideals and Methods.

Nine illustrations, 12mo, Cloth, net $1.25.

"The Student Movement" says: "It is likely to dominate the thoughts of the missionary thinker for many years." Devoted largely to experiences in Egypt and lessons gathered on this field—it tells of a man who devoted his intellectual powers to thinking out the wider problems of the evangelization of the world and the spread of Christian institutions in Mission lands.

GEORGE HAWKER

The Life of George Grenfell,
Congo Missionary and Explorer

Illustrated, 8vo, Cloth, net $2.00.

"This may be regarded as a companion volume to Sir Harry Johnston's 'George Grenfell and the Congo'—it was, indeed, originally arranged that Sir Harry Johnston and Mr. Hawker should collaborate in a single volume as a memorial to one of the greatest names in the annals of equatorial Africa."—*London Times*.

REV. JAMES WELLS, D. D.

Stewart of Lovedale

The Romance of Missions in Africa told in the Life of James Stewart, D. A., M. D., F. R. G. S. With forty-two illustrations and two maps. 8vo, Cloth, net $1.50.

"We may heartily congratulate Dr. Wells on having written a book that will live, and more than that, a book that will create life wherever it is read."—*Dr. Robertson Nicoll, in the British Weekly*.

Poland, the Knight Among Nations

With Introduction by Helena Modjeska.

Illustrated, Cloth, $1.50 net. LOUIS E. VAN NORMAN

Poland is worth knowing—it is interesting. How could it be otherwise when it gave us Copernicus, Kosciusko, Chopin, Paderewski and Sienkiewicz. Not much has been known about the people because they have been hard to get at. Mr. Van Norman went to Cracow, won the hearts of the people, was treated like a guest of the nation and stayed till he knew his hosts well, and he here conveys an extensive array of information.

The Continent of Opportunity: South America

Profusely illustrated, $1.50 net. FRANCIS E. CLARK

Dr. Clark writes from a thorough-going tour of examination, covering practically every centre of importance in South American continent, Panama, Chile, Ecuador, Peru, Argentine, Brazil, Paraguay and Uruguay. Dr. Clark's prime object has been to collect information of every sort that will help to understand the problems facing Civilization in our sister Continent.

China and America To-day

12mo, Cloth, $1.25 net. ARTHUR H. SMITH

Dr. Smith is one of America's ablest representatives at foreign courts. He is not so accredited by the government of this country, but rather chooses to be known as a missionary to China. In this capacity he has learned much of China which in another relation might be denied him. Being a statesman by instinct and genius, he has taken a broad survey of conditions and opportunities and here presents his criticisms of America's strength and weakness abroad.

Ancient Jerusalem

Illustrated. In press. HON. SELAH MERRILL

This work will immediately be recognized as authoritative and well nigh final. Dr. Merrill, as the American Consul, has lived at Jerusalem for many years, and has given thirty-five years of thorough, accurate study and exploration to this exhaustive effort. It contains more than one hundred maps, charts, and photographs.

Palestine Through the Eyes of a Native

Illustrated, $1.00 net. GAMAHLIEL WAD-EL-WARD

The author, a native of Palestine, has been heard and appreciated in many parts of this country in his popular lectures upon the land in which so large a part of his life was spent. His interpretation of many obscure scriptural passages by means of native manners and customs and traditions is particularly helpful and informing.